D0852669

THE CHOCOLATE TRUST

Milton S. Hershey (*Special Collections Research Center, Temple University Libraries, Philadelphia, PA*)

THE
CHOCOLATE TRUST

Deception, Indenture and Secrets
at the $12 Billion **Milton Hershey School**

BOB FERNANDEZ

CAMINO BOOKS, INC. / PHILADELPHIA

1 2 3 4   18 17 16 15

Library of Congress Cataloging-in-Publication Data

Fernandez, Bob, 1965-
  The chocolate trust: deception, indenture and secrets at the $12 billion Milton
Hershey School / Bob Fernandez.
    pages cm
  Includes bibliographical references.
  ISBN 978-1-933822-59-4 (alk. paper)
  1. Milton Hershey School (Hershey, Pa.)—Corrupt practices. 2. Milton Hershey
School (Hershey, Pa.)—Finance. I. Title.
  LD7501.H47F47 2015
  371.826'940974818—dc23   2014048646

ISBN 978-1-933822-59-4 (paper)
ISBN 978-1-933822-60-0 (ebook)

Interior design: Kate Nichols
Jacket design: Jerilyn Bockorick

This book is available at a special discount on bulk purchases for promotional,
business, and educational use.

Publisher
Camino Books, Inc.
P.O. Box 59026
Philadelphia, PA 19102
www.caminobooks.com

CONTENTS

ACKNOWLEDGMENTS

MY THANKS go to Hershey School alumni, former students, parents, former and current employees, insiders, attorneys, law professors, editors, colleagues and friends who helped me with this book. Sadly, at least three of the Home Boys with whom I spoke about their childhoods at the Hershey Industrial School died before this book's publication.

The Chocolate Trust would not have been possible without the alumni rebellion of the 1990s and early 2000s when Joe Berning, John Halbleib, Ric Fouad and others brought attention to the troubled Hershey School and the machinations of the Trust itself, sometimes at great personal cost. Craig Stark, who grew up in Hershey and is an encyclopedia on the town and the Trust, was invaluably helpful.

I spoke with many experts and interested individuals, including Robert Sitkoff, the John L. Gray Professor at Harvard University; James Lytle, practice professor at the Graduate School of Education at the University of Pennsylvania; Michael J. Hussey, associate professor at Widener Law School; Randall W. Roth, law professor at the University of Hawaii; John Schmehl, partner and chair of the tax group at Dilworth Paxson LLP; Pablo Eisenberg, columnist with the *Chronicle of Philanthropy,* and private attorney Mark Schwartz.

My thanks to *Philadelphia Inquirer* business editor Brian Toolan, who edited my Trust stories, and to Mike Leary, the persistently curious former managing editor at the *Inquirer,* who kept on asking about Hershey, and

Vernon Loeb, former deputy managing editor for news, who was a strong advocate for the stories about the Trust. Thanks to Bill Marimow, the *Inquirer* editor who published the Wren Dale golf course and Charles Koons stories, and to Stan Wischnowski, the *Inquirer* editor when the newspaper published several other Trust stories. My thanks to Karl Stark and Avery Rome, who worked with me as I reported on the student care at the Hershey School. And thanks to *Inquirer* reporter colleagues Jane Von Bergen and Diane Mastrull, who read early versions of chapters.

I would like to thank my agent, Anne Devlin, who found me a publisher; to development editor Miriam Seidel and Camino Books editor Brad Fisher, who smoothed the text and guided this project; and to Camino Books publisher Edward Jutkowitz, who believed in me and didn't waver as I missed deadlines.

I take full responsibility for the contents and observations in this book that contradict the overpowering and decades-long narrative of a multi-billion-dollar American institution dedicated solely to helping orphans and poor children with chocolate profits.

My thanks to Gil Gaul for his conversations about the title, and to Rocco Mancini, who listened to my Hershey stories at the bus stop.

Finally, true thanks to my wife Mae, who didn't question the wisdom of putting so much energy into a book project about an orphanage. And thanks to my sons Zack, Luke and Seth for only minimally complaining about the hours I spent in the basement and not with them.

INTRODUCTION

MOST AMERICANS don't think of poor kids when they hear the name Hershey. Their first thought is of Hershey chocolate bars. Others may think of roller-coaster rides at HersheyPark, or the bucolic charm of dairy farms that dot the area around the town of Hershey in Central Pennsylvania. But those of an older generation do remember the school Milton Hershey began over a century ago for poor, white fatherless boys.

Milton Hershey, the founder of the massively successful Hershey Chocolate company, set up a trust in 1909 after he and his wife Kitty couldn't have children of their own. In a time of widespread poverty and limited social services, starting an orphanage was a generous act but not unprecedented.

What would be unprecedented was the scale of Hershey's generosity. In 1918, the widowed Hershey vastly expanded the terms of his charity, putting the entire assets of the Hershey company—along with the Hershey mansion, Cuban sugar plantation, thousands of acres of Pennsylvania farmland and the town of Hershey itself—into the huge and sophisticated legal trust "exclusively devoted" to his orphanage, that was to exist into perpetuity.

Milton Hershey did not foresee the results of this sweeping gesture. This book will show how, ironically, the prodigious amounts of cash generated by Hershey's assets and put exclusively in service of a rural school for orphans created huge spending dilemmas—as well as temptations for those overseeing the trust, who found ways to persistently steer funds away from the intended beneficiaries, orphans and impoverished children. At the same time, his trust created an unusually intimate connection among Hershey's for-profit enterprises, the state government, the local court and the charitable entity—one that over the years, led to many instances of overreaching, flawed oversight, and a decades-long history of bitter confrontations with reformers.

THE NATION'S CHOCOLATE KING lived for almost three more decades after setting up the trust, and his chocolate-funded orphanage would be one of the nation's most celebrated charities of the first half of the 20th century—featured on the front page of the *New York Times* and in national magazines. When he died in a rural Pennsylvania hospital in 1945, governance of the complex organization passed to interlocking and self-perpetuating boards of businessmen and confidants, the so-called Trust.

Handpicked successors heeded Milton Hershey's dictates to nurture orphans with chocolate profits through the late 1940s and 1950s. But as the orphanage model for helping poor children declined throughout America, the Milton Hershey School struggled with shrinking enrollment, in the face of continuing huge profits funneled through the trust from the mass-appeal chocolate brand. In the early 1960s, a new generation of Trust leaders privately negotiated with state officials and the local court to divert tens of millions of dollars into a new giant medical center to train doctors and treat patients, establishing a pattern of deploying orphanage assets in ways that would benefit central Pennsylvania's economic development. The Trust's businessmen leaders believed—and state officials agreed—that there weren't enough orphans in America to help using Hershey's chocolate profits. The Trust later leveraged orphanage assets to build roller coasters in an ambitious expansion of the old Hershey amusement park, and would bail out the Trust-owned Hershey Entertainment & Resort Company when the company disastrously over-extended Hershey-branded hotels.

But the Trust couldn't abandon its original child-care mission altogether. In the early 1920s, the Internal Revenue Service had approved of Milton Hershey's charitable scheme to harness his businesses to his orphanage, allowing the businessman federal tax benefits. The Hershey name itself, in a brilliant marketing coup, was now synonymous with chocolate and orphans. The Trust gradually loosened restrictions on admission to the school so that by the mid-1970s any healthy, impoverished child of whatever race or gender in America was welcome to apply. The Trust also spent hundreds of millions of dollars on construction projects to modernize and upscale the campus. But student numbers fell so steadily that by 1999, enrollment was only two-thirds of the stated capacity of the early 1960s and about the same level as the late 1930s. Meanwhile, Hershey's medical center boomed with thousands of employees. Millions of tourists visited Hershey, the "Sweetest Place on Earth," with open wallets. The town prospered.

I heard about this secretive, chocolate-funded charity as a business reporter for the *Philadelphia Inquirer.*

Where had the generations of chocolate profits to help orphans and poor children gone?

Where were the kids?

Who were the educational leaders?

Why hadn't I heard more about this multi-billion-dollar school for poor kids, right outside one of the most impoverished cities in America, Philadelphia?

One of my early stories in 2010 described the Trust's purchase with school funds of a luxury golf course for two or three times its appraised value from local executives, doctors and lawyers. The story asked whether orphans and poor kids needed a fourth golf course, particularly since the Hershey School didn't have a golf team.

I wrote of a three-million-dollar Trust settlement with former students who had been molested by a serial pedophile on campus, and an online pornography collector nabbed on campus. I detailed the soaring compensation on the Trust's complex of boards as state Republican power broker LeRoy Zimmerman presided over a vast charitable enterprise, with holdings including 10,000 acres of land, the Hershey Entertainment & Resort Company, control of the Hershey Company's chocolate manufacturing, and a multi-billion investment portfolio.

Representatives of the Trust called me vindictive and wrong. But poor mothers and concerned alumni lit up my phone. They told me stories of expelled children, attrition, harsh care, untrained houseparents, medicated kids, kid-on-kid sexual abuse and hiring favoritism.

Parents who had been dazzled by the Hershey School's promotional literature, the multi-billion-dollar endowment and the allure of the Hershey brand told me that when they called the Pennsylvania Office of Attorney General desperate for help, officials at the state's top law-enforcement agency told them to hire private attorneys. But they didn't have thousands of dollars to retain a private attorney. When they called other state agencies or elected state officials, they were told there was nothing those officials could do—it was a private school.

During the years spent researching and writing this book, scandals continued to emerge.

A Philadelphia advocacy lawyer sued the Hershey School in 2011 for rejecting for admission a teenage boy with HIV. The Trust fought her and the boy in the courts and on its website. A Justice Department investigation revealed that the institution had violated the Americans with Disabilities Act. The Trust settled in 2012 with the Justice Department and the boy, agreeing to pay him $700,000 and posting an apology on its website.

In June 2013, tragedy struck: an impoverished 13-year-old Hershey School student hanged herself in the second-floor bedroom of her home after being asked to leave the school. Abbie Bartels had come to the Hershey School as a kindergartner. She loved cats and listened to Selena Gomez. The Hershey School banned her from her eighth-grade graduation and from the campus for depression and suicidal thoughts. Her mother Julie believed the child-care school quickly targeted Abbie as a liability and washed its hands of her. After the girl's suicide, the Trust paid for Abbie's funeral in the Trust-owned Hershey Cemetery, but alleged there had been nothing wrong with her treatment.

Some believed that Abbie's death, or one like it, was inevitable. Though unreported publicly, the school's own data showed that the institution that marketed itself as a nurturing haven for poor youth had treated many poor and vulnerable children roughly. Over a recent decade, far more poor kids dropped out or were kicked out for misbehavior than graduated—even though the institution had selected them for its lavishly funded program.

In May 2014, teen students at the Hershey School dialed 911 after finding a hidden digital camera in a dorm shower. Police investigated a Hershey School staffer. He had three loaded handguns in his campus apartment.

It didn't sound to me like Hershey was the "Sweetest Place on Earth" for these kids.

I FELT THAT the full story of the behavior and broken promises of Milton Hershey's Trust needed to be told. In the chapters that follow, I begin by looking more closely at Milton and Kitty Hershey, the charity's creation and evolution, American orphanages, and failed reforms at the Hershey School over the decades. I go on to cover the institution's current child-care failings and dangers. Later chapters tell the story of the Trust's flawed governance and oversight, including recent actions by the current Pennsylvania attorney general Kathleen Kane.

Finally, I explore the Trust-controlled Hershey Company's complacency in eradicating slave child labor or forced child labor in West Africa's cocoa industry, a major source of cocoa for Hershey's chocolate bars and Reese's peanut butter cups. This sad and still-developing story takes on ironic overtones in view of Milton Hershey's grand vision of using his profits to help poor children better themselves. In an epilogue, "Hershey's Shame," I suggest what lawmakers and regulators might do to help fix this deeply troubled, $12 billion institution and one of the world's richest philanthropies.

I

THE HOMESTEAD

Milton, Kitty, and Orphans

A STUNNING cut-glass torchière graced the entrance hall of the $100,000 High Point mansion when it opened with fanfare in the rural hills of Pennsylvania's Lebanon Valley in 1908. Milton Hershey had first spotted the dazzling floor lamp at the Chicago World's Fair, and architect C. Emlen Urban designed the mansion's three-story entry hall for it. Windows flooded the cut glass with sunlight. In high Gilded Age fashion, Milton and Kitty Hershey had purchased more than a dozen oil paintings at a New York gallery for High Point's walls, and they joyously filled its 22 rooms with furniture and china collected during travels to American and European cities. The minimally educated, hard-driving Milton Hershey occupied the Gold Room. Kitty had the one with pink walls and pink carpet. A fireplace in the living room blazed with gas logs, while a full-time staff, housed in servants' quarters, catered to the wealthy couple's needs and whims—a demanding and challenging task that would require a new housemaid every six months or so. Milton and Kitty had everything they could have wanted in their unconventional marriage except for the one thing: children.

Now in his early fifties, the multi-millionaire Chocolate King couldn't deny it any longer: Kitty, 15 years his junior, was barren. There would be no heirs to whom he could pass his fabulously profitable chocolate company. More troubling, Milton realized that Kitty's health was irreversibly declining even as he spent a small fortune seeking specialized medical care for her. What should they do with the chocolate business, with his namesake town, with all the money? Kitty talked about helping orphans, and Milton couldn't say no to her. He too thought it was a good idea. There is no record of conversations between the Mennonite husband and his Catholic wife about their plans, though Milton repeatedly said in later years that the orphanage was Kitty's idea. He gave this simple explanation to the *New York Times*: "Well, I have no heirs—that is, no children. So I decided to make the orphan boys of the United States my heirs."

They filed the Deed of Trust to create an orphanage on November 15, 1909, endowing it with about 500 acres of dairy farms, but with the potential to add assets over time. The document specified that the boys had to be fatherless, white, healthy, between the ages of four and eight, and good companions. In that time of limited social services, the plight of millions of orphans and homeless children had become a focus of national attention. *The Delineator*, a national fashion magazine edited by novelist Theodore Dreiser, published photos and stories of orphans, publicizing their plight to its readership of American women. The same year the Deed was created, Teddy Roosevelt hosted the first White House Conference on Children to address issues related to neglected children.

In the early 20th century, widows often struggled to provide for their young children. Some had little choice but to send sons and daughters to orphanages, already crowded with children who had no parents. Many orphanages were bleak institutions, hardly better it seemed than the almshouses that had preceded them, in which children had been housed alongside adult debtors, homeless or the deranged. Other children were placed on trains to the Midwest to be adopted by the first family that would take them.

Milton and Kitty's vision was a more hopeful one. The boys whom they accepted would be housed in home-like group cottages; they would live in the healthy environment of a rural farm setting looked after by Mennonite women, and would have the benefit of basic education and practical training. Milton Hershey had been inspired by Girard College, the school for poor fatherless boys founded in 1833 by the early American merchant and shipper Stephen Girard in Philadelphia; his commitment to educating orphan boys was groundbreaking in its time.

While they may have been responding to a progressive focus on the plight of children, one aspect of Milton and Kitty's plan harked back to earlier times: before the Hershey Industrial School would accept a boy, their widowed mothers had to sign indentures. Centuries old, these were typically contracts for labor servitude; Pennsylvania was then among about a dozen states that still allowed such legal arrangements so charity-case children could work off their debts. And, indeed, the fatherless orphan boys who enrolled with the Hershey Industrial School would be expected to work hard: milking cows, shoveling manure, pitching hay, picking strawberries and potatoes, and cleaning turkey coops on Hershey-owned dairy farms. Milton Hershey, who had been apprenticed in his early teens, claimed that the indentures allowed him to raise the boys without mothers or other family members interfering.

The *Lebanon Daily News* published an item on the new orphanage in the summer of 1910 and impoverished widow Mary Wagner of Mount Joy brought her sons Nelson and Irvin to be considered for admission in early September. Everyone in this part of Pennsylvania had heard of Hershey—first as the Caramel King and now the Chocolate King. She confidently penned her signature on Nelson's indenture with the final "r" spilling into the seal area. Nelson would be the first Home Boy. Milton Hershey also signed the document. Other fatherless boys trickled into the orphanage. Calvin Mader showed up on the 8th of September, and Guy and Jacob Weber on the 12th. October brought Carl Smith, John D. Grief and Charles Schaup.

Neither Milton nor the ailing Kitty took direct responsibility for caring for the boys—that task fell to farms supervisor George Copenhaver and his wife Prudence, who looked after them at the Homestead, Milton and Kitty's residence before they moved into the High Point mansion. The deeply religious Copenhavers instructed the boys on manners and Christian behavior. George cut hair and taught. Prudence laid down rules. One of those rules: no sports on Sunday.

Not surprisingly for the era and his background, George Copenhaver's views on child behavior and psychology could be harsh. A memo he wrote to Hershey and the School's Board of Managers about one young child, LeRoy Metzel, reveals the punitive, sin-laden perspective that informed the handling of those first students. "It becomes my very unpleasant duty," he wrote, "to report to you that LeRoy has earned for himself such an unenviable record that I consider him no longer entitled to the benefits of the school and an unfit associate for the rest of the pupils here. The boy has been here more than three and one-half years and he has not missed six nights during this time that he did not wet his bed. This is so offensive that we must keep him in a room by himself and none of the help can wash his bed clothes on account of the stench. He is absolutely void of the truth… He is a natural born thief. He has stolen money from a bureau; at one time from a box containing the boys' savings; twice from pocketbooks; once from the governess's church fund and once from another boy's pocket, and at another time he stole a dollar bill belonging to John Daniel and after tearing it to shreds, threw it into the waste basket. He also stole clothes out of trunks, even women's clothes. We have done all in our power to correct this boy. We have admonished him, we have punished him, and we are now at wit's end. If this was a reformatory we could probably punish him as he deserves; but this school cannot go to such extremes."

Copenhaver described LeRoy's "spells" and noted the boy's mother "was just as he is, and he has probably inherited his wayward ways." The Board of Managers voided the boy's indenture and sent him away.

A LOOK AT Hershey's own early life, marked by poverty and instability, offers some insight into his motivations for establishing the Hershey Industrial School. He was born in 1857 to a Mennonite couple, Fanny and Henry, in rural Derry, Pennsylvania—where he would later found the town of Hershey and the orphanage. Henry's father failed both at farming and at wildcatting—digging for undiscovered oil in western Pennsylvania. The family sold berries and brooms door-to-door, trying to make ends meet. After a while, the pious Fanny didn't seem to want to have anything to do with Henry. The final straw may have been the death of their daughter Sarena. They didn't divorce; but Henry and Fanny lived mostly separate lives. Milton dropped out of school after fourth grade, and his parents apprenticed him first to a printer, and then to Lancaster confectioner Joe Royer.

Because of his sporadic and shortened schooling, Milton may have been illiterate. Lebanon Valley College English professor Paul Wallace noted after interviewing hundreds of people for an unpublished authorized biography for the Hershey Trust Company in the 1950s that "what has made these researches unusual is the almost complete absence of anything written by Mr. Hershey himself....He kept no diaries and prepared no memoirs. He did, however, leave a vivid impression on the minds of all those who were near him."

Hershey always attributed the idea for the orphanage to Kitty. She was born Catherine "Kitty" Sweeney in 1871 in upstate New York to Irish parents. Hershey met her at A.D. Work's Confectionery in Jamestown, New York, on a sales trip with chocolate executive William Murrie, according to the Hershey Community Archives. Kitty's sister recalled the meeting between Milton and the flirty Kitty: "She was not selling candy. The girls used to congregate there and mess around. So Mr. Hershey was there with Mr. Murrie, and of course the girls introduced him to my sister."

Michael D'Antonio tells a very different version of the early relationship between Milton and Kitty in his 2006 biography, *Hershey: Milton S. Hershey's Extraordinary Life of Wealth, Empire and Utopian Dreams*. D'Antonio, who had extensive access to Trust archives and the cooperation of archivists, suggests that Kitty may have been a prostitute when Milton Hershey met her—not in small-town Jamestown, but in vice-ridden Buffalo. D'Antonio based this conclusion on Kitty's medical treatment records and a surviving transcript of Wallace's interview with a close family friend. Wallace interviewed Mrs. Thomas Chambers in 1954. She said that Milton and Kitty "met in Buffalo. She went to Buffalo to work. It was awful....He was crazy about her." As for what Kitty was doing in Buffalo away from her family, Chambers told Wallace, "I would not tell. Her mother didn't complain because her mother wanted the money. Mrs. Sweeney, she was awful for money."

Kitty relocated to New York to work in a department store, and she and Milton married a year later in a private ceremony on May 25, 1898 in the rectory of St. Patrick's Cathedral on Fifth Avenue. The wedding shocked Milton's family and business colleagues. Milton's pious mother, Fanny, who dressed plainly, did not get along with her new daughter-in-law. As wife of a rich chocolate industrialist, Kitty could afford the best medical care, and she traveled to Germany where she was treated by Wilhelm Erb, who had established modern standards for treating and diagnosing syphilis and related nerve damage. D'Antonio concludes that the "weight of the medical evidence leaves little doubt" about Kitty's illness: the advanced stages of syphilis, a disease most commonly transmitted through sexual activity. A woman who knew Kitty described the illness as a "creeping paralysis." Those in Hershey, D'Antonio writes, maintained a polite silence on the matter for more than a century.

When Kitty's health sharply deteriorated after 1910, the couple sailed to Europe searching for medical care and visiting exotic destinations. During these travels or at other times, they visited Wiesbaden, Aix-la-Chapelle, Monaco, Nice, Salzburg, Luxor, Alexandria and Cairo. They rode the Paris-Orient Express, the Vienna Alpiner and the Milano-Roma rail lines. Hershey bought tickets on the *Titanic* but didn't sail the doomed luxury liner.

Paralyzed by the end of 1914, Kitty died on March 25 1915 at the Bellevue-Stratford Hotel in Philadelphia, after a trip to Atlantic City. Milton Hershey ran out for a glass of champagne. When he returned to her hotel room, she had died. He broke down in tears, and paid for chocolate company workers to travel by train to her funeral. She was 42. The Reverend Francis J. Clark said Mass for Kitty at the Oliver H. Bair Funeral Home in Philadelphia on March 27th. Milton temporarily interred her at the city's West Laurel Hill Receiving Vault, and then relocated her to the Hershey Cemetery.

BY THE TIME of Kitty's death, Milton Hershey had been head of two highly successful candy-manufacturing enterprises for almost 30 years. He launched the Lancaster Caramel Company in 1886 with borrowed funds. He sold the business in 1900 for one million dollars, believing caramels to be a fad. But Hershey retained ownership of Lancaster Caramel's fast-growing chocolate division as part of the deal, and negotiated to supply the purchaser, American Caramel Company, with chocolate coatings. He described the transaction as a "daddy-longlegs exercise, in which I kept one foot on first base while I stole second."

Chocolate had long been a luxury treat in Europe, and Hershey initially copied the European model. He marketed chocolate novelties as Bijous, Vassar Gems, Le Roi de Chocolat, Le Chat Noir and Chocolate Blossoms. Hershey's Lancaster plant listed 114 of these products for wholesale in the late 1890s. But the businessman's longer-term goal was to bring milk chocolate bars to the American mass consumer market, ensuring profit by attaining manufacturing efficiencies. He envisioned making a good profit selling a nickel chocolate bar—a small luxury accessible to anyone, poor working people included. To do this, however, would be a huge project. He needed to develop chocolate-manufacturing processes, build a factory, hire workers and access the raw materials—importantly, fresh milk.

Hershey decided early that he wouldn't build his new chocolate company in Lancaster, where his first company was located. Some say he had been asked for a political contribution for the local Republicans and refused, which led to higher property assessments. Hershey looked for a new start and evaluated alternate sites for his new chocolate factory in four different states, including Maryland and New York, before deciding on the region where he'd been born, the "bowl of the Lebanon Valley, with Lebanon and Lancaster Counties in reach—one of the great milk regions of the country."

He bought the Hershey family's ancestral home—as the Homestead, it would become a Hershey landmark in southeastern Dauphin County—for $10,310 even before the Lancaster Caramel transaction had closed. Hershey added thousands of acres of dairy farms contiguous to or near the Homestead, along with milk-supply depots, and a Lebanon creamery. His plan for a factory mushroomed into a plan for an industrial town as Hershey's vision broadened. Workers installed the first telephone line for what would be the town of Hershey in 1903, and broke ground on the chocolate factory the same year. The Hershey Park Dance Hall and the Cocoa House opened in 1905.

A Hershey Press book articulated Milton Hershey's paternalistic concept of lodging orphan boys on his dairy farms. Hershey planned a "chain of farms tributary to the new industrial town. ...Now all the farms and dairies are organized by the Hershey Industrial School." Hershey was, more than anything, a shrewd businessman, and one can imagine he saw this synergy between the school and the business as an ingenious example of capitalist virtue in action. There was no public record of how many gallons of milk the orphan boys produced on Hershey's farms. A *Wall Street Journal* article said many years later that the school's excess milk production was contributed to the chocolate factory.

Hershey insisted on clean streets and orderly behavior. In his town, there were to be no taverns, piggeries, glue, soap, candle-making, lampblack factories or blacksmith shops in the residential areas. Hershey hired farmers, laborers for construction projects, relatives to help manage the company and, sometimes, children for his factory. Margaret Clark, 13 years old, earned five cents an hour in the Hershey Chocolate wrapping room. She walked to the factory and clocked about ten hours a day. Hershey was everywhere, Margaret Clark recalled years later, "and I don't mean just everywhere in the world. I mean everywhere *around here.*" Clark recalled Milton Hershey visiting the candy-wrapping room and losing his temper when he thought she was packing too many chocolates into a box.

THE CHOCOLATE PLANT grossed $10.3 million the year of Kitty's death. It was entering a period of rapid revenue growth as manufacturing capacity exploded and the nation developed a sweet tooth for chocolate. The company sold the classic flat chocolate bar, the chocolate bar with almonds, and Kisses. Hershey also supplied other candy makers with bulk chocolate to manufacture their own products—a big business.

The chocolate company's potential for growth enabled Hershey to leverage his assets into other ventures. He covetously viewed chewing gum as an area in which he could grow his business. Hershey created a subsidiary and developed a gum, marketed as Easy Chew. Copying his chocolate marketing, he priced a six-stick pack for a nickel. But Hershey quickly ran into fierce competition from gum magnate William Wrigley Jr., based in Chicago. The two businessmen briefly engaged in a game of who could outdo the other. Wrigley purchased a minority share of the Cubs baseball team, offering him a great marketing opportunity. Hershey offered $250,000 for the Phillies, but he couldn't reach a deal with club owner John Myers, who asked for $350,000. The ill-conceived chewing-gum venture ran into more problems. Hershey appointed a cousin to run it, and costs mounted when the U.S. government insisted on war-related taxes on chewing gum ingredients. Easy Chew Gum cost the Chocolate King an easy $2.5 million in losses.

The five-cent chocolate bars required three main ingredients: cocoa, milk and sugar. Hershey controlled his milk supplies through the Pennsylvania dairy farms; now he aggressively pursued a risky multi-million-dollar scheme to control his sugar supplies. He first visited Cuba with his mother Fanny, who wintered in Havana—where local residents initially took her plain Mennonite garb for that of a Catholic nun. Hershey thought the Cuban climate could be ideal for sugar production, and he investigated purchasing land. He would be the first large-scale sugar producer there.

In 1916, Hershey established the Hershey Corporation in the state of Delaware, to buy or lease sugar plantations in Cuba. He then purchased tens of thousands of acres for sugar cane cultivation, anchoring the business around Central Rosario, Central Carmen, Central San Antonio, Central Jesus Maria, and Central Juan Bautista. "All the old-timers at Central Hershey remember Mr. Hershey's early morning cigar, the corona he lighted after breakfast as he stepped out of the octagonal dining room and walked across to the Sugar House two or three minutes away," wrote Lebanon Valley's Paul Wallace.

Hershey also disastrously purchased high-priced sugar futures while waiting for his Cuban sugar production to develop. When the sugar bubble burst after World War I, Hershey's futures plunged to pennies on the dollar. He lost an additional two million dollars. Hershey Chocolate had been hugely profitable, but it lost $395,739 in 1920. A stunned National City Bank appointed an overseer to look after its loan exposure. The bank's R.J. DeCamp relocated to Hershey. The chocolate company rebounded with profits of three million dollars in 1921.

The two money-losing ventures—gum and sugar futures—didn't come as a surprise to those who knew Hershey. He had lost early candy retail businesses in Philadelphia and New York when he over-extended himself with borrowings. He courted risk "with an obsessive ardor," observed author Charles Castner in his regionally published Hershey biography, *One of a Kind*. "The record shows that…one personal characteristic that played a big part in both strings of winning and losing was directly tied to a trait [Hershey] inherited from his Papa. He was a gambler, and he didn't know when to quit."

This personal characteristic found its outlet in other ways. Hershey traveled periodically under the alias "M.S. Hall," requesting wires of $500 to $5,000. Hershey's chauffeur confided to Hershey's doctor and friend Herman Hostetter that Hershey liked horse races and would bet on every horse in a race, guaranteeing himself a winner. On a visit to Monte Carlo, young beauties nicknamed him "Mr. Maximum" because Hershey placed the highest-allowed casino bets. "He had a taste for Cuban cigars, tropical fruits, and champagne," wrote D'Antonio. "As time passed, he would spend hundreds of thousands of dollars in casinos and at racetracks. He would also become so comfortable with who he was in Cuba that he made no effort to hide his habits."

IN INTERVIEWS, Hershey explained that he gave his businesses to the Hershey Industrial School because of the institution's good work and he had thought about the decision since Kitty's death three years earlier.

In November 1918, Milton Hershey transferred ownership of the chocolate company, the undeveloped Cuban sugar lands, his non-chocolate diversified businesses, dairy farms and the town of Hershey itself to the existing trust fund for the orphanage and school, vastly broadening its asset base. All these businesses were contained within one corporate entity and stock certificate: for the chocolate company. Sam Hinkle, President of Hershey Chocolate from 1956 to 1965, noted in an unpublished memoir that within only a few days, Hershey leveraged the chocolate company to borrow millions of dollars to expand into Cuba, and placed the chocolate company into the trust for the orphanage. What this meant was that just as Hershey was taking huge risks with his chocolate company by borrowing millions of dollars to develop a Cuban sugar-refining complex, he was giving the leveraged chocolate company away to his orphanage. Why?

Hershey also informed the Internal Revenue Service in 1918 that he had contributed his assets to the charity. The recent War Revenue Act had allowed for the nation's first charitable tax deduction.

Those who have looked at Milton Hershey's finances speculate on additional motivations for his generosity beyond just philanthropy. Hershey, or his longtime attorney John Snyder, realized the financial risks of the Cuba venture, and that Hershey's businesses needed special legal protections. Placing the chocolate company inside a trust fund for an orphanage would make it nearly impossible for creditors to seize if Hershey's leveraged business dealings faced bankruptcy. Moreover, Hershey didn't have anything to lose. He was now 61 years old, childless and a widow. He apparently had no intention of remarrying and would gain substantial, perhaps inflated, federal tax benefits with the charitable contribution under the new federal law.

As a practical matter, Hershey also wouldn't face any diminished lifestyle even though he had given virtually everything he owned away to the orphanage. His legal and tax maneuver meant that control of his business and personal assets, including the town of Hershey, were subject to the dictates in the 1909 Deed. The Deed named the Hershey Trust Company as legal trustee of the orphanage's assets. Milton Hershey owned the bank and chaired its board—thus, he continued to control his companies and assets through it.

The 1909 Deed also addressed oversight of the orphanage. Hershey didn't have to worry about losing control here either. The Hershey Trust Company board appointed the orphanage's Board of Managers. And this bank's board, based on the Deed, could only select those Managers from a very small pool of candidates: themselves!

So the two self-perpetuating and interlocking boards—one for the Hershey Trust Company as financial fiduciary for the orphanage's assets, and the second for the orphanage's administration —were composed of the same men, headed by Milton Hershey. The highly contrived charitable scheme, with near total power over the organization aggregated in the board of the for-profit Hershey Trust Company, still exists today.

Before 1918, Hershey ran his companies as any other private businessman would, and privately bankrolled the Hershey Industrial School. After 1918, Hershey ran his businesses as a fiduciary for the orphanage, whose teenage students lived on what had been his dairy farms and milked what had been his cows. Now those dairy farms and cows were part of the orphanage trust that Milton Hershey controlled through the dictates in the 1909 Deed. Profits from the Hershey businesses rolled into the Hershey Trust Company. Milton Hershey dispersed the profits to the orphanage, or to his businesses as capital.

Hershey's organization was unique in American industry, with for-profit businesses hitched directly to a charity—an arrangement that mostly likely would be rejected today by the Internal Revenue Service. The convoluted structure drew the attention of the IRS even then. It was only in the early 1920s, after several years of investigation, that the IRS approved Milton Hershey's charitable donation of his companies and land to the Hershey Industrial School. Over time, the fiduciary marriage of the Hershey companies and the charity would be the source of problematic deals and conflicts of interest, and the sources of mismanagement and scandal.

At the time, though, it appeared to the public as an act of corporate generosity of historic proportions. The *New York Times* splashed Hershey's story on its front page on November 9, 1923 with the headline, "M.S. Hershey Gives $60,000,000 Trust for An Orphanage," adding, "Pennsylvania Chocolate Manufacturer Transfers His Entire Wealth." The orphanage at this time was mostly a collection of dairy farms with about a hundred boys who attended public high school.

Hershey told the newspaper of his plans and philosophy in a lengthy feature published on November 18: "I am 66 years old and I do not need much money. My business has been far more successful than I ever expected it to be. If I should drop out, what would become of the business, the capital, the earnings? As matters have been arranged, the business will go right on, a considerable part of the profits to be used for the Hershey Industrial School. The capital, of course, remains intact. Well, I have no heirs—that is, no children. So I decided to make the orphan boys of the United States my heirs. The orphan boy has a harder time than anybody else, you know. There are always relatives or outsiders to take an orphan girl. Girls are useful in the home and people are glad to get them. But boys are likely to be looked upon as a nuisance."

Hershey continued: "Our boys are our finest possession. With them must rest the realization of all those high hopes held by this generation. They are the future itself, growing up before our eyes. And we do not give them the kind of care they should have. Often we hear it said that 'children are not what they used to be.' Well, I have an idea the children are just about what they always have been. Sometimes I wonder if the parents are not different. The biggest influence in a boy's life is what his dad does. He watches him at the dinner table, going off to work, coming home. He knows exactly his dad's way of life and most of his thoughts. When his dad is a fine, brave man, bearing his part of the struggle like man should, the boy is going to be the same sort of man. But if his dad happens to be shiftless or mean or weak, the boy at his side is shaped the same way. Every boy, good or bad, high or low, feels that his dad is the model of life he should follow. I wish every dad could get that idea into his mind and see what it would do for him. And when a boy doesn't happen to have any sort of dad he is a special mark for destiny. I am afraid that most of our orphan boys have a bad time of it and that many never get the right start. They tell me that the youngsters who go to prison never had a chance. Well, I am going to give some of them a chance, in my way."

The story was a marketing coup for the Hershey chocolate brand, now associated with orphans and philanthropy. Neither the *New York Times* nor the other newspapers reported on the complex of interconnected boards that allowed Milton Hershey to retain control of his companies and industrial school. The *New York Times* also didn't mention the indenturing practice. Some of the boys—who are now very old men—say their indentures weren't mentioned by houseparents or teachers. Some of the boys didn't even know of the indentures until many years later when they heard of the contents of the 1909 Deed. School officials told the boys that the farm chores taught them responsibility and a good work ethic.

Inevitably there were whispers of cheap labor. Through the first decades of the 20th century, child-care advocates sought to end the persistent indenturing of charity case children. The U.S. Children's Bureau, headed by child-labor activist Grace Abbott, noted that Pennsylvania was one of only a few remaining states to allow indenturing. These children typically worked off the cost of their care through their indentures.

A March 1926 article by Raymond Clapper of United News, headlined "Child Indenture Brought Out in Bureau Report," said some indentured children were virtual servants. "The underlying principle of all these laws which are inherited from the enlightened days of Henry VIII," Clapper wrote, "is that a farmer or housewife can obtain cheap help by supplying board and room to indentured children."

In Wisconsin, a bureau agent observed an indentured 12-year-old girl who helped care for three children, prepared meals and milked five or six cows a day. But "the man who had her under contract told the federal investigator 'he would not take another child unless I can get one young enough so I can break them into work.'"

The report mentioned an unidentified Pennsylvania County where the Bureau found children who "are under indenture contracts that keep them virtual peons until 1938 or 1940." The orphan boys at the Hershey Industrial School would remain indentured through the early 1950s.

2

BOYS ON THE FARM

The Depression

"I was old enough to realize that one less mouth to feed would be good for the family." —ALUMNUS JOHN "MAC" AICHELE

HE CIGAR-CHOMPING Milton Hershey, short, stout and ruddy-faced, witnessed the heyday of his orphanage in the Depression of the 1930s.
Cars brought boys by the hundreds to the Hershey Industrial School from Baltimore, Philadelphia, Scranton, and Pennsylvania's coal-mining and mill towns. Nurses examined each one, and admitted the healthy ones. The school officials sent the mothers away and banned visits for a month. Boys bawled in kitchens, or bedrooms, or swinging on swings when the reality sunk in: they'd be separated from brothers and sisters, grandmothers and grandfathers, aunts and uncles. Single Mennonite women looked after the younger boys in group homes with as many as 30 boys, and married couples looked after the older boys on working farms.

Hershey constructed homes or bought new ones to keep up with the greatly increased need. Hershey's pace quickened as banks and factories closed in the Depression's economic vise-grip. The Pinehurst home opened in February 1931, and that year a small group of thankful Home Boy alumni held their first formal banquet in the Walnut Room of the Hershey-owned Cocoa Inn.

Hershey added the Willow Wood home on Crest Lane in September 1931 and Cloverdale, at the intersection of Meadow Lane and U.S. 322, in November. Broad Acres opened in January 1932 and Bloomingdale in May. Men-O, named after a distant cousin, opened in September. There were now 464 orphan boys enrolled at the school.

The number of orphans in American orphanages hit a high of 144,000 in 1933; an additional 150,000 children roamed cities and small towns as homeless vagrants. Well over 10 million Americans were out of work. The unemployment rate in Detroit, Cleveland and other industrial cities approached 50 percent. The Dow Jones Industrial Average hit a high of 386 on September 3, 1929 and then dropped like a rock. It bottomed out at 41 on July 8, 1932, having lost 90 percent of its value. Frank Walker, president of the National Emergency Council, captured the nation's mood when he observed of the nation's economic calamity, "I saw old friends of mine—men I had been to school with—digging ditches and laying sewer pipe. They were wearing their regular business suits as they worked because they couldn't afford overalls and rubber boots. If ever I thought, 'There, but for the grace of God'—it was right then."

Milton Hershey opened the Silverbrook and Longmeads homes in early 1933, then Maple Lawn, followed by Midvale, followed by Arcadia, Englewood, and Venice. That year, Hershey also responded to this massive crisis of need by expanding the potential applicant pool, when he raised the maximum age for admission from eight to fourteen. Hershey also opened the institution to boys whose mothers had died, though he preserved his racial and gender restrictions—no black orphan boys and no girls. That fall of 1933, there were 604 boys at the school, double the number of 1930.

The boys of the Milton Hershey Industrial School had been attending public high school. Now Milton Hershey financed the construction of Senior Hall, spending $2.5 million so that the orphan boys on his farms could be educated separately from the public school children. A trolley transported the boys from their group homes, up the hill and directly into the school, which had such unheard of amenities as an indoor swimming pool. Robert Evans, a '32 graduate, penned the school's alma mater to the tune of *Anchors Aweigh*. The expansion continued through the eve of World War II, when in 1939 enrollment hit 1,018.

The school and orphanage ran like a clock during these years: a self-sustaining village of farms, orchards, dairy herds, trade school and commercial kitchen. School staff assigned each teenage boy a Hershey-owned farm and cow, or cows, to milk. By now there were more than ninety farms with names and numbers such as Broad Acres (1), Arcadia (20), Oakleigh (38), Bonniemead (50) and Rolling Green (61).

Younger boys lived in family-like group homes near town. They were looked after by Mennonite women. The boys played outside on sunny days, and in the basements on rainy ones. Sherwin Brady recalls the separate kitchen building located near the junior homes. When the housemothers finished, they called out, "Carry the cans!" Boys dropped their baseball bats or jumped off swings and ran to hoist metal cans of fruits and vegetables to a storage basement.

The teenage boys milked before school, and after school. "Three [cows] in the morning, and three [cows] in the afternoon," one told me in an interview. A truck picked up the milk and transported it to the Hershey Dairy. Home Boys shoveled manure, cut hay, washed Sunday dishes and polished silverware. Some farms were two or three miles from school. Boys couldn't be late for milking. A Home Boy who was late for milking had to run, his arms and legs pumping, along a country road to get there on time.

John "Mac" Aichele enrolled in 1935. "You know you weren't allowed family visits for a month. And when my mother came to see me, I cried like a baby and mother said, 'I'll take you home.' But I said no. I was old enough to realize that one less mouth to feed would be good for the family."

Charles Bofinger lost his father on the railroad. Bofinger's two brothers had gotten into Girard College, the Philadelphia trade school and orphanage that Hershey used as a model for his charity. He couldn't. It was Hershey for him. "Our neighbors had a car, and it was the first time I was in a car. Then when we got near Hershey I saw all these farms." Charles was checked over by a nurse. "My mother was there and she said 'Take care of yourself,' and she said, 'Goodbye,' and that was it." That was 1936. He estimated that during his childhood in Hershey he milked 13,000 cows on Hershey farms.

Philip DiPietro's father had choked on mustard gas in the World War I battle trenches and, with weakened lungs, later died of tuberculosis. Philip rebelled at home; one day he punched a kid in his Reading neighborhood. He sprinted into the street to get away without looking, and got sideswiped by a car. In 1929, his family dropped him off on the front porch of the Hershey School, DiPietro remembered. "That was about it. Miss Barker came out and took charge."

His mom remarried and seemed to forget about him. Philip thought all kids were raised in an orphanage. He slept in a small room, "the size of a closet" with no roommate because he had trouble getting along with other boys. "Everyone was on the farm working their ass off. We had cows. We had mules. We had to carry a lot of shit." Milton Hershey checked on the Midvale farm and the other farms during unplanned visits. "He stayed for a few minutes and smoked his cigar through the hallways," said DiPietro, who graduated in 1940. "It was fragrant. Cuban."

Ken Brady's father Frank had been a traveling salesman. He died in 1929 at age 36, wasting away from terminal cancer in a row home in West Baltimore. Ken was seven years old at the time. He has two recollections of his dad: a joyful day trip to the centennial celebration of the B&O Railroad in 1927, and visiting him as he lay dying in a curtain-drawn second-floor bedroom. The cancer drained the family's savings, and the widowed Elsie abandoned the row house for a two-bedroom apartment. Relatives helped out with food. A grainy picture at the time shows five older Brady children: the eldest girl, Flordrid, dressed in a white tunic dress, with her hair styled in a flapper bob, standing in a confident, hands-on-hips pose. Beside her was Ken in knickers. Next in line was a hatless Sherwin; then Frank in a striped tie and jacket, and, finally, Jeanette in a white poncho.

The December after Frank Brady's death, Ken's Aunt Irene and Uncle Walter drove Ken and his brothers north into Pennsylvania. The humming Model A crossed the Susquehanna River and speeded into Hershey. Snow covered the barns and farm fields. Ken wouldn't forget the date: December 9th. "When we got to the home, they left us very quickly," said Brady of his aunt, uncle and mother. "I really didn't give it much thought. It was such a change of life, going from a family to the industrial school. Some boys missed their mothers and cried, but I didn't. We really didn't have a home to go back to." Brady, who graduated in 1940, says of the farm work in his teen years, "I just took it as a form of life and I did it. It was a pleasure if you got a cow who gave a lot of milk. We were always assigned the same cow. If you were assigned cow No. 32, you always got No. 32. When the cow stopped giving milk you got a new one. The ones that just had heifers always gave the most and you wanted one of those. It was a thrill to fill the bucket. It was routine if you had half a bucket. I have no idea whether the farms made much money. But they kept us busy."

Teenage boys worked hard on the farms, but there also was time for them to entertain themselves. One Hershey Industrial School alumnus wrote a letter to me of his memories, still vivid after many decades: "One I have is of Saturday morning barn cleanup. There was a track system with suspended carts that were used to carry the manure from the barn to the pit where it was accumulated until it could be spread on the fields. After cleaning the cart of manure, someone would get into the car and others would give it a strong push so it would sail out of the barn, turn the curve over the pit, and if lucky, be able to be pulled back," so the boy in the car could disembark. "The less fortunate would make the curve and the cart would dump the 'passenger' into the manure pit! It was all in fun and all had many laughs.

"In the fall, there were hikes to the surrounding area to pick up hickory nuts or black walnuts. In the case of Men-O, the housemothers would bake cakes or cookies with nutmeats. At other times, the housefather would supervise the older boys in the making of homemade walnut ice cream. Another enjoyable event was making homemade root beer"—supervised by houseparents, who would oversee the home brew and help put it in bottles. "This we enjoyed at a Fourth of July bonfire along with hot dogs and other picnic stuff sent from the central kitchen."

IN THE MIDST of the Depression, Hershey spent millions of dollars—some estimate easily tens of millions of dollars—on construction for the town of Hershey with money from the orphanage trust. Most of this money came from profits at his Cuban sugar operations, which was now hugely successful.

The Hershey Park Golf Course and Clubhouse opened in July 1930. The next year, Hershey completed the luxuriously appointed Hershey Community Building, with its locker rooms, gymnasium, swimming pool, library, social room, two theaters, twelve classrooms, lodging for 125 men, hospital and nurse's quarters.

Hershey returned from a vacation in the Mediterranean with a postcard of a 35-room hotel, and told his builder, D. Paul Witmer, "I like this hotel; I want you to build one just like it on top of the hill." Only he didn't want a 30-room hotel. He wanted a 200-room hotel, but settled for 150 rooms. The Moorish-themed Hotel Hershey opened in May 1933 with a circular dining room so that everyone had the same panoramic view of the Lebanon Valley. The just-built Hershey Community Theater held its first performance several months later, on September 1, 1933, with New York stage revue acts. Milton opened Senior Hall, the junior-senior high school, in 1934. Hershey expanded his pet project, the Hershey Zoo, with a bird house.

Early on, Hershey set aside land for the Hershey amusement park as entertainment for local residents and a tourist attraction. It was unfenced, and people or Hershey School boys paid for individual rides. Many mothers of orphan boys met there during these hard economic years. The park drew tens of thousands of visitors a year, and was part of the orphanage trust. It would be transformed into HersheyPark in the 1960s and 1970s.

In 1935, the chocolate company opened a new office building on Chocolate Avenue—built with no windows, in order to maximize worker efficiency. That was one of Hershey's innovations that never caught on. The Hershey Sports Arena opened in late 1936, and the Hershey Gardens in 1937.

Hershey employed more than 6,000 workers in central Pennsylvania during the Depression. Some believed that Hershey spent so heavily to take advantage of Depression prices for construction materials and labor, creating large projects at low cost. This issue was still a sore spot in the 1990s, as revealed in a public talk on the Trust's history by Trust board member William Alexander. He drew the attention of his audience, a group of local officials, to the number of cars parked adjacent to the arena project in a photo from the 1930s, pointing them out as evidence of workers' relative prosperity. "Both Mr. Hershey and Mr. Witmer felt that skilled manpower should be paid a wage commensurate with the skill and talent that they brought to the project irrespective of the high unemployment rate in the country....These workers lived well as indicated by the quantity of cars in this picture."

The business magazine *Fortune* published an article in 1934 that praised Hershey's philanthropy, but raised concerns about his quasi-feudal sway over the town and its economy. The author's tone was biting: "On windless summer days the town of Hershey is permeated by what the Pennsylvania Dutch farmers of the neighborhood call 'da chockle shtink'—the sweetish, cloying smell of milk chocolate in the making. The moral atmosphere of the town is pervaded by a similar aroma—the sweet and oppressive odor of charity....To give too much outright saps a community's self-reliance and injures its pride. Not only has Mr. Hershey made gifts without inviting the cooperation of the town, but he also has kept control entirely in his hands. His school owns everything and his men, not the community's, manage everything....He has a strong will, the ego, and limitations of many another self-made man."

WITH ECONOMIC FORCES destabilizing the town, Hershey agreed with Derry Township public school officials that the town needed a junior college to keep jobless young men and women out of the pool halls, and off the streets. According to *The Rise and Demise of the Hershey Junior College* by Richard Russell Klotz, the number of two-year colleges in the United States rose by about one-third between the late 1930s and the mid-1960s, from 556 institutions to 719. Public schools or universities ran these institutions, which were similar to today's community colleges.

Hershey created a separate trust fund within the M.S. Hershey Foundation and endowed it with 5,000 shares of chocolate company stock to finance the Hershey Junior College. Because this new trust fund also was administered by the Hershey Trust Company, it also fell under his ultimate control—just like the orphanage trust. The M.S. Hershey Foundation had a separate board, and would share board members with the Board of Managers and the Hershey Trust Company board.

The idea of a junior college appealed to the practical, work-focused Hershey: a boy or girl could advance their education after high school at minimal costs, or they could earn credits toward a four-year degree. Hershey calmed concerns among the five area four-year colleges, telling them that the Hershey Junior College would be a "feeder school" for them and would send their institutions better-educated students.

The Hershey Junior College was free to Hershey boys or girls, though they would pay $25 to $40 in books and supplies. Because it was a commuter school, students didn't board there and could pursue academic, business administration and secretarial, or industrial studies. The initial plan called for nine faculty members, with classes held in the Hershey Community Building.

The local public school superintendent J.I. Baugher explained the mission in the *Hotel Hershey High-Lights* in June 1938: "Mr. Hershey, in keeping with the needs of the time, feels that it becomes the duty of communities to provide profitable employment for our young people, that if industry has no work for them until they become 18, 19 or 20 years of age, then education of a realistic and practical nature must fill the gap."

On September 14, 1938, Milton Hershey and others attended the opening day ceremonies for the Hershey Junior College in the Little Theater in the Hershey Community Building. There had been some jitters about how it would go off. Hershey residents seemed skeptical that the institution would open. Posters advertised the opening of the junior college, and registration hours were extended from eight in the morning to eight at night for shift chocolate factory workers, because few people had pre-registered. But by late September, the official registrar's tally showed 66 full-time and 65 part-time students—more than 120, and higher than expectations. Milton Hershey, a fourth-grade dropout, now was financing two educational institutions with his chocolate profits: the Hershey Industrial School and the Hershey Junior College. As the nation descended into World War II and Milton Hershey himself into old age, the Hershey Junior College would be Hershey's last big new charitable project

EARLY ON, Hershey had held all his assets under one umbrella: the chocolate company. But as the chocolate company became hugely profitable, and its activities diversified, this became economically inefficient. In 1927, Hershey attempted to divide the holdings optimally by separating his business empire into chocolate and non-chocolate entities. He incorporated the non-chocolate entities in the nearby town of Lebanon, as Hershey Estates. The companies within Hershey Estates included the Cuban sugar operations, the Pennsylvania farms, Hershey Abattoir (Hershey Meats), Hershey Baking Company, Hershey Cold Storage, Hershey Community Inn, Hershey Country Club, Hershey Dairy, Hershey Department Store, Hershey Feed and Grain, Hershey Farming Implements, Hershey Greenhouse and Nursery, Hershey Laundry, the Hershey amusement park, Hershey Sewerage Company, Hershey Telephone Company, Hershey Transit Company and the Hotel Hershey. These would remain privately owned by the Trust.

Milton Hershey then sold shares in the chocolate company to Wall Street investors in an initial public offering, or IPO, in 1927. The company had just introduced pourable Hershey syrup as well as the popular Mr. Goodbar, and the twenties economic boom had jazzed stock market valuations to a historic peak. The Trust retained majority voting control of the chocolate company.

In 1929, Hershey negotiated a three-way merger with Kraft Cheese and Colgate-Palmolive. The new consumer products company would be called International Products Corporation, and would be capitalized with $100 million in a first round of financing. Hershey's orphanage would own 40 percent of International Products. Sixty percent of the ownership would be split evenly between Kraft Cheese and Colgate-Palmolive shareholders.

Local residents feared that Milton Hershey would lose control of the chocolate company. But Hershey withheld ownership of the Cuban sugar operations, then valued at $70 million. At the time, Hershey considered himself a tycoon in two industries: sugar and chocolate. Hershey Cuba efficiently produced sugar for export not only to Hershey Chocolate, but also to Coca-Cola and other U.S. corporations. The business owned Cuban National Railway Bonds and traded tobacco, mahogany, hemp and cocoa. Ships transported Hershey sugar to the United States, and Pennsylvania anthracite coal to Cuba. During a second round of financing for International Products, Hershey could borrow against the Cuban operation to raise the funds to acquire 55 percent majority control of International Products. The deal was reminiscent of Hershey's sale of his caramel company in 1900, when he'd retained his chocolate division and then negotiated a chocolate supplier agreement with

American Caramel. Hershey circulated the papers for the three-way merger on October 28, 1929. The stock market crashed the next day.

The nation's economy was about to descend into the Depression. The International Products deal fell apart. Thousands of companies went bankrupt in the hard times that followed, but the chocolate company with its five-cent chocolate bars wasn't one of them. Hershey officials also began using the orphanage to cast its commercial dealings in a better light. Two events show how Hershey's charitable venture was wielded to throw a cloak of legitimacy over the company's activities. When federal regulators proposed new rules that could harm Hershey's Cuban sugar operations, Hershey executive and confidante Percy Alexander "P.A." Staples testified in August 1933 before the Agricultural Adjustment Administration, saying, "The Hershey Corporation is an American corporation, completely owned and controlled in the United States and held in trust as part of the endowment in a fund which Mr. Milton S. Hershey, of Hershey, Pa., has established for the maintenance and education of orphan boys, and we are asking that this juvenile group of American stockholders be not discriminated against in favor of any group of American stockholders as proposed by in this tentative draft of Proposed Marketing Agreement." Staples' comments weren't totally accurate: the orphan boys themselves may have benefitted from Hershey's corporate entities, but they had no direct ownership in the companies.

At the chocolate plant, labor activist chocolate worker Russell "Bull" Behman waved a red handkerchief on April 2, 1937, and fellow chocolate workers joined him in sit-down in the plant. A pro-company, anti-union flyer distributed to the community framed the sit-down strike as an insult to Milton Hershey, declaring in bold lettering:

SIT-DOWN IS A STRIKE AGAINST ORPHAN BOYS
AIMS OF M. S. HERSHEY WHO BROUGHT HIS COMMUNITY
THROUGH THE DEPRESSION WITHOUT A SLUMP BASED ON
LONG-TERM PLAN—GAVE ENTIRE WEALTH FOR
BENEFIT OF ORPHANS

The flyer praised Milton Hershey's "metropolitan air." "Today, this 79-year-old gentleman, as president of the Hershey Trust Company, is watching every dollar spent for the happiness and contentment of the people of Hershey.... Hershey was the only town in America that the wolf of depression did not enter after the colossal crash of the stock market in

November 1929. More than 6,000 people were employed between the chocolate plant and Hershey Estates, workers coming from Palmyra, Swatara, Hummelstown, Annville, Campbelltown, Elizabethtown, Middletown, Lebanon, and other towns within a radius of 15 miles." It concluded: "He is working to benefit the community, and a sit-down strike is really a sit-down strike against the orphan boys he is educating."

The strike ended violently in mid-April when an antiunion crowd of about three thousand, armed with baseball bats, pitchforks and lead pipes, stormed the factory and beat some of the striking workers. Some say Milton Hershey aged overnight: in his paternalistic worldview, he must have felt the workers' strike as a personal betrayal.

HERSHEY'S PRESENCE loomed over the orphan boys of the Hershey Industrial School. Alumni with whom I spoke still have vivid memories of the man from the 1930s and 1940s, conjuring the chocolate magnate driving around town with a nurse or chauffeur, handing out diplomas, visiting student homes and attending sporting events.

Ralph Wolf, who was 92 years old in 2012, remembered meeting Milton Hershey several times, and reported the older man's exact words to him as he graduated in 1937: "You did a good job, Ralph." Wolf emphasized his own name in a baritone voice. Wolf received his diploma two months early in 1937 to take a job in a Lancaster machine shop. "How do you like them bucket of apples?" Wolf asked, savoring the memory. He laughed and then repeated his impersonation of Mr. Hershey: "You did a good job, Ralph."

Levi Filepas was eight years old when a car pulled up outside his student home. He and other boys were playing baseball. Milton Hershey sat in the back seat and asked if they'd like a ride. "We all packed in the car." They drove several miles to Erb's Corner at Route 322 near the Masonic Hall, and then returned to the ball field.

Another time, Hershey walked into the gym in Senior Hall during a basketball game. Filepas was sitting near the scoring table, and jumped up to make room for him. "I thought it was the right thing to do," he said. "He took me and my brothers out of real poverty." Before Filepas came to the Hershey School, life had been hard: his mother Vera had died of pneumonia and dad Obrad lost his job at Bethlehem Steel in Lebanon during the Depression. Some nights, Levi and brothers George and Michael shared a can of beans for dinner. "We burned our furniture to keep warm."

Ralph Hetrick and Artie Jugel had been walking down Homestead Road when the big blue-gray car pulled up ahead of them, and they ran to catch up. A nurse was driving. She asked if they wanted a ride. Jugel opened one back door and Hetrick opened the other. An old man shifted his seat to the center to allow room. "He had on that homburg hat, that's how I knew it was Milton Hershey," Hetrick said. They chatted about the afternoon's football game. Hetrick was fired up over losing. "I was put out about it but Mr. Hershey said, 'Oh, that's just a game.'" Hershey's nurse drove them part of the way to Bonniemead, and they walked the last mile.

Around Christmas, Hetrick and other glee club boys caroled downtown. "We would stop at a corner we thought was good and we would sing," said Hetrick, who graduated in 1947. "It was softly snowing. It was beautiful. People would stop and listen. We might have walked that night two or three miles around town." The orphan boys sang traditional Christian holiday songs: "Hark! The Herald Angels Sing," "Silent Night"—no "Jingle Bells" or other pop culture holiday songs. Director Jay Atlee Young suggested they sing for Milton Hershey at his High Point mansion. Hershey looked down on them from the second floor, wearing his smoking jacket.

Hershey's death in October 1945 didn't come as a surprise. He was 88 years old, and failing. He became mischievous in his older years. He played pranks and didn't listen to his nurses. He drank champagne and ate caviar. "He would fiddle around for two hours finding excuses not to go to bed," one of his nurses, Susan Spangler, was quoted as saying in D'Antonio's biography. He'd turn up the brim of his hat like a Vaudeville comedian. "He looked like a man without a cent," Spangler said. School officials told the boys that whatever happened they could continue their studies, because Milton Hershey had provided for them. "I heard the church bells" that rang when Hershey died, said William Weaver of Lock Haven, one of Hershey's orphan boys. "We were out in the field making corn. We knew what happened. We stopped and we walked back to the farm."

Others heard of Milton Hershey's death on a Boy Scout hiking trip or from houseparents. The news bounced around the globe on radio. On the liberty ship SS Carl Schurz, which was ferrying troops between the Aleutian Islands and Seattle, Ralph Boettger awoke in his bunk to the radio. "They said Hershey, Pa., and I knew right away it was an announcement of Milton Hershey's death because I knew how old he was. I think it was October 13," said Boettger, who himself was then 88 years old.

Stationed at the Chanute Air Force Base south of Chicago, Levi Filepas asked for emergency leave from his commanding officer. Filepas walked and hitchhiked to Central Pennsylvania. "I was in a cattle truck in the beginning and, boy, did that stink. And then I got a ride with a Navy ensign who was going to New England, and he picked me up."

Principal W. Allen Hammond told the boys at the memorial service that Hershey was "practical idealist" who lived by the Golden Rule. "The greatest example of his practical idealism can be seen in his financial success and what he did with his wealth. You know the story. You are living characters on his stage. Actors will come and go throughout the years. You need not pack up and leave now that he is dead, because he has made provision in his will to care for you and to give you training for life." The Reverend John H. Treder of the All Saints Episcopal Church eulogized at Milton Hershey's funeral ceremony attended by state officials, community leaders and friends in the big high school he built for his orphans and near the luxury Hotel Hershey: "Today we are gathered in this school room on a Pennsylvania hillside in tribute to a man, who by God's grace was brought to his spot, somehow to build this community....When Mr. Hershey began to reap his harvests here he left not only the forgotten sheaf in the field for the father-less; he gave not only the first fruits to God, but virtually all the sheaves; and the lives of hundreds of boys who have passed through these halls; they are the great monument that has been reared and that will go on abuilding as others come from broken houses into the care and guidance of the school." The boys' choir sang A.H. Malotte's "Lord's Prayer" and Bach's "Come Now, Sweet Death," the young male voices wafting in the hushed auditorium.

Once over, the casket was wheeled off the auditorium stage to a car that would carry Hershey's body to his cemetery to lie near his wife Kitty, his parents Fanny and Henry, his longtime attorney John Snyder, and his other confidants.

At the Sunset farm, Elwood Scheib had learned several days before Milton Hershey's funeral that he'd be one of eight pallbearers. He didn't and still doesn't know how the school chose him, but he was nervous. "It was clear day because when we made the turn off Route 743, we could see all the way to the high school. And when we looked back we could see the cars leaving the school parking lot and we were already at the cemetery," said Scheib, then 82 years old. "We were in a limousine. Everybody was pretty serious. There was no goofing around." At the cemetery, the farm-hardened boys shouldered the casket and solemnly walked to the gravesite.

3

POST-MILTON

"What We Know" and "How We Feel"

N OCTOBER 1944, anticipating the need for a successor, Milton Hershey picked Percy Alexander "P.A." Staples to lead the organization, with its novel combination of for-profit businesses and an orphan charity. Hershey died the following year at the age of 88. Staples, trained as a utility engineer, had successfully reorganized Hershey's money-losing Cuban sugar properties in the early 1920s. When he was done, the 60,000-acre complex of railroad lines, cane-growing fields and refining facilities produced three times more sugar than Milton Hershey needed for the Chocolate Avenue chocolate factory. Hershey rewarded Staples by appointing him to a succession of Trust-related boards: the chocolate company in 1927, Hershey Estates in 1929, and the Hershey Trust Company in 1930. As a member of the Hershey Trust Company board, Staples automatically qualified for the school's Board of Managers.

Still, it was a surprising choice. Many had believed that Hershey would tap William Murrie, who at the time of Hershey's death was president of the chocolate company. Hershey had hired Murrie, a former telegraph operator, as a salesman back when he still ran the Lancaster Caramel Company in the late 1890s. Murrie sold 200 barrels of chocolate in his first week; he was soon promoted to general manager. Murrie was a character who lived big. He owned the biggest mansion on East Chocolate Avenue. A chauffeured Packard Roadster transported him daily the 150 yards between the mansion and the chocolate plant; he got there punctually to watch employees streaming inside. He spoke like a character out of Sinclair Lewis' classic novel *Babbitt*: Money was "dough" and the government "that outfit." When offered the opinion "the Hershey bar doesn't taste like it used to," Murrie dismissed the criticism, replying, "It never did." When a Catholic official told Murrie he should show favoritism and hire Catholics, Murrie reportedly blurted, "Father, I'm running a business here, not a charity." Murrie had grown sales to more than $100 million a year by the mid-1940s, though a significant portion of it was low-margin bulk product. But Murrie was getting old, and his prospects for leading the company were not helped when his son Bruce began working with a competitor, the Mars Candy Company, launching the popular M&M's with rationed chocolate during World War II (M&M stands for Mars and Murrie).

P.A. Staples had a different personality. He was a workaholic with little taste for ostentation. Having worked for years in Cuba, he now lived with his wife in rented rooms at the Hotel Hershey. He was devoted to Milton Hershey, and printed a heartfelt tribute to his former boss after Hershey's death, in *The School Industrialist*: "Central Hershey, Cuba is as great a monument to his creative ability, his sense of orderliness, and his concern for a well-rounded economy as is Hershey, Pennsylvania, which most of us know so much more intimately. There he opened and made proper a vast undeveloped area by the construction of a railroad and the creation of many industries. Thus he developed in Cuba the same type of contribution to well-ordered living as he has in the United States."

But Staples wasn't a sentimental businessman man. A year after he took over, Staples sold the Hershey Cuba operation for about $30 million, seeking to diversify the Trust's assets and fearing political unrest. Cuban-Atlantic Sugar Company bought the giant sugar operation, and two Hershey representatives joined the Cuban-Atlantic board. The money was redirected to the orphanage trust. What had been the Hershey's sugar operations were later nationalized under Castro's Communist regime. Staples also closed the Hershey Estates-owned trolley lines, and fretted over post-World War II spikes in cocoa bean prices.

The number of boys at the Hershey Industrial School had fallen to 620 in 1945 from the all-time high of 1,018 boys in 1939 because of wartime rationing, which made it hard to feed so many children, and World War II-related labor issues. Yet at the same time, the Trust was rolling in cash— millions of surplus dollars—because of Hershey Chocolate's wartime contracts to supply the Army's ration D bar, the Emergency Accessory Packet, the 10-in-1 ration, K-ration and C-ration. By 1945, the company's three pro-duction lines manufactured around-the-clock a total of 24 million ration units a week. With the Japanese and German surrender, Staples swung open the doors of the orphanage in the mid-1940s, attempting to renew the orga-nization's commitment to the dictates of Milton and Kitty's 1909 Deed of Trust. By 1950, the Hershey Industrial School's enrollment had grown to match the late 1930's levels, and four more group homes were opened.

In 1951, the Trust filed with the Orphans' Court for its first Deed modi-fication. It was a modest one: to change the school's name, from the Hershey Industrial School to the Milton Hershey School. When Milton and Kitty first started the school, it was one of about 50 such industrial and manu-al training schools in the country: a 1908 directory listed similar schools including the Manual Training and Industrial School in Bordentown, New Jersey; the Charles N. Schwab Manual Training School in Homestead, Pennsylvania; Girard College in Philadelphia; South End Industrial School in Roxbury, Massachusetts, and the State Normal and Industrial School in Ellendale, North Dakota. But by the 1940s and 1950s, the term industrial school carried associations to a reform school for delinquents, an impres-sion that the Trust wanted to avoid.

About the same time, the Trust also ended indenturing—although this was done without seeking court approval. Without a court filing, there was no discussion as to why the Trust had indentured orphan boys through the 1930s and 1940s. The indenturing language remained in the Deed until 1970.

Trust law goes back centuries. It's meant to allow someone to transfer wealth to a beneficiary or beneficiaries. A private trust benefits a specif-ic person or charitable entity. A charitable trust benefits a class of similar individuals such as the blind, or members of a religious order. The Hershey Trust was a charitable trust benefitting fatherless boy orphans. The individ-uals who comprised the Trust's interlocking boards—one for the Hershey Trust Company and the second for the school's Board of Managers—had day-to-day decision-making control of the organization, along with the responsibility to preserve the Hersheys' financial estate for current and future beneficiaries. The 1909 Deed was considered the roadmap for how to spend Milton Hershey's estate assets.

The government had oversight and regulatory powers—as it would other similar charitable entities—through the attorney general and the Coun-ty-level Orphans' Court. But those powers were minimally defined, and the attorney general or the court could be expected to interfere only in case of serious disagreements or evidence of malfeasance. Generally, Trust leaders had to demonstrate that the organization was fulfilling its charitable mission of helping orphans without wasting assets or self-dealing. Minor issues, such as the change of the school's name, could be dealt with administratively between the Trust and Orphans' Court. If the Trust believed it needed to radically alter Hershey's 1909 Deed because of a so-called charitable failure, it would file a *cy-près* petition, which allows the courts to amend the terms of a charitable trust while staying as close as possible to the original intention of the testator to prevent the trust from failing. As we will see, more major modifications would be undertaken, and in some cases imposed on the Trust in future years.

Going along with the name change, School administrators undertook a makeover of the school, including buying black-and-white TVs for the student homes in the early 1950s and distributing brochures describing life there as "country living—family style—amidst the foothills of the Blue Ridge Mountains." Boys were expected to remain at the institution through childhood, with the school taking responsibility for their education, health care, lodging and clothing. Family could visit monthly. Boys had a two-week summer vacation. They trained for blue-collar jobs, but with good grades and academic aptitude, could qualify for scholarships to go to the Hershey Junior College.

The 90-page *Guide for House Parents*, published in the late 1940s or early 1950s, contained a campus map and organizational chart. It explained terms of employment for houseparents, the boys' lives at the school, and the institution's philosophy. "Realizing day by day the substitution of *synthetic love for genuine parental love* is a difficult task, we are editing this booklet with the hope that you will study same carefully and be guided by its contents," the guide began. "We have advanced far enough in the field of experience to know that our farm-home life is a success and fulfills Mr. M.S. Hershey's idea which was to replace the old-fashioned cooperative family of bygone days."

Housefathers could be called for help during harvest season. Housemothers canned fruits and vegetables for the orphanage's consumption. But their most important responsibilities were teaching orphan boys honesty, integrity, fair play and social skills. The guide instructed boys on how to remove floor wax, what to wear, and how many minutes it should take to walk here or there. Even dinner had rigid order. According to the guide's section on Minimum Standard Table Etiquette:

All boys should be seated at the table at the same time.

Boys should leave the dining room in individual table groups.

Dishes should be started at the head of the table and passed to the right.

Slices of bread should be broken prior to spreading and eating.

When eating soup, the spoon should be dipped away from the eater.

The knife should be placed across the plate after use.

Napkins are to be used at each meal and boys should place them across their laps.

Elbows should be kept off the table.

Meals should not be eaten in a hurry.

Congenial conversation should be carried on at each meal, but boisterousness should be avoided.

Knife, fork and spoon should be placed in parallel in the center of the plate when finished eating.

Everyone should begin eating dessert at the same time.

Eating and chewing foods should be done in a quiet manner.

Pitchers should be passed with the handle toward the receiver.

It is always improper to dunk bread, cookies, etc. in liquids.

The fork, never the spoon, should be used in eating all foods from the plate, except in the Junior Division.

The makings of sandwiches at the table should be considered proper only when using cold sliced meats or cheese.

Leave the table during the meal only when absolutely necessary, and at such times ask to be excused.

On the day of his father's accident in 1948, Terry Wright remembers, his father had called him into the small living room of their home in the Ohio River town of Baden with a surprise gift: a Hershey chocolate bar. "Strange," Terry "Toe" Wright says today. That night, the rail car brakeman slipped at the Crucible Steel plant, and rail cars rolled over him. There was nothing left of him by the time they stopped the train.

Terry and his brothers Leon and Larry had no place to go after Crucible. "We were like trailer park trash. Nobody could take a lady and three kids. My aunts would keep me for a week or two and then I would go to a foster home. I was shoveled around. My brothers lived like vagrants. My mom's dad didn't want anything to do with her. He said, 'You made your bed.'"

Wright got to the Hershey Industrial School on September 7, 1949. He was four years old. They gave him his clothes in a laundry basket in the "Old Main" and assigned him and Larry, who was five years older, to the Evergreen student home. "I don't remember being homesick because so many things were going on and it was so new," Wright says. "I became institutionalized pretty quickly, basically."

He slept in the same bed every night, and ate three meals a day. He learned what was expected of him and he did it. He had what he needed, but there was little personal attention in a home with 30 boys. "Once a year you would get a cake for your birthday. They would send it with the meal," Wright says. "The housemother would slice it up, and you would get a slice. You would like more but you were just damn happy to get that cake." A Santa visited the student homes with the younger boys. They pulled at the pillow in his belly or kicked him in the shins.

The boys at Hershey called him "Toe" because he was from western Pennsylvania. His favorite team was the Cleveland Browns, and they had a kicker who kicked straight-on. The media called him Lou "The Toe" Groza.

The school was changing in the 1950s, Wright recalled. It was the Hershey Industrial School when he enrolled, and the Hershey School when he graduated. He didn't know his mother had signed an indenture: "The school didn't talk about indenturing. I never heard houseparents, teachers, other students, anybody, even talk about indenturing." Then someone sent him his indenture in the late 1990s to show him what it said. "I said, holy shit." He thinks he might have been one of the last white boys indentured in America. Some boys Terry's older brother knew thought the farm work wasn't only about charity, but about cheap labor for the farms. Wright wouldn't go there: "One of Old Man Hershey's things was, he wanted to teach his boys respect for labor. There was nothing wrong with dignity of manual labor."

In the mid-1950s, the Hershey School opened an "intermediate division" for sixth, seventh and eighth graders. Those boys didn't have to board with teenagers who might bully them. Later in the 1950s, the school lightened the farm work load for the boys. Boys were getting hurt around the farm machinery, and child-labor laws were evolving.

A boy had to learn how to survive and what to expect at Hershey, Wright says. You didn't rat anybody out. You stood your ground. You did what you were told. Houseparents didn't hug you. Housefathers might hit you with belts or ping pong paddles. Some of the houseparents were nice, and some were sons of bitches. "If Old Man Hershey had understood it better," Wright says, "he would have provided more social workers or more psychologists."

Wright bounced around the Hershey campus. He lived, in addition to Evergreen, at the Habana, Meadowbrook, Cloverdale, Sunnybank and Sunset homes. Wright thought he should have more say in his life and he rebelled when he got tired of the bullshit. The school finally placed him in a home he liked. Early on, the housefather there told Wright to call him Berk; Wright told the housefather to call him Toe. They got along great. "We had guys who hated the school," Wright says, "but when they ran away, they had no place to go. I mean if you made it home, they would say to you, 'What the hell are you doing here?' and send you back. Then you had your houseparents mad at you, and the administrators mad at you."

When his mother Ethel remarried, she asked Terry to come home. Leon was graduating. Larry hated Hershey, and he did return home. Wright stayed in Hershey. "I told her I don't know any other lifestyle. I had done seven years and I had seven more to go. I did not relate to the outside world."

He graduated in 1963. He'd been there 14 years. His mother told him that Crucible Steel had promised her it would hire her sons because of their father's accident. But when Wright applied, a Crucible manager in a suit and tie told him he had to serve the military first. Wright enlisted in '64 and did his tour in 'Nam; he was discharged in '68. The GI bill paid for him to attend the University of North Carolina. He retired after several decades from the South Carolina Department of Corrections.

AS WRIGHT was growing up on Hershey's rural campus, the old-timers of the Hershey organization inevitably aged and retired one by one in the late 1940s and 1950s.

D. Paul Witmer had been hired as a draftsman in 1924. He designed and helped construct a gas-filling station and auto-repair shop with 75 garages and two apartments on West Chocolate Avenue. Milton Hershey appointed him in 1925 to run the Hershey Lumber Company that manufactured boxes to ship chocolate products, which in one year sawed about 13 million feet of poplar and gum. The lumber company later diversified into family furniture—drum tables, end tables and the like—sold through New York, Cleveland, Pittsburgh and Washington department stores. Witmer's biggest assignments came in the 1930s, heading construction projects worth millions of dollars. "When he wanted something, and many little things, I'd drop everything and take care of Mr. Hershey," Witmer said in an oral history for the Hershey Community Archives. "As soon as he was through, I'd go back again and get on with my job....He sort leaned on me."

Hershey was living in the Witmer-built Hotel Hershey on the hill overlooking his town when George Copenhaver died in 1938. Someone now had to run the orphanage and school. Hershey called the trusty lumber company manger for a talk in the hotel's mezzanine. He asked Witmer to step in and take over the school. Witmer recalled the winter day as cold and sunny. He didn't want to—he wasn't trained or prepared to run an institution educating and raising orphan boys. Hershey insisted, and after several months Witmer agreed. For more than a decade, he ran the lumber company and the orphan school. Witmer relinquished the school position in 1951, and retired from all his positions in the Hershey organization in 1959.

Earle Markley had trained as a machinist in the Williamson Trade School near Philadelphia, and taught vocational education in Hanover. Boys there alternated training for two weeks with studying for two weeks. During the summer of 1929, Copenhaver had called Markley for a job interview. They met in the Hershey Inn lobby and walked outside to talk with Milton Hershey in his chauffeured 12-cylinder Cadillac with Cuban license plates. The number of students was growing at the Hershey Industrial School, and Hershey believed he needed to offer the orphan boys more rigorous job training. Hershey asked Markley if he knew of a highly regarded trade school. Markley told Hershey of one in Merchantville in South Jersey. Hershey told him they'd go and visit it that day, and they hauled out of Hershey in the Cadillac. "We just went in," Markley said of the Merchantville school visit. "We didn't have a date. Why, those people treated Mr. Hershey like he was king, you know. They were very proud to have him."

The entourage returned to the Hershey Inn in the evening. Hershey asked, "Now, Mr. Markley, do you think you could get me a trade school?" Markley replied, "Mr. Hershey, if you give me a chance, I'll either do it or hang myself."

Markley purchased $45,000 worth of vocational equipment for a trade school program for the Derry Township public schools. When it opened, there were about eighty public school boys and ten to fifteen orphan boys who enrolled in it. Markley then executed a grander plan for the trade school program at Senior Hall for the orphan boys at the Hershey Industrial School, based on the one in Merchantville. Hershey "had it in his mind to teach the boys to work," Markley recalled. The trade school program taught the orphan boys one thing: "How to work and the value of working and knowing what production means, and I think we were doing a pretty good job." Markley ran the trade school program at Senior Hall through the 1930s and 1940s, even training women for factory engine work during World War II. He retired in 1958.

Hershey didn't speak with Markley of his aspirations for the boys, but would call him to the mansion for lunch to talk about the trade school program. "He had a certain cigar that he smoked, and he never smoked a different one," Markley said. "He always passed those out. In those days, I was smoking. I thoroughly enjoyed his cigars. And Mr. Copenhaver, he smoked cigars."

Hershey Industrial School principal W. Allen Hammond published a memoir, *A Man and His Boys*, in which he described a conversation between Clyde A. Lynch, president of Lebanon Valley College, and Milton Hershey during which Hershey disclosed to Lynch why he established the orphanage and trade school: "(1) he wanted the satisfaction of seeing how his money could do good while he was living and (2) he hoped that other men of wealth, seeing his project, might follow his example."

Hammond told of the Hershey Industrial School's ethos and policies with chapters titled "Education for Character," "Spirit," "What We Know," "How We Feel" and "What We Will." Farm work, household chores and sports forged the male character. Home, heredity and spirit were "three facets of the same gem of human personality. They are so inextricably tied up together and so fused into each other to make up an integrated person." The school frowned on shirkers and those with inflated egos. The vocational program over time had earned a national reputation, and companies recruited boys out of the classroom, Hammond wrote. "The fact is that a lazy boy is most unhappy at our school," said Hammond. He retired in 1959.

STAPLES WAS OBSESSED with running Hershey's businesses and orphan charity in the late 1940s and 1950s. He hadn't fit easily into the insular and clubby culture of Hershey, and insisted that Hershey Chocolate minimize low-margin commercial and bulk chocolate sales and concentrate on higher-margin retail sales with candy bars. He took work home with him, and worked in bed in the Hotel Hershey. On weekends, he worked at the Hershey Trust Company offices. Rumors swirled that Staples was thinking of selling the chocolate company to diversify the Hershey Industrial School's assets. He had appointed the first outsider to the chocolate company board, New York lawyer William Radebaugh. But Staples died unexpectedly in 1956, resulting in a broad reorganization of the Hershey entities.

The Trust publicly committed itself to Milton and Kitty's orphan-caring mission, but privately its businessmen leaders realized the institution had to be modernized. How? Who would decide? And what should the super-rich orphanage do with the tens of millions of dollars that it had banked from the sale of the Cuban sugar operation and operating surpluses?

The Trust appointed a three-person expert panel for ideas. Leading the panel was Leonard W. Mayo, who specialized over decades in the care of delinquents, orphans and crippled children. His father had been the director of the Berkshire Industrial Farm in Canaan, New York, and Mayo's first job out of Colby College was at the Opportunity Farm in the backwoods of Maine, which opened around the same time and was strikingly similar to the Hershey School.

Opportunity Farm founder F. Forrest Pease told the public of his project in the October 1911 edition of *Work with Boys*, published by the Federated Boys' Club in Massachusetts. He wrote: "I have moved on to a 10-acre farm in the town of New Gloucester, Maine. I call it 'Opportunity Farm.' I propose to train boys to be 'A No. 1' farm help and supply to a slight extent the great demand for intelligent farm help. Carpentry work, blacksmithing, and gas engineering will become strong departments in this boys' trade school. I will omit other details of my vision and get down to facts." The farm, with its six fireplaces, had room for 50 boys. Every boy had to come with clothes and return fare home.

Willard Wallace, a Wesleyan University history professor, described it in a memoir. "Opportunity Farm was a tightly organized institution and, to a large extent, self-sustaining," he wrote. "The larger and middle-sized boys carried on the barn and field work. In the winter they also felled trees for wood and sawed it into furnace and stove lengths, and kept the outside area of both farms orderly and clean—Mr. Mayo would not tolerate a lack of tidiness. The smaller boys, under the direction of Mrs. Mayo, were responsible for the housework. Although every boy made his own bed, the smaller boys washed and dried the dishes, and, in summer, helped with the weeding and the gardens, picking the peas, beans and berries, and husking corn."

Leonard Mayo then held jobs at the Maryland Training School for Boys outside Baltimore and the Children's Village in Dobb's Ferry. Over time, he helped shape U.S. policies on child welfare, mental retardation and physical disabilities. He served on four White House Conferences on Children and Youth from 1930 to 1960, and advised the Truman, Eisenhower, Kennedy, Johnson and Ford administrations. He attained such recognition for his expertise that the *New York Times* published his obituary at his death in 1992.

Frederick Allen was the director of the Child Guidance Clinic in Philadelphia, and chaired the board that certified child psychiatrists in the United States. A Trust official called him "the father of guidance centers." He was the second person appointed to the committee to evaluate the Hershey School's programs.

The third was Helen Hubbell, Pennsylvania's "Miss Child Welfare Social Worker."

The three individuals met with Hershey School officials and spoke with students, teachers and administrators. Their 105-page *Report of the Anniversary Committee in August 1960* concluded that there was still a place in society for the Hershey School, if it hired more staff, professionalized child-care delivery, and reconsidered admissions of very young boys.

Milton and Kitty Hershey had restricted enrollment to the orphanage in 1910 to white boys between the ages of four and eight years old. Fifty years later, the panel thought the institution should refocus admissions on boys between the ages of 10 and 14 years old. At this point, a huge body of research had shown that separating a young child from his mother would be painful and perhaps counterproductive, emotionally and psychologically, for the parent and child. Plus, state and federal welfare programs could keep those young families together at least for a few years. "It is the Committee's belief that almost any mother would and should hesitate to send a four- to eight-year-old into a boarding school situation. The twofold trauma of loss of a parent and separation from home can be an especially damaging experience for younger boys," they wrote. The Trust didn't embrace this recommendation then or later despite its continued difficulty finding mothers or fathers who would agree to part with their very young children and continued research indicating that separating a young child from a parent could be damaging to the child.

Mayo, Allen and Hubbell thought the Hershey School could offer subsidies to the parents of young boys. Those boys could relocate to the Hershey campus when they got older. The experts also thought the orphanage should be more flexible and allow family to visit in the first month to ease homesickness.

The report had a section titled "The Serious Overcrowding." The Hershey School's lodging was based on "cottage-style" homes with thirty boys. That was too many boys to a home. The institution should halve the ratio. This was so important, the panel believed, that the institution should halt new admissions until new homes could be opened and staffed. Maximum enrollment at the Hershey campus should be 1,500 boys, with perhaps an ideal level at 1,200.

Mayo, Allen and Hubbell believed the institution had to hire more counselors and professionals and review salary schedules to ensure "the employment of high-grade staff." The school had relieved housefathers of farm work, but also cut their pay. The panel indicated that this sent the wrong message to houseparents, who also now had long periods, 11 days, without a weekend break. It was too long. They unanimously told the panel they had to care for too many boys.

Despite grousing by students about the farm work, Mayo, Allen and Hubbell panel found that alumni universally praised the farm work that had been required of them as teens at the Hershey School, saying milking cows and the other chores had given them a sense of self-worth. Mayo, Allen and Hubbell also believed the Hershey School was remarkably patient in dealing with boys with sexual and other deviant behaviors. "The Committee is impressed with the desire to help these boys rather than discharge them. This attitude, while not universal, strikes us as one of the fine features of the Milton Hershey School. The absence of punitive attitudes toward 'deviant' boys lays such a fine foundation for helping him. As counseling services in the various forms are made more available, more of these troubled boys will be helped to overcome their difficulties."

Mayo, Allen and Hubbell thought the Hershey School could be a national institution for research into educating the economic underclass and boys with learning disabilities. It should hire a research director and affiliate with a major university in Philadelphia to direct research projects. "So many of these boys come to the Milton Hershey School with many educational deficits," the report noted. "Our public schools are being overwhelmed by the so-called slow learner. Many such, even with normal intelligence, are admitted here and these problems are detected in the orientation group. The opportunity for planned research on both the etiology and the correction of these deficits is available here."

The Trust embraced some of the ideas, and rejected others. The institution constructed many new student homes in the 1960s to ease the overcrowding. But it didn't raise the minimum age of boys who could be admitted, and it didn't affiliate with an independent researcher or university, even though the Hershey School's orphanage model deviated substantially from evolving mainstream child-care trends toward child adoptions and family-based foster care.

ON TV it looked like poverty had been licked in America in the 1950s, an era of traditional families, conformity, the baby boom, nukes, the Cold War and Ike's toothy smile. William J. Levitt perfected the concept of the planned suburban development. Tens of thousands visited his sample homes, which were later mass-produced and sold with 30-year mortgages.

Author Michael Harrington presented a different view of the nation with his best-seller, *The Other America: Poverty in the United States.* "Mr. Harrington estimates that between 40 and 50 million Americans, or about one-fourth of the population, are now living in poverty," wrote Dwight McDonald in a 14-page review of the book in the *New Yorker.* "Not just below the level of comfortable living, but real poverty, in the old fashioned sense of the word—that they are hard put to get the mere necessities, beginning with enough to eat."

Many of the nation's poor were now blacks in the South and Appalachian whites. And the seeds of future poverty were being sown. Blacks were migrating to the North for high-paying manufacturing jobs. But northern factories hiring them were closing, and production relocating to low-wage states in the South that were emptying of blacks. As the factories closed, northern cities became hollowed-out racial tinderboxes about to burst into flame with race riots.

How would the Trust—the nation's richest orphanage—respond to these social changes to help vulnerable children with its vast wealth?

4
LOOTING THE TRUST
A Political Deal to Divert Tens of Millions from Orphans

*"I could see the orphan population dwindling somewhat,
on the downgrade, and I began to wonder what Mr. Hershey
would do if he himself were living."*
—HERSHEY CHOCOLATE PRESIDENT SAM HINKLE

B Y 1962, the Milton Hershey's trust fund surplus had swelled to $96 million—the equivalent of $740 million today. The bulk of this massive surplus, $72 million, came from dividends or profits from the Hershey companies, with an additional $24 million earned by investing the $72 million into stocks and bonds.

How did this happen? The Trust had been building surpluses since the 1920s, as the company's profits piled up faster than the School could spend them. Then came the lucrative military contracts during World War II. Hershey made the Army's ration D bar, the Emergency Accessory Packet, 10-in-1 ration, K-ration and C-ration. The company's three production lines manufactured around-the-clock 24 million ration units a week by 1945. Profits gushed. In the 1950s and 1960s, strategies including diversification and focusing on the consumer market led to continued healthy profits and corresponding growth in the surplus.

The unusual charitable dilemma of figuring out what to do with such a huge surplus had its roots in Milton and Kitty's 1909 Deed. The Deed had created a permanent endowment or "corpus" consisting of ownership of Hershey Chocolate and Hershey Estates, including the 10,000 acres of dairy farms, Like a modern-day college endowment, corpus assets generated dividends that flowed into a second "income account" intended to pay for costs of running the orphanage: textbooks, clothing, teacher salaries, administrator salaries, student homes and the like. Under no circumstances was the corpus to be liquidated to pay the orphanage's bills. The Hershey School was to operate within the budget of the income account that held the dividends of the chocolate company and Milton Hershey's other companies. But what if the chocolate company and other corpus assets produced surplus profits for the income account, more than was needed to pay for the orphanage's daily bills? Milton and Kitty's Deed had an answer: Admit more orphans.

Yet during the booming World War II years, the Hershey School actually cut the number of orphans almost in half as the nation mobilized to fight the Nazis and the Japanese. Thanks to a combination of lower operating costs and higher corporate profits, the orphans' fund surpluses swelled by $10 million. After the war, the Hershey School added students, but couldn't grow the school at a pace anywhere near what could have soaked up the surpluses, which continued to mount in the consumer-driven economy of the 1950s.

This pattern of mounting surpluses, with more money flowing into the income account than the Hershey Trust Company expended on the orphanage and school, became the norm. In 1953, the Trust spent $2.8 million on orphans and parked $2.9 million in the income account as surplus. In 1956, the Trust dished out $2.9 million for orphanage bills, and still saved four million dollars in the income account. The gap widened in 1959, with $3.4 million spent to operate the Hershey School, and $5.1 million placed in the income account as surplus.

As of 1962, the surplus that Milton and Kitty Hershey's orphans' fund had accumulated before investment returns, $72 million, was now greater than the $62 million the Trust had spent to educate, lodge and feed orphans during its entire half-century of existence. The total value of Hershey's orphans' fund topped $395 million, or three billion dollars in 2014 dollars, in 1962, and the surplus accounted for almost one-quarter of it.

The 1909 Deed said the income account surplus was to be "*exclusively devoted*" to the Hershey School. The Deed had spelled out other requirements, most of which were still being followed in 1962. The admission requirements limited admission to fatherless white boys. The school's location was specified as Derry Township, with admissions based on a geographic hierarchy: orphan boys in Dauphin, Cumberland and Lancaster Counties got first preference, next came boys from the rest of Pennsylvania, and then boys from throughout the United States.

Orphans weren't the national crisis in the 1950s that they had been when Milton and Kitty filed their Deed. Poverty also had faded from public view in an era of post-World War II confidence, optimism and prosperity. Yet child-care specialists who tracked the statistics and economic desperation of young Americans still saw millions of orphans and needy children that the Hershey School could help. The federal Children's Bureau estimated that in 1961, three million children had lost a mother or father, including 55,000 children who were full orphans without a mother or father. Children's Bureau research director Helen Witmer noted critical demographic changes. Yes, there were fewer orphans than in America's pre-Depression society. But an additional three million children were now born out of wedlock, and four million children lived with only a mother or only a father because of divorce, desertion or separation. Taken together, the orphan children, children born out wedlock and children raised in one-parent households because of abandonment or divorce amounted to 10 million children—15 percent of the nation's child population. At the time only about 300,000 got government assistance.

As we've seen, in the late 1940s and 1950s the Hershey School did take steps to increase the school's capacity. The campus was modernized, and the institution marketed itself with brochures and a free film, *A Living Heritage for Boys*. Trust officials publicized the orphanage's story thousands of times on thousands of visits. They gathered the names of 9,000 potentially eligible boys on trips to welfare offices, service clubs and community leaders. But, even with a school population of rising to 1,080 boys in 1960 from 620 boys in 1945, the Trust was not operating at capacity. But this was far lower than the Trust's own enrollment goal of 1,500, set in its special report from 1960. And the surpluses in the Trust kept growing.

Trust officials now spoke privately of a charitable failure of Milton and Kitty's 1909 Deed, with its never-ending flow of chocolate profits into the orphans' fund. Options to modify the original deed began to be quietly considered. This would mean deploying the old legal doctrine of *cy-près*, which has the meaning of "as near as possible" or "as near as may be." A charity seeking to change its mission in order to stay viable would need to propose a new mission "as near as possible" to the intent of the original one.

If the Trust truly couldn't find enough orphan boys to help, there were some easy fixes it could propose that would immediately widen the admissions pool. It could broaden the definition of orphan in Milton and Kitty's Deed to boys or girls of single mothers or single fathers, a growing population in the 1950s and '60s. The Trust also could open its doors to include black orphan boys, or to black girls.

Another *cy-près* option, some believed, would have been to modernize the tuition-free Hershey Junior College, or convert it to a low-cost, four-year university. This wouldn't be "as near as possible" to Milton and Kitty's charitable mission of helping orphans, but it would be a service to children of poor families. And the junior college was popular with local residents. An upgraded junior college, moreover, could benefit orphan graduates of the Hershey School who could live near the school where they'd spent their childhoods as they attended the orphan-friendly post-secondary educational institution.

And the Junior College had a direct connection to Milton Hershey, who had founded and funded it in the late 1930s. Hershey's friend and personal physician Herman Hostetter provided evidence of Hershey's personal commitment to the Junior College. In his self-published 1971 book, *The Body, Mind and Soul of Milton Snavely Hershey,* Hostetter quoted Hershey telling an official with the state universities, "In 20 or 25 years the demand for trained mechanics will be so great that the schools will not be able to supply the demand. So I am going to build a Technical-Vocational School that will surpass any other institution of its kind in the world. I am going to build a new Junior College and when the time comes, we will change the Junior College into a four-year college and there should be plenty of money here to do it. I will take the ground between Cocoa Avenue, Governor Road and Homestead Road and make a campus for these schools."

But the Trust didn't take any of these actions. Instead, the president of Hershey Chocolate pushed his own idea of what should be done with the surpluses. His idea didn't involve impoverished children at all, but another project that would, if implemented, offer a huge boost to the region's economic development.

SAM HINKLE took over as Hershey's President in 1956, but he had been involved with the company since 1924. As Director of Research, he had been responsible for the introduction of such iconic products as Hershey's Chocolate Syrup, Krackel and Mr. Goodbar. He later remembered how Milton Hershey inadvertently contributed to naming Mr. Goodbar: "'Someone said, 'That's a good bar.' And [Mr. Hershey's] hearing being a little bad, he thought they said Mr. Goodbar. So he named it Mr. Goodbar." A confident leader, Hinkle also paved the way for Hershey's diversification into other foods and services.

Hinkle explained his approach to the Trust's charitable dilemma, in grainy black-and-white footage available on YouTube. Hinkle told others seated at a table about the Trust's dilemma: "I could see our fund in the Hershey School accumulating. I could foresee if business kept on the upper trends as it has for years, the fact that we would have the funds that we wouldn't need to take care of orphans. I could see the orphan population dwindling somewhat, on the downgrade, and I began to wonder what Mr. Hershey would do if he himself were living…with the accumulation of money that he didn't need for his orphans. What would he do?"

Hinkle privately expressed his reservations toward expanding the Trust's child-care mission. "If we were to ask the court's permission for trust modification…to…admit boys from broken homes for example," he wrote in a private letter, "it seems that we immediately would be inviting criticism of our methods…and in no time our worst fears of 'The line forming on the right' would be realities." The town of Hershey, in other words, would be hosting and educating many more poor boys—exactly what the Deed says should be done if the funds were available, but that Hinkle was now lobbying against.

To avoid his doomsday scenario, Hinkle speculated that Milton Hershey would agree that the orphans' fund surpluses should be devoted to new purposes that would lead to "new and better remedies for the relief of human suffering—probably traceable to the untimely death of his wife, *although he seldom mentioned her years of degenerating illness* for which he could find no cure." [Italics added.]

Hinkle wrote a letter to Trust board chairman John B. Sollenberger. In the letter, dated May 25, 1959, he proposed diverting the surpluses into the construction and operation of a new medical center to treat sick patients and train doctors. Hinkle added an appendix to the letter offering his ideas on how to modernize the Hershey School.

Sollenberger had headed the Trust board since the sudden death of P.A. Staples in 1956. Sollenberger rose through the ranks of Hershey Estates, the corporate entity that held ownership of the non-chocolate Hershey companies, heading it from 1949 to 1962. Over the years he had booked bands at Milton Hershey's entertainment venues, managed Hershey Park amusements, organized a national golf tournament at the Hershey Country Club, and brought minor league hockey to Hershey. "[Milton Hershey] tried to invest money into the town as a destination, and in a way that the whole community would benefit and enjoy," Sollenberger said. "I heard him say many times he never went nuts on any one thing, but liked a little music and a little sport."

WHEN JOHN SOLLENBERGER RETIRED in 1962, he had not acknowledged the receipt of Hinkle's letter, with its bold proposal to build a medical center.

Sam Hinkle revived the medical center idea with the new Trust chairman, Arthur Whiteman, a School alumnus who had enrolled in 1916. His father had died in a coal mine, and his mother sewed in a Harrisburg shirt factory. Horrified one day to find four-year-old Arthur and his six-year-old sister playing in the Susquehanna River, she sent him to the Hershey Industrial School. Whiteman thought he might be a painter. But he also was a whiz with numbers and was hired to work for the Hershey organization in a banking capacity. Whiteman responded positively to Hinkle's idea of a medical center.

Though the forceful Hinkle speculated that Milton Hershey might approve the Trust's providing the money to build a new medical center, someone who knew Hershey well over many years recalled otherwise. Herman Hostetter, Milton Hershey's friend and physician, recounted years later how Hershey had rejected proposals for a medical school when he was living. "At least on two occasions [Milton Hershey] told me he was approached about building a Medical Center in Hershey. [Hershey] said, 'This I would not do because it is not a place for a Medical Center,'" Hostetter wrote. "The only time he ever gave any thought or consideration to building any other hospital than the community hospital was when Dr. Chambers from the Hospital for Crippled Children at Elizabethtown approached him about building a hospital for crippled children in connection with the Milton Hershey School."

Initial opinions from the Trust's New York law firm were not encouraging toward the medical center idea either, indicating that the diversion of assets had no precedent. Trust funds by law were to be conservatively managed and administered—they didn't veer into new, unintended directions. Hinkle then turned to the chocolate company's politically connected labor lawyer, Gilbert Nurick, to take the project.

Nurick had published a 16-page book on Pennsylvania court procedures and had represented Allstate Construction Company before the Supreme Court in 1953 after Allstate failed to pay overtime to employees. Though he lost the case, Nurick showed Pennsylvania business leaders that he could champion the state's business causes at the nation's highest court. He also would be the first Jewish attorney to head the Pennsylvania Bar Association, in the late 1960s. His offices were located less than 10 miles away in Harrisburg.

Nurick brought charm and deviousness to his work and felt challenged with legal ramifications of the proposal. Hinkle knew that obtaining the funds for the medical center would require opening the "iron-bound gates of a trust for the avowed purpose of drawing of a huge sum of money to be diverted for another purpose." The Harrisburg attorney, Hinkle noted, would have to be "masterful" to do it.

Nurick accepted the project, saying, "I've always operated on the theory that if what a client wants to do is basically good, ethically and morally sound, expends their money, and serves a great public purpose, the law ought to be slow to impair the implementation of that desire."

Nurick acknowledged it would take "a lot of stretching" to bust open the orphans' fund for a planned medical center, and he set about developing his legal argument and political strategy.

On the face of it, the need for a new medical center could be demonstrated. In 1959, a U.S. Surgeon General report estimated that the United States would need an additional 20 to 25 medical colleges and graduate 11,000 doctors by 1975, as compared with the current 7,400 new doctors because of a growing population, underinvestment in medical colleges, specialization, higher incomes and urbanization. So there was a national need for what the Trust was proposing.

But did Pennsylvania need an additional medical center to train doctors? The state already boasted six medical schools, more than any other state except New York, which had 10. Pennsylvania taxpayers subsidized the education of these medical students—many of whom eventually practiced in other parts of the nation—with about $3,000 per student a year. "Regions which need medical schools the most," the U.S. Surgeon general report noted, "are those with inadequate medical opportunity for their young people and few physicians in relation to population. The needs of those areas must be weighed against their ability to give adequate support to new medical schools." Nine states had no medical schools.

Independently of the Hershey plan, the Pennsylvania General Assembly introduced bills in 1961 and 1963 authorizing a new medical center for Pennsylvania State University, a project that would elevate its "cow college" status and put it on par with colleges in Philadelphia and Pittsburgh. Launched just before the Civil War as Farmers' High School, the institution in its early years sounded very similar to the Hershey Industrial School, only without indentured orphans. Over the years, the farm-based Farmers' High School changed its name and modernized its curriculum, expanding in the

20th century with branch campuses in Altoona, DuBois, Erie, Hazleton, Ogontz and Pottsville. In the mid-20th century, Penn State hired Milton Eisenhower, Ike's brother, as president and began a quest for national recognition, adding engineering and technical programs, and military research. Eisenhower's successor, Eric A. Walker, headed the university's Ordnance Research Laboratory. Walker set the theme for his administration in his inaugural address in the mid-1950s, saying, "We must strive for quality and quantity. Our challenge is the challenge of mass excellence."

Penn State's blueprint called for an enrollment of more than 25,000 in 1970. Colleges of Business Administration, Engineering, Liberal Arts, Chemistry and Physics, and Education would absorb the new students, and there would be a higher ratio of graduate students to undergraduates. Walker planned to invest $168 million into new buildings on the main campus and between 1957 and 1962.

Eric Walker didn't publicly encourage the idea when lawmakers introduced bills authorizing a Penn State medical center. In Hershey, meanwhile, Sam Hinkle—a '22 Penn State grad who had been awarded its Distinguished Alumnus Award in 1957—had his mind set on diverting the orphans' funds into one.

On April 23, 1963, he telephoned Walker and formally offered the funds to Penn State—the "$50 million phone call." The Trust would build a medical center in Hershey and lease it to Penn State for one dollar a year rather than spending the money on more orphans. An important condition was that the medical center be constructed in Derry Township. "You never saw eyes light and anybody drool like that in all your life," Nurick wryly observed of Walker's reaction. Nurick also graduated from Penn State. Walker later said that the Trust might have given him $60 to $70 million in orphans' funds if he'd asked.

IF THE TRUST was to succeed in its plan to divert funds from their intended purpose of educating orphan boys, it would do so without telling the public, other charities or other attorneys. Not only would public disclosure of the plan most likely lead to opposition to the plan in court, but it would bring up questions of fiduciary duty, conflicts of interest and whether the Trust was abandoning orphans. "If you let the public know that you had $50 million available for charitable purposes," said Nurick, "the Orphans' Court would conduct a hearing to determine how it should go, well that would be a lifetime career for all the lawyers in Dauphin County."

Also, many Hershey residents—and businesses—could financially gain from the massive construction project, and the transformation of Hershey into a health-based economy. The Trust's secretive approach was typical of the smoke-filled backroom politics of Harrisburg at that time.

Nurick assigned recent Columbia Law graduate Jack Riggs to the task of researching legal arguments and precedents that could be presented to the Orphans' Court and the attorney general, who had *parens patriae* responsibility, the power granted to the state allowing it to intervene so as to protect potential orphan beneficiaries of Milton and Kitty's fund.

"We even kept it a secret in the office," Nurick noted, "because a leak like this could've, well, it would have been suicidal. Jack spent days and nights in researching and he'd come up with an idea, and we'd discuss it at night and see what's wrong with it and knock it down. Finally after months of research, Jack and I were able to fashion at least an argument."

Gilbert Nurick's final argument was straightforward: He claimed there had been a *pro tanto* failure of Milton and Kitty's orphans' fund—in other words, a partial failure. The petition proposed that the Trust would provide benefits to the white male orphans who could be served in Hershey, Pennsylvania, estimated at 1,600, while diverting $50 million into the medical center. The medical center qualified under the *cy-près* doctrine as being "as near as possible" to Milton and Kitty's original charitable intent because it was consistent as an educational institution with the Hershey School for orphans and the Hershey Junior College. Based on this, Nurick claimed in the petition "that the creation of a fully equipped medical school in and about the town of Hershey, Derry Township, appropriately named to commemorate [Milton Hershey], would best fulfill [Milton and Kitty's] charitable intentions and scheme while providing Pennsylvania and the nation with urgently needed medical educational facilities."

Nurick and Hinkle wined and dined the Harrisburg power brokers to talk about the exciting plan. They consulted former attorney general Robert Woodside, then a Superior Court judge, at the Hotel Hershey on a Sunday afternoon in January 1963. "His reaction to our concept of a medical school in Hershey was immediately enthusiastic," Hinkle recalled.

Holding to his maxim of no public disclosure, Nurick kept the Trust's plans private as he discussed the plan with Attorney General Walter Alessandroni, who was legally obligated to protect the beneficiaries of Milton and Kitty's orphans' fund—orphans.

Nurick believed he could legally avoid actual public disclosure, by arguing that privately informing Alessandroni that the Trust was about to bust open the orphans' fund for another purpose was equivalent to filing public court documents on the Trust's *cy-près* petition in the Dauphin County Orphans' Court. This meant that critics wouldn't hear in advance about the repurposing of the money and have the option of offering alternatives in a court proceeding. They wouldn't be able to argue that the orphans' fund should be refocused on the modern needs of the child-care system. A public airing of the medical center plans also would allow experts to consider the Trust's cost estimates, not to mention the demands of the Pennsylvania health-care industry, and whether the state really needed a new doctor-training hospital.

"We thought it through and figured, well, if the Pennsylvania Attorney General is the sole and exclusive representative of the public in matters of charitable trusts and if the attorney general would go along," Nurick said, "the notice to him would be a notice to the public."

WAS INFORMING Attorney General Walter Alessandroni, who harbored dreams of someday being elected governor of Pennsylvania, the equivalent of informing the public on a plan to divert money from a fund for orphans to a new medical center that would create thousands of jobs?

Could Alessandroni be counted on to protect beneficiaries of Milton and Kitty's trust fund—orphans who didn't vote—instead of going along with the desires of hugely influential Trust organization and Harrisburg power brokers?

Walter Alessandroni began his political career under Philadelphia mayor Robert E. Lamberton in the late 1930s and continued his service under Mayor Bernard Samuel, who would earn distinction as the longest-serving mayor in the city's history. Samuel also was the last elected Republican mayor, as his corrupt administration ushered into existence the reformist administrations of Democrats Joseph Sill Clark and Richardson Dilworth.

After serving in the U.S. Marine Corps Reserve during World War II, Alessandroni returned to Philadelphia and became known as a McCarthy-era communist baiter, through his involvement with the American Legion as chairman of its National Committee on Un-American Activities. Drawing attention to his fierce views, in 1951 he criticized the release of communist leader Steve Nelson on $20,000 bail. Alessandroni called on federal officials to re-arrest Nelson. He declared Nelson's release a "travesty of justice, if not corrected, occurring at the birthplace of freedom," which would "help prove Russian propaganda that we are a weak, vacillating and confused people." Alessandroni believed that communists should be banned as teachers in public schools, because a few of them "in the right places" could control the minds of tens of thousands of children.

He had soaring political ambitions and growing connections. As head of the Philadelphia Housing Authority, Alessandroni administered an agency with 9,500 homes and 40,000 residents. In 1958, he became the youngest chancellor in history of the legendary Philadelphia Bar Association. President Dwight Eisenhower appointed him U.S. Attorney in Philadelphia in 1959.

Alessandroni seemed to realize that he had gone as far as a Republican could go in the reformist era in Philadelphia. He explored a bid for the GOP gubernatorial nomination in 1961, but bowed out for "harmony" GOP candidate William Scranton. The media branded Scranton as a "Kennedy Republican" because of his good looks and support of civil rights. Scranton ran with former Crawford County District Attorney Raymond Shafer. Ever the good Republican soldier, Alessandroni managed the victorious Scranton/Shafer ticket against Philly mayor Richard Dilworth.

Once elected, Scranton rewarded Alessandroni by appointing him state attorney general, issuing the news from his vacation home in Florida. A 1966 magazine article noted of Alessandroni, "He's made a science of forming mutually beneficial alliances with the right people. He's a pragmatist, a Machiavellian in the best tradition. In a game that most people consider dirty, Alessandroni has kept his reputation as immaculate as he keeps those conservative business suits he wears."

The article's author continued, "He has a knack for allying himself with the right people and the right causes. He does so with instinctive caution, in a nearly colorless, subdued manner. He's intelligent and politically motivated to the point that he impresses some as being cagey. He's aloof but charming when he has to be. His alert efficiency got him up the backstairs of politics."

Alessandroni supported the Trust's medical center plan, and consented to keep it confidential. Gilbert Nurick then told Dauphin County Orphans' Court Judge Lee F. Swope of the medical center, and of Alessandroni's support. Swope "realized that the medical center would be a tremendous benefit to the public," Nurick gushed.

Nurick still had no intention of disclosing the plan to the public. "We worked up a large number of legal memoranda, to show not only that *cy-près* would be proper in this situation but that the court had the right to issue a decree without notice to the public other than the Attorney General and without holding a formal hearing."

Presented with the plan and its array of support, Governor Scranton approved the Hershey medical center. On August 23, 1963, Swope signed the order to divert $50 million in orphans' funds—about $375 million in today's dollars—and to allow the transfer more than 500 acres of Trust-owned dairy farms, once worked by indentured Hershey School students, to the proposed medical school. Those farms consisted of Gro-Mor, 37-A; Eastmoor, 53; Long Lane, 37-B; and unnamed farms 55 and 56.

Swope's three-page order showed how extensively the orphans' fund assets could be used for the medical center. "The fund awarded in this decree," the judge wrote, "shall be applied and expended for planning, construction, operation, equipping, administration and maintenance of a medical school to be located in Derry Township, Pennsylvania, with all of the necessary or appropriate components including but not limited to, land, grounds, buildings, structures, appurtenances, equipment, supplies and any other property, real or personal... providing adequate teaching facilities, a teaching hospital, dormitories, residences, dining, recreational...."

HARRISBURG NEWSPAPERS celebrated the news. "Area To Get Medical College" read the seven-column, front-page banner headline in the Harrisburg *Patriot*. Three front-page articles jumped to A-2, while A-3 was fully devoted to coverage with photos, stories, sidebars and a map. Stories crackled with civic pride. Stunned was the reaction among legislators who had no idea of the project. One local congressman, Representative John C. Kunkel, said it seemed as if an atomic bomb dropped on Harrisburg. On vacation, Governor Scranton issued a statement saying it was a "source of real gratification that the Hershey interests have provided the necessary private funds to establish a medical school which should prove to be one of the finest centers of medical learning and research in the world." Alessandroni added, "This is a momentous occasion, not only for this area and state, but perhaps the country."

The medical school would educate 200 to 300 doctors in a 200- to 300-bed hospital, and it would require no state subsidies. About $20 million of the $50 million would be used to construct the medical college. The other $30 million would generate about one million dollars a year to operate the facility. Even in these early hours of the announcement, some were speculating that the $20 million wouldn't cover the construction costs of a modern hospital to train doctors. One expert said it could cost $40 million.

A page-three story in the newspaper's front section captured the buoyant mood and knowing winks. "I'm so grateful to Sam Hinkle," said Penn State's Eric Walker, "who we had the foresight to name as a distinguished alumnus a few years ago and who we had the foresight to name as a trustee last June without any of the people who voted for him knowing a thing about this, which was on fire, and I'm sure they'll all say we had it in the bag, Sam, but we didn't, did we?" Hinkle played along at the press conference, chuckling.

A *Patriot* editorial praised the civic virtues of the medical college, and asked Penn State to advance a plan for a graduate school in Harrisburg. A follow-up news feature carried the headline: "Fantastic! Wonderful! Extremely Logical!"

As part of it political bargain for the medical center project, the Trust said it would spend $21 million to modernize the Hershey School and ease overcrowding. The orphans' home and school would hire 30 new houseparents, 11 teachers, a naturalist and two assistants, as well as a planetarium director, high school counselor, vocational education counselor, research director, consulting counselor and others as it aimed for an enrollment of 1,600 students.

On the Hershey School campus, orphan sixth-grader John Mardula heard about the *cy-près* action in a school assembly of orphan boys. Born in 1951, he had lived in Lilly, Cambria County, with his mother, who cleaned houses, after his coal miner dad died from a lung disease when he was two. "We weren't making it, Mardula said later, "and the teacher in our little school heard about Milton Hershey and talked to my mother about it." He recalls the assembly in which plans for the Medical Center was announced to the boys and the school staff. A teacher leaned over and, cryptically referring to the $50 million, asked him, "Wouldn't you rather have that money for college?"

NOW THE MEDICAL CENTER PROJECT entered a new phase. Architects had to be hired. Designs had to be approved. Contractors had to be told what to do. Cement had to be poured. Costs had to be watched. The Trust itself now seemed about to transition from orphan care and operating a junior college with Milton Hershey's estate to providing health care and training doctors to the region.

And the mechanism of the transfer had to be worked out. Swope's decree allowed the Hershey Trust Company to transfer $50 million of surplus orphans' funds to the M.S. Hershey Foundation, the separate trust fund that Milton Hershey had created in the 1930s to finance the Hershey Junior College. These funds would be used to construct and operate the medical center, which would remain an asset of the Trust.

Through its existence, the modest Hershey Junior College had collected accolades and accreditations. The State Council on Education approved the institution in 1939, and the Middle States Association of Colleges and Secondary Schools accredited it in 1943. Students could enrich themselves with extracurricular activities by participating in the Hershey Junior Players, Junior College Choir, Russian Culture Club, Student Christian Association and Newman Club. The golf team went undefeated in 1954, and the men's basketball team won the Pennsylvania Junior College Athletic Association tournament in 1962. But there were no days off for football games, and it wasn't a "place for playboys," noted one observer.

The Hershey Junior College shared space with other groups in the Community Building, and Hershey residents found it hard to beat the free tuition. Those who qualified for admission included Derry Township public school graduates, sons and daughters of Derry Township teachers, the sons and daughters of employees in Trust-controlled businesses, and Home Boys. The full-time enrollment expanded from 70 students in 1950 to 97 in 1952. Except for one year, the number of students rose annually through the 1950s.

But in 1963, Pennsylvania lawmakers enacted the Community College Act, authorizing school districts and towns to sponsor community colleges. The first city to apply was Harrisburg, and the State Board of Education approved of the Harrisburg Area Community College, or HACC, in February 1964. All of a sudden, the Hershey Junior College had competition 10 to 15 miles away.

The Trust, responsible for the construction oversight of the medical center complex through the M.S. Hershey Foundation, also now had a convenient reason to exit the junior college business. The official announcement that the Hershey Junior College would close and merge with the new Harrisburg institution came in April 1964. The M.S. Hershey Foundation attributed the decision to costs and competition. Under a negotiated arrangement, the students and faculty would transfer to HACC.

Hershey residents protested. They asked how the Milton Hershey's foundation could abandon the free local junior college that the Chocolate King created with his money, while financing the medical center that he had nothing to do with.

More than 200 students and faculty staged a mock funeral. A hearse carrying signs led about 60 cars in a funeral parade. Signs on the hearse and cars said, "First the trustees killed our college. Now we have to bury it," and "Good colleges never die; they're just given away." Another noted, "Money is the root of all evil." The students planned a mock burial at Milton Hershey's grave, but the junior college faculty dissuaded them.

SAM HINKLE retired as president of the chocolate company in 1965, but stayed on as a member of the Trust board. Groundbreaking for the medical center happened on February 26, 1966, with the symbolic photo-op of the project's leaders, Walker and Hinkle, thrusting shovels into snow.

Complexities associated with building and operating a medical center in rural Hershey hadn't been anticipated in the secret meetings to divert orphan money into the project. The town lacked housing and a social scene for nurses, doctors and administrators. The Trust had no experience with such a big project.

Even local geology placed obstacles in the project's path. Limestone caverns honeycombed the region's bedrock, forcing contractors to dig test holes eighty feet down to find solid ground. Project bosses recruited laborers from Philadelphia, and paid hole-diggers extra wages. Earthmoving during the blazing summer of 1966, one of the hottest on record, kicked up dust plumes that could be seen 10 miles away in Harrisburg. Grit seemed to land everywhere, even when one closed the windows and drew the curtains. On February 23, 1967, the fifth floor of a science wing caught fire when a burning tarpaulin ignited a propane tank. Some parts of the project finished on time; others didn't.

Keeping the project moving forward fell to J.O. Hershey, the head of the Hershey School. J.O.—no direct relation to Milton and Kitty—had been a part of Hershey since 1938 when he was hired as a houseparent, on two conditions: that he could farm and that he had a wife. J.O. hitchhiked to Detroit and married his college sweetheart Lucille. They started as substitute house parents in January 1939, the youngest and first college-educated houseparents at the institution. On his second day there, J.O. hauled manure on the orphan-staffed dairy farm.

J.O. had no intention of hauling cow shit for his entire career, and quickly climbed the organization's ladder. He disciplined boys, helped admissions and taught. His mother had died in childbirth, and he'd been raised by an aunt. J.O. acknowledged late in life, "I had no practical understanding of what it's like to have a father or a mother. All I can do is fantasize about all of that." Still, the Trust appointed him to head the orphanage that was seeking to replicate a loving home life. And over time, he became as indispensable to the Trust and its monumental new project as Gil Nurick. He phoned contractors, watched costs and acted as an intermediary between the Trust and Penn State officials.

The medical center project quickly threatened to drain additional millions of dollars, perhaps tens of millions of dollars, out of Milton and Kitty Hershey's orphans' fund. As some feared early on, the Trust had significantly underestimated the project's cost.

Penn State lacked the financial resources to close a budget gap, and Penn State president Walker had informally promised state lawmakers that he wouldn't seek state subsidies for the medical center. The financial crunch threatened the viability of the project, and made it look like a boondoggle. "Those of us on the faculty were aware of some of the financial problems but certainly not to the extent of their magnitude," wrote C. Max Lang, one of the early hires at the medical center. "This was probably wise because if these problems had become widely known, they would have had a disastrous impact on recruitment and retention of faculty and staff."

Where could the money come from to finish the project? One important source of funds, Penn State and Trust officials realized, could be the federal government. In 1963—ironically, the same year the Trust diverted money from the orphans' fund into the medical center—President John Kennedy had signed the Health Professions' Education Assistance Act. This made available massive amounts of federal funds for the construction of medical centers.

It seemed as if federal funds were the answer to their prayers. But there was a hitch: Penn State and the Trust couldn't apply for them. Because of Judge Swope's 1963 order, the medical center's underlying assets—the land and the buildings themselves—were owned by private M.S. Hershey Foundation. As long as this private foundation continued to own the medical center's assets, the federal expected the foundation to pay for its construction. But Penn State, as a university, could qualify for the federal funds. The Trust's Mr. Fixit, Gil Nurick, returned to Swope's courtroom to transfer ownership of the medical center to Penn State. In one swift action, he had scandalously washed the Trust's hands of the ballyhooed and unfinished project after only five years.

Swope agreed to the Trust's request, with a vague explanation of his reasoning in a December 17, 1968 decree: "and it appearing that certain problems in the administration of the Trust have developed as a result of the scheme adopted...and it appearing that the administrative scheme adopted in the 1963 Decree is not essential to the charitable purpose...and, on the contrary, has inadvertently and unnecessarily impeded the achievement of those purposes; and it appearing that the administration difficulties encountered by the present trustee and the Pennsylvania State University would be substantially reduced and, to a large extent, eliminated, if the funds and assets were removed from the M.S. Hershey Foundation...."

Swope didn't hold the Trust accountable for low-balling the project's cost and failing to consider the ownership ramifications. Nor did Swope consider that the Hershey School could have opened its admission to black orphan boys or orphan girls in 1963, which would have undermined the argument for diverting $50 million into a medical center.

One has a hard time not viewing the medical center project as a $50 million gift from Milton and Kitty's orphans' fund to Penn State by two alumni boosters, Gil Nurick and Sam Hinkle. Penn State finished the medical center construction with the help of federal funds, and subsequently ran the hospital and teaching school without Trust interference. Lang estimated that the construction of the medical center cost $63 million through the early 1970s—more than three times the original $20 million estimated budget. Some believed that the Trust initially projected $17 million because it based estimates on a hospital complex for patients, instead of a teaching hospital for patients and teaching.

The M.S. Hershey Foundation continued to exist, but without the Hershey Junior College or the medical center to finance. Instead of educating Derry Township residents, the foundation subsidized Hershey's tourism industry.

A glowing marketing brochure for Nurick's law farm years later boasted of Nurick's "approach to lawyering." The firm was a "shadow of Gilbert Nurick, whose influence continues to be felt. A leader in his community and his profession, Gil Nurick built a great firm and endowed it with the traits he personified: integrity, persistence, intelligence, toughness and civility. But most of all, he championed a belief that a lawyer's role is not to be a naysayer; a lawyer's role—at McNees, Wallace & Nurick—is to find a way to accomplish...the desired result."

Diverting assets into a medical college "was an impossible thing to do. Gil Nurick did not accept this," the brochure continued. "With his colleagues at the firm, he developed a theory and supported it with an ancient precedent that if there is more money in a charitable trust than is necessary for its basic purpose, then that excess may be used for purposes consistent with the charitable philosophy of the donor. A medical school in Hershey fit within that concept. The firm was able to persuade the court that this concept was valid and applicable, and the rest, as they say, is history."

The brochure doesn't tell the whole story: How the '63 *cy-près* process overlooked other options that would have served the still pressing needs of poor children; how the project's cost was wildly underestimated; and how a legal maneuver succeeded thanks to secrecy and backroom dealing.

Nurick noted in an oral history that the medical center was one of the nation's largest *cy-près* actions. But did it set precedent? "Since there was no appeal taken, since there was no opinion written, since it was not reported in any of the official reports, I don't know whether it has made an impact on the law of *cy-près* or not," Nurick admitted, adding "certainly anybody researching the question would never come upon it unless they knew about the situation."

Dauphin County Orphans' Court Judge Warren Morgan revisited Lee Swope's decision many years later, in 1999. The Trust came to Morgan seeking again to divert money away from the orphans' fund in a new *cy-près*, this time to create a research institute with orphans' funds. By then the Hershey School had changed its student qualifications and could admit any healthy poor child in America, giving it a potential applicant pool of many millions of kids. Morgan refused the Trust's request, and commented on Swope's 1963 actions: "That proceeding was not contested; the Attorney General joined in the petition. There was no public notice of the pendency of the matter, no hearing was conducted, and no Opinion filed to support the decree."

Even J.O. Hershey seemed to regret some aspects of the medical center that diverted chocolate profits away from orphans. "The one thing on the master plan that never developed, that I was so sorry about, is that I had several million dollars in there for a research center to find out why kids' IQs seemed to advance anywhere from 10 to 40 points after they're here for several years. I'd love to have found out to what extent certain dietary foods affect learning. I would have loved to have done certain kinds of very selective research with the medical center. It had been my dream in the beginning, of course, that we would have used the money for the most outstanding child health center in the world to specialize in all kinds of things in research that relate to the health of children and learning, all that sort of thing."

5

WINDS OF CHANGE

Girard College Finally Admits Black Boys; So Does Hershey

HE EARLY 1960S at first looked to be a continuation of the optimistic, conformist 1950s. But the civil disobedience of civil rights activists, both in the south and the north, would have an explosive effect on the country, bringing longstanding inequalities to the surface, and forcing major institutional shifts in response. Philadelphia, the big city nearest to the small town of Hershey, went through its own upheavals in this period, which would have a ripple effect on the Milton Hershey School as well.

One of the city's epicenters of conflict over racial equality was Girard College. Despite its name, it was a boarding school serving children from elementary through high school. Established by the incredibly wealthy Stephen Girard in 1833 and opened for students in 1848, Girard College was intended to provide education for poor, white, fatherless boys—a radical idea for its time. Girard, who like Milton and Kitty Hershey died with no direct heirs, had made his fortune in shipping and banking, and was believed to be the wealthiest man in America at the time of his death. The terms of his will allowed for the construction of an imposing 43-acre campus filled with massive neo-classical stone buildings, surrounded by a tall, forbidding stone wall.

By the mid-20th century, Girard College was surrounded by poor black and working-class row house neighborhoods. Nathan Mossell, one of the first black doctors in Philadelphia, had railed against Girard College's whites-only admissions restriction for decades, but he died in 1946 without seeing any change there. The landmark 1954 ruling of the Supreme Court, mandating desegregation of the nation's public schools, emboldened those who had hoped to open Girard to black children. The Brown plaintiffs had told the high court that "separate but equal" treatment for white and black students institutionalized second-rate public schools for blacks. The same year as the *Brown v. Board of Education* decision, Philadelphia's Board of City Trusts rejected six black boys who applied for admission to Girard College. Years of court challenges ensued.

In 1965, in an atmosphere of continuing frustration combined with raised hopes, thanks to successful civil rights actions, protesters organized demonstrations in the streets around Girard College. On the first day of those protests, in May, several dozen picketers encountered about 1,000 Philadelphia police. The next month, the protesters jumped the Girard College walls and were arrested. Later that summer, the Reverend Martin Luther King spoke to 5,000 protesters from a flatbed truck, comparing the Girard walls to the Berlin Wall that separated Democratic-controlled West Germany from Communist-controlled East Germany. "At this stage of the 20th century," King shouted to the crowd, "in the city that has been known as the cradle of liberty, the Girard College wall is like the Berlin Wall. This wall, this school, is symbolic of a cancer in the body politic that must be removed before there will be freedom and democracy in this country."

Newspapers tracked the seesaw battle with headlines. "Girard Granted Stay in Negro Admissions," said one headline. "U.S. Court Upholds Girard on Exclusion of Seven Negroes," said another. "Negroes Lose Appeal Round in Girard Case." The Association for the Preservation of Wills and Private Schools warned Pennsylvania Governor Raymond P. Shafer in 1967 "that it would try to close Girard College if the school is forced to admit Negroes." But this was a statement of desperation, as headlines now pointed to victory. "Eisenhower Hits Girard Will," said one. "Negro Boys Upheld in Girard Case," read another. Finally: "Negroes Hold Victory Rally at Girard College."

Philadelphia widow Marie Hicks witnessed the grandeur of Girard College while attending a Boy Scout badge-awarding ceremony for a son. "When I saw how beautiful everything was," Hicks recalled, "it made me even more angry that no black boys were allowed in. I figured I would never get in there again." A Philadelphia newspaper called her the "Rosa Parks of Girard College."

A jubilant crowd of 450 gathered at the Girard College walls in June 1968. The U.S. Supreme Court refused to intervene in the case, and let stand a lower court ruling forcing the orphanage to admit black boys. "We're going to turn those walls as black as they were white," thundered Cecil B. Moore, of the local chapter of the National Association for the Advancement of Colored People. He added that he was forming a new group, the Black Independent Alliance, "to teach people to vote black, buy black, build black, think black and learn black."

Girard College admitted the first black boys in August. One carried a chess set as he walked through the gates. "There will be a new dawn now with me as chairman of admissions," a Girard official promised the public. "No more discrimination by race, I can assure." Seven hundred white boys boarded at Girard in 1968. The school had room for 103 black boys.

The Trust in Hershey had to decide what to do—follow Girard College in accepting black boys, or fight integration. The Philadelphia government controlled Girard, and the federal courts determined the orphanage fell under the equal protection clause of the U.S. Constitution's Fourteenth Amendment that prohibited racial discrimination by state or local governments.

But did the equal protection clause apply in Hershey? Very possibly it did not. The Trust operated with private money—Milton Hershey's money. But did the Trust want to risk antagonizing the NAACP? Did it want a repeat of Girard College, with street protests and court challenges in conservative Hershey? Probably not.

But the institution also couldn't just let black boys into the school. The 1909 Deed on file with the state still contained the whites-only restriction. A white supremacy group might seek to enforce the restriction if the school opened its doors to black boys.

The Trust's go-to lawyer Gilbert Nurick appealed privately to the attorney general to extricate the organization from this legal and public relations jam. The Trust had gotten the medical center plan through the state government and the courts without telling the public. Nurick now sought to solve the racial restriction without telling the public. This would be a pattern in subsequent decades—the Trust dealing privately with the orphans' court and the attorney general, and foreclosing debate on Milton Hershey's charitable intent.

Nurick drafted a 17-page legal opinion, dated May 13, 1968, arguing that the private Trust had become so entangled with state government that it legally fell under the equal protection clause itself, and should immediately admit black boys without formally modifying the Deed. This was another one of Nurick's "stretches."

Milton Hershey had deliberately placed the future governance of the

Hershey Industrial School in private hands, unlike Stephen Girard who had handed over responsibility to the now-corrupt Philadelphia city government. It was one of the ways that Hershey believed he improved upon Girard's organization. Nurick cited a "galaxy" of ways in which the Hershey School intersected with the state and local government. "Mr. Hershey was a sophisticated businessman and was undoubtedly quite knowledgeable in the advantages of corporate existence and the nuances of corporate operations," Nurick wrote. "It is significant that in the Deed of Trust he specifically provided for the authority to incorporate the institution and for said corporation to enjoy all the benefits of the laws of the Commonwealth of Pennsylvania relating to this status. This factor assumes special importance because this power to incorporate was exercised on December 19, 1919 when an application for charter for 'The Hershey Industrial School' was filed by the [Board of Managers] and was approved by the Court of Common Pleas of Dauphin County, Pennsylvania as of that date. It is noteworthy that Mr. Hershey was one of the managers who participated in that proceeding. Thus, the School achieved corporate status and material benefits therefrom through the application of the state legislature and the action of the state judiciary. We do not suggest that, under the present state of law, this action alone was sufficient to activate the proscription of the Fourteenth Amendment, but it is a significant event which must be included in considering the total scope of state involvement and participation."

Nurick added that the Departments of Labor and Industry, Agriculture and other state agencies regulated the institution. The orphans' court had approved Deed modifications in 1933 and 1951, allowing the diversion assets into the medical center, and the lease of Trust land to a supermarket.

Under Gilbert Nurick's argument, just about any organization in Pennsylvania—or any private business incorporated in the state or that interacted the state departments—would fall under the equal protection clause, which was not what the courts intended.

That didn't seem to concern Attorney General William C. Sennett, who agreed on June 4th with Nurick's expansive interpretation. Rejecting black boys, Sennett wrote, could "constitute State action prohibited by the said equal protection clause." Sennett concluded his letter in a high-minded fashion, saying, "I confidently predict that the elimination of the color restriction will enable the School to continue its invaluable service to orphan boys, who obviously were so dear to the heart of its illustrious Founder, Milton S. Hershey."

The Trust deceived the public in diverting $50 million from the trust fund in 1963, looted the orphans' fund for a job-creating medical center, and for decades deprived black orphans of the charitable services of the Milton and Kitty's trust fund. Nonetheless, Attorney General Sennett praised the organization as "judicious." The whites-only restriction in the Deed would be quietly removed in 1970.

DURING THE SAME MONTH as Sennett's letter, June 1968, a young black mother in the M.W. Smith housing projects in Harrisburg, Joyce Waters, died of cancer, leaving 11-year-old twins Terry and Jerry in the care of an aging father. Jerry, who is now an executive with the Liquor Control Board, pointed out his fifth-floor window during a 2012 interview to a bridge crossing the Susquehanna River. Blacks in the 1960s, he said, didn't cross it and enter the West Shore neighborhood. Jerry and Terry visited family in Virginia in the summer of '68. When they returned to Harrisburg, their 61-year-old father drove them the 10 miles to Hershey for intelligence and behavioral tests. "We didn't want to go," Jerry said, but "most kids who were 11 years old in the sixties did not question their parents."

The boys passed the tests, were accepted and assigned to the Habana student home of 15 boys. "Unequivocally I felt welcomed," said Jerry of his houseparents. His Hershey housefather "was true to his word" when he told his birthfather that he would look after two black boys as if they were his own.

Terry's first roommate was a boy named Francis Bacon, who helped him with his studies. "He was the main reason I caught up so quickly in terms of class work," Terry said. "It was definitely more challenging than what had been handed to me in the Harrisburg public schools."

Terry saw the word "nigger" written on the bathroom stalls. One time a houseparent called him one. "I remember vividly a math teacher…who made no secrets that he was NOT happy to be teaching me. He always seemed to call on me when I didn't have my hand raised to answer a question, but never ever called on me when I did," Terry said in an email. Terry recalled one man who told his father on parent weekend that "they are good kids. They will never be real smart kids, but they are good kids." His dad just said, "Uh, huh."

SOME SLIGHTS were undoubtedly real. Others might have been perceived. The Hershey baseball coach cut Terry, who thought it could have been because he was black. "I played and started on a championship team in Harrisburg," he said. "I guess they didn't want a black who had a little swagger with him on the team."

Hershey hired a black counselor, Gray Johnson, a former military officer. The black boys called him Colonel, though no one seemed to know his official rank. White students viewed Johnson as helping the black students integrate; black students viewed him as an informant for the administration. One Saturday after school let out for the summer, a boy pushed Terry off a little walking bridge. "They said it was an accident and that the kid was joking." Nothing happened to the kid who'd pushed him. "But I hopped on one leg the entire weekend. A substitute houseparent who was the farm dairyman would not take me to the hospital. Finally Monday morning Mr. Stout [the regular houseparent] took me to the school hospital." Terry had broken his ankle in three places.

Freshmen in the farm homes were called "dirt." "It was 'dirt get this; dirt get that.' They would take you and put your head in a toilet and flush it. It was called a 'whirly,'" Terry said. "Well I wasn't having it." He never was subjected to it, nor to other hazings that included peeing on an electric fence.

There were no black girls in Hershey—or very, very few. A religious instructor who coached basketball, and was one of the first black housemothers, drove black girls from Harrisburg to Hershey in a station wagon for the dances.

More blacks enrolled. By the early 1970s, they began speaking out. "The school barbers where all white," said Terry. "They did not have a clue how to cut a black person's hair. Also this was the time of the afro, and they wanted to keep [black kids'] hair in line with the white students. Finally I refused to get my hair cut by a white barber. I was allowed to get my hair cut when I went home. Anyway there were issues with stuff like combs. Blacks needed afro combs or hair picks at that time, and we were issued the same small six-inch black combs as the white students and told to use them. There was tension because more blacks were at the [high school] and speaking up. It should be noted that Jerry and I were the first blacks to go through the three years at the middle school [grades six through eight] and then the four years at the high school so we saw pretty much all of it."

6

THE SOUL OF THE ORPHANAGE

Upscaling the Institution; Call Them
Scholarship Winners

BY THE LATE 1960S and 1970s, the classic Hershey-style orphanage had been marginalized as a component of the nation's safety net for neglected children. A dwindling number of orphanages cared for 43,000 kids in a nation of 200 million people. This reflected a major sea change in attitudes about child development, and about best practices for needy children. Some experts view Theodore Roosevelt's 1909 White House Conference on the Care of Dependent Children as a turning point marking the dawn of modern child care, with its recommendation that government should do all it can to keep families together instead of consigning children to orphanages. This idea inspired child advocates, although it was not until more than two decades later, in the depths of the Depression, that the federal government enacted welfare payments for impoverished parents with children as part of the Social Security Act of 1935.

Researchers versed in newer psychological theories also specialized in neglected-child issues beginning in the 1930s and 1940s. The work of Britain's John Bowlby had its roots in personal experience. His upper-class Victorian mother had believed her love and affections would spoil him. A nanny raised the boy until he could attend boarding school. Bowlby later famously observed, "I wouldn't send a dog away to boarding school at age seven." The World Health Organization commissioned Bowlby to write a report on the mental health of homeless and displaced children in post-war Europe, which was published as *Maternal Care and Mental Health* in

1952. Anna Freud, Mary D. Ainsworth and others pursued similar research topics. Michael Rutter, often called the father of child psychiatry, eventually published his classic book, *Maternal Deprivation Reassessed*. These researchers had a huge influence on child-care models.

As part of a separate intellectual vein that involved orphanages, sociologist Erving Goffman published *Asylums: Essays on the Social Situation of Mental Patients and Other Inmates*. In this 1961 book, Goffman introduced the concept of "total institution." These were "places of residence and work where a large number of like-situated individuals, cut off from the wider society for an appreciable period of time, together lead an enclosed, formally administered round of life." Goffman looked at the physical indignities and psychological humiliations forced on individuals in total institutions, applying the concept to mental hospitals, monasteries, prisons and orphanages. Mental hospitals in particular seemed to reinforce chronic mental illness. Ken Kesey portrayed these indignities in his novel, *One Flew Over the Cuckoo's Nest*.

Increasingly, social workers counseled against placing children into orphanages—total institutions that deprived a child of a mother's affection and love. Foster care boomed. Adoptions drained children out of the orphanage market. The National Center for Social Statistics reported that the number of children adopted increased from 91,000 in 1957 to 135,000 in 1964, to 169,000 in 1971. "Large institutions were especially out of favor and in most states...were used as little as possible by public agencies," wrote Marshall B. Jones of Penn State University in a history of American orphanages between 1941 and 1980. "If a children's home was to exist at all, it should be professional and treatment-oriented, as small and as integrated with the general community as possible."

The remaining orphanages cared for problem kids. But the Child Welfare League of America observed that the aging and mostly underfunded institutions were poorly prepared for new child-care realities of kids with emotional and psychological problems. A 1960 league report described an orphanage in York, Pennsylvania, where the staff "has not been prepared by training or experience to meet the emotional problems; so despite their hard work and interest in the children, their therapeutic help is seriously limited. Their methods of solving problems have been limited to 'a good, firm discipline,' ignoring the behavior with the hope that it will disappear, diverting the child, keeping him busy at work or play, finding relatives or friends for him. These methods frequently eliminate the symptom but leave its causes untouched. When these methods fail, children who are a threat to the group's equilibrium have to be removed. Without trained staff and without casework services, an institution has no other choice, and yet it is these very difficult children who most need group care."

The Trust acknowledged that modern child-care trends diverged sharply from its away-from-home institutional care model in rural Hershey. In its 1963 *cy-près* petition—the one that modified the Deed of Trust, allowing funds to go to a new medical center—the Trust admitted that professionals tended to "disfavor institutional care of healthy children in favor of institutional foster care in their local communities and, where institutional care is indicated, to disfavor placing students in institutions which are located long distances from their local communities in favor of placing them in institutions reasonably near their homes so that close contacts with surviving family members can be maintained."

This was a legalistic way of saying that the school should be located near kids' families. But the Trust buried the comments deep in the court document. The issue of the Hershey School's care model never became a public issue because there never were any public hearings on the *cy-près* petition. Doing so—talking about the care model—would open a can of worms. What should the alternate care model be? The Hershey School could take delinquents away from home. But the school didn't want to be viewed as a reform school for delinquents. It wanted to enroll good, poor boys. The Trust could relocate Hershey educational facilities closer to cities. Expenditures of the Hershey School assets, Milton and Kitty's chocolate-enriched trust fund, would then be applied to other geographic locations. The local businessmen who sat on the board of the Hershey Trust Company and controlled the charity's expenditures didn't want to do this.

The easiest way to deal with this dilemma was through some judicious rebranding. J.O. Hershey, the head of the Hershey School, lobbied to tell mothers or fathers they were offering extremely generous scholarships to orphan boys. He spoke of centralizing the campus so that it would look like a New England prep school. The Trust constructed Founder's Hall, opening the domed monument to Milton Hershey in the early 1970s on Route 322. Trust leaders appeared to have copied the idea of an expansive and architecturally adventurous building from Girard College. Stephen Girard had specified the construction in his will, and banker Nicholas Biddle managed the project. The architect who designed Founder's Hall at Girard College, Thomas Ustick Walter, had designed the dome of the United States Capitol.

Trust officials didn't disclose the cost of Founder's Hall, but estimates at the time ranged between $15 million and $25 million. Gubernatorial inaugural balls would be held in the Founder's Hall lobby.

Other modernizations at the Hershey School wowed its visitors. New carpets covered the classrooms and hallway floors, and more TVs were added. The Trust purchased 14-seat station wagons for houseparents, and enlarged the auto shop at Senior Hall with an open pit to teach front-end alignments. The Trust renovated or opened dozens of student homes between 1962 and 1969: Monroe, Fulton, Adams, Buchanan, Eisenhower, Madison, Jefferson, Washington, Lincoln, Logan, and so on.

JOE BERNING'S EXPERIENCE at Hershey reveals some of the dangers of institutionalizing orphan children. His mother had died of a cerebral hemorrhage when he was in first grade: "I ran in and all I remember is grabbing her foot and shaking her and trying to wake her up. And then the life squad came and took her away, and it was a blur after that, and the neighbors helped out." The traumatized boy started having trouble in school. He crawled and snorted in the classroom. He chased girls into elementary school bathrooms. Administrators ended up kicking him out of two schools. Then his father married the housekeeper. "She whipped us and beat us, and my dad thought it was great because he thought she was whipping us into shape. My brother and I were scared shitless." His father told Berning he would have to go either to Milton Hershey or a reform school because of the expulsions. They packed the '61 Ford Falcon for Central Pennsylvania.

"The car was so overloaded that it dragged, and when you'd hit a bump, the back universal joint would hit the metal," Berning recalls. They traveled for hours. "I had to piss so bad and my stepmother handed back a juice bottle and said, 'Piss in the bottle.' So anyway, I pissed in this bottle. I emptied it out of the car. I rolled down the window and emptied the bottle"—here Joe made a motion of extending his arm out a window and shaking a bottle. "I got piss all over the side of the car. Well, she just turned around and beat the snot out of me. That was my trip to Hershey."

When they got to town, Joe heard his father tell his housefather that the housefather had his permission to beat his son if he misbehaved. "My brother was four years older than me and he had not been enrolled. Honestly, I had contact once a month. I would get a five-minute phone call and they were so paranoid that they would time the call. My dad didn't want the long-distance phone bill. So it would be five minutes and I would be talking and he would say you got two minutes, you got one minute. Say goodbye. And I would write letters, but I stopped after a while because I would get no response."

Joe Berning liked Hershey. Houseparents didn't have to hug him and tell him he was a good boy—and he didn't expect it. He wanted to be treated fairly and the same as other boys. And he was. Everything was distributed equally, even the clothing. Home Boys had five sets of clothes: play clothes, house clothes, school clothes, second-best clothes and Sunday-best clothes. They wore big white "barn socks." One boy wore his barn socks with his shiny brown Milton Hershey School track uniform to track meets. "We'd say, 'Homey, you look like an orphan,'" Berning remembers, laughing. They called him Orph. "There was a routine that everybody did. Shower time was the same time for everybody. Snack time. Bed time. Everything was scheduled and everybody did it. So you didn't feel like they were picking on you. That's my definition of institutionalized."

Hazing and bullying could be brutal and ritualized in an orphanage where boys sought power over peers, and control in an institution where they had little say. "I just considered that this is what you did. You had to pay your dues," Berning recalled. "The boys had the freedom run. Older boys gave you a head start so you could find a place to hide in the cornfield. You might be forced to piss on an electric fence. You could be thrown in the manure spreader."

Berning learned to fix cars as part of the trade school program. He played football in the fall, and he cut weight to wrestle at 185 pounds in the winter. "It was just a way of life. I was completely institutionalized at that point. I still got into trouble. I got in a couple of fights and I got caught stealing tools from the auto shop, and they tried to kick me out for that." House parents and coaches stood up for him. He stayed.

After his '73 graduation, Berning went home to Cincinnati, but found he couldn't make a go of things on the outside, even living near his family, who were strangers to him. He returned to Hershey in two weeks: "It didn't work out [in Cincinnati]. I had no place to live. Nothing. I had a pickup truck with a camper cap on it, and I drove it up to Camp Milton and parked it there and slept in my truck until I made a contact. A buddy

RATHER THAN RESPOND to the societal and demographic shifts of the time with substantive reforms to the School, the Trust had diverted a huge portion of its assets to the medical center. In its petition to the Attorney General and the Orphan's Court in 1963, the Trust's argument rested on the claim that it had more money than it needed to provide care to America's white orphan boys. It told court and state officials that it could finance both the modernization of a 1,600-student orphanage and the construction of a medical center with cash surpluses, both of them massive projects. As it turned out, this represented a monumental miscalculation of construction costs and the Trust's spending power.

The chocolate business was changing rapidly. Mars Inc. was overtaking Hershey as the nation's leading chocolate manufacturer with its popular M&Ms, Snickers and Milky Way bars. Other companies, including W.R. Grace, National Dairy Products, Lorillard, Standard Brands and Pet Inc. had entered the chocolate business. Hershey Chocolate bought Reese's peanut butter cups, which eventually became bigger than the traditional Hershey brand. But Hershey itself hadn't introduced any new blockbuster products for decades, and still viewed itself as a "flat bar" chocolate company as the consumer market was heading toward bars with nougat, caramel and other ingredients. It still didn't advertise on television. Meanwhile, cocoa prices spiked 200 percent in the 1960s on a commodity cycle. This was particularly bad for Hershey, because it couldn't offset the cocoa spike with the sugar-based ingredients in its chocolate bars. What to do? The company diversified into pasta and prepared foods, and built a California plant to help slash national trucking costs by a million a year. It also bought 5,000 acres of almond groves for a cheaper supply of nuts.

Still the economic tide washed over Hershey. *Time* published "Chocolate's Drop" in February 1968, in the midst of the construction binge in Hershey. Other national publications jumped on the story. "Big Chocolate Maker, Beset by Profit Slide, Gets More Aggressive," the *Wall Street Journal* told its business readers in a front-page story in 1970. Reporter Jack H. Morris visited Hershey and summarized the issues: "Plunging profits have forced the firm to discontinue the nickel candy bar, long its best-selling product. Aggressive competitors have nibbled away at Hershey's share of the candy market." A plant in Canada—Hershey's first manufacturing venture outside Pennsylvania—was not doing well. "And although Hershey executives refuse to discuss the matter, knowledgeable sources say the company lost a bundle on the cocoa market—which Hershey allegedly controls."

Hershey Chocolate profits fell to $12 million in 1969 from $25 million in 1966. The 1969 financials included seven million dollars in the cocoa-market losses. Squeezed by Nixon-era cost controls aimed at containing inflation, along with the soaring cost of raw materials and aggressive competitors, Hershey Chocolate cut its stock dividend—not once, but twice.

Those dividends were the source of the Hershey School's operating budget to educate and lodge orphans, and the corporate hardship had an immediate impact on orphans. The 1909 Deed mandated that the Hershey School couldn't operate with deficits, and it couldn't liquidate the "corpus," or permanent endowment. The Trust ordered new-student enrollment cutbacks. John "Mac" Aichele, an alumnus and head of the school's business operations in the 1970s, told me: "The nice part was we did not have to fire anybody. We were loyal to our employees and we could keep the students we had. It did take a while to get the money back."

The Trust, with a fiduciary responsibility to orphans, should have been expected now to hunker down and do all it could to deliver charitable services during the economic crisis—tighten belts and sacrifice. Instead, the only ones to sacrifice seemed to be orphans. The Trust functioned as if nothing was wrong and, in fact, took an action at this point which loosened the financial protections on the trust fund and reinforced the Trust's evolving economic-development mission around the town of Hershey.

In 1970, the Trust's attorneys petitioned the Orphans' Court to allow a number of modifications to the 1909 Deed. One of its provisions barred anyone with a financial interest in the charity from serving on the Trust board. This included school administrators, consultants, lawyers and construction contractors. Milton Hershey had inserted the conflict-of-interest provision into the Deed in the 1930s, because he didn't want those who could financially benefit from the orphanage's assets having power over the trust fund itself. On December 24, 1970, Orphans' Court Judge Lee F. Swope agreed with the Trust's request to weaken— some thought gut—that provision. Because Swope released the decision on Christmas Eve, few people outside of the Trust or legal community knew of it. Activist alumni discovered the change two decades later as they exhaustively researched the institution's legal history. Within months of Swope's 1970 decision, attorney Gilbert Nurick of the Wallace McNees firm joined the Trust board. Nurick and Samuel Hinkle were the two men most responsible for diverting the Trust's orphan assets into the medical center.

But that was not all. At the same time, Judge Swope granted the Trust's request to do away with the Deed's land-sale restrictions. The 1909 Deed had dictated that Trust had to reinvest the proceeds of land sales into new land purchases for the orphanage. This seemed to reflect Milton Hershey's

Mennonite upbringing; Mennonites placed great value in owning land. Swope said that the organization didn't have to abide by the restriction anymore, which allowed the Trust to liquidate parts of its land holdings—such as parcels on busy roads—without finding replacement land. Many believed this added up to an economic development boon to the town by making land available for stores, homes and tourism. A month after Swope's decision, the Antique Automobile Association bought the Rolling Green orphan farm. Millions of tourists would visit the association's annual car show over the years.

The Trust closed or sold many of the legacy Hershey Estates businesses and utilities connected with running the town of Hershey: telephone lines, the sewer system, the drug store and the department store. Instead of putting money into the Hershey School to maintain enrollment, the Trust reinvested the capital into tourism projects, such as the Hershey Motor Lodge and the Hershey Convention Center. The largest meeting space between Philadelphia and Pittsburgh, the facility opened in 1974 as the Hershey School itself was retrenching.

Trust Chairman Arthur Whiteman asked J.O. Hershey to split his duties between running the budget-tightened Hershey School and modernizing HersheyPark, an asset meant to benefit the school. "So I went over," J.O recounted. "What do I know about a park? I don't know anything about a park. But I went over and walked through it with management." J.O. flew around the nation to speak with top amusement park executives. "So to make a long story short, I come back with a pretty high price tag, many millions of dollars to redo the park. We remodeled and expanded the park into the style it is today." The SooperDooperLooper roller coaster opened in April 1977. Trust officials broached the idea of a Pennsylvania Turnpike exit to Hershey attractions.

The Trust now believed it could go national with its orphan-subsidized Hershey-branded tourism business. It renamed Hershey Estates as the Hershey Entertainment and Resort Company. The company developed multi-million-dollar trophy properties, even as enrollment at the Hershey School remained far below the target of 1,600 students. There was a Trust-owned Hershey Philadelphia Hotel on South Broad Street, a Trust-owned Pocono Hershey Resort, and a Trust-owned Hershey Corpus Christi Hotel in Texas. The company also bought a run-down amusement park in Connecticut. But the debt-dependent national expansion didn't advance the mission of the Hershey School with cash dividends. Instead, the Trust ended up bailing out the near-bankrupt, mismanaged entertainment company with $15 million in school funds in the late 1980s.

SOMETHING HAD to be done about the lame chocolate cash cow. Bill Dearden, a 1941 graduate of the Hershey Industrial School, took over as CEO in 1976, and began implementing sweeping reforms. He de-emphasized the flat chocolate bar, and heavily marketed Reese's peanut butter cups with TV ads using the pitch, "two great tastes that taste great together." He diversified the candy business by acquiring the rights to Good & Plenty, Jolly Rancher, Twizzler, Kit Kat, Rolo, Heath, York Peppermint Patties, Payday, Milk Duds and Whoppers, recapturing the top market share position in the U.S. chocolate business.

On the corporate side, Hershey Foods recapitalized its financial structure in 1984, dividing the company's equity into two share classes. Class A shares paid a higher dividend but carried one vote in governance matters. Super-voting Class B shares carried 10 votes but paid a lower dividend. The Trust retained voting control of the company by transferring its ownership into Class B shares. The shrewd recapitalization benefited the chocolate company with a war chest for acquisitions, and benefited the Trust with cash that could be reinvested into higher-yielding government bonds. Cash surpluses again flowed into the Trust's income account for the Hershey School's operating budget. Finally, the Hershey School seemed destined to realize its potential. The Trust had cash surpluses because of the recapitalization of the chocolate company. And it had widened its applicant pool tremendously: in 1976, the Trust abandoned the strict "orphan" requirement in the Deed, and opened admission to all qualified poor kids, including girls. The Trust called these kids "social orphans;" traditional orphans would all but disappear from the school's enrollment.

But even with this greatly broadened eligibility, the Trust couldn't reach the long-sought 1,600 students on which it had based the 1963 *cy-près* petition. In fact, enrollment fell. Hershey School statistics tell the story. In 1965, the Hershey School enrolled 1,378 boys as it opened new homes and modernized the campus. Student numbers peaked at 1,553 boys in 1971—about the time of the crisis at the chocolate company. Enrollment then dropped steadily to 1,216 students in 1976, 1,033 students in 1987, and 1,024 students in 1989.

The town of Hershey got its medical center—eventually one of the largest employers in central Pennsylvania—and a big tourism industry, thanks to the expansion of HersheyPark, the construction of the Hershey Lodge on orphan land, and more. What did the orphans and poor kids get? Because the Hershey School consistently didn't attain its 1,600-student goal between the early 1970s and the mid-2000s, one of the nation's wealthiest charities effectively failed to enroll about 14,000 orphans or poor children—which was the difference between 1,600 students and the actual enrollment over those years. This doesn't take into account the explosion of Trust assets, which should have pushed the enrollment target substantially higher than 1,600 students in the late 1980s and 1990s.

NO GOVERNMENT AGENCY or media organization in Pennsylvania seemed to understand the Trust or what it was doing during the 1960s and 1970s. But in Nebraska a very similar charity, Boys Town, had come to the attention of crusading newspaper publisher and investor Warren Buffett.

Boys Town was founded in 1917 by Father Edward John Flanagan as a home for homeless boys between the ages of 10 and 16. Located west of Omaha, Nebraska, The City of Little Men, as it would be known, had a mayor, a post office, a chapel, a school and its own zip code—quite like Hershey. The 1938 Hollywood film *Boys Town,* starring Spencer Tracy, publicized the charity to the nation. Tens of millions of dollars poured into the organization's coffers through appeals for contributions even after Flanagan died in 1948. Flanagan had insisted on caring for hardcore delinquents. He'd even take juveniles charged with murder. His successors, though, screened out emotionally disturbed boys, mentally challenged boys and serious delinquents, instead seeking out homeless boys with no significant emotional or physical problems. By the early 1970s, the institution employed about 600 staffers to care for 665 boys, and, as with Hershey, its "institutional approach of housing boys in isolation from the surrounding community, with a custodial, even prisonlike atmosphere, had begun to seem out of date," wrote Alice Schroeder in *Snowball,* her biography of Warren Buffett,

Buffett had purchased the *Omaha Sun* chain of seven weekly newspapers in the late 1960s. The papers published news in the Omaha suburbs, and Buffett encouraged the editors to look into the sacrosanct Boys Town. *Sun* editor Paul Williams obtained a report showing that Boys Town sent between 34 and 50 million mailings a year—a staggering national charitable appeal. Buffett had the insight to tell reporters to obtain Boys Town's tax filings with the Internal Revenue Service. The documents revealed a donation-supported orphan charity with a net worth of $209 million that was growing by $18 million a year, four times more than it spent on its operations. When asked to justify the fundraising appeals to the American public when it was flush with cash, 74-year-old Reverend Monsignor Nicholas H. Wegner replied, "We're so deep in debt all the time." The *Sun* published the story on Boys Town on March 30, 1972 and won a Pulitzer Prize for it a year later. In response to the public backlash, Boys Town enacted reforms.

BY THE 1980S, the Hershey School's famed vocational education program—the jewel of Milton Hershey's vision for his boys—was suffering from lack of student interest. The job shops were "like a ghost town," recalled a retired school administrator. "Nobody wanted to be an electrician or a plumber. They all wanted to go to college or be a CEO"—partly, perhaps, driven by a more selective admissions department. And attrition was becoming a problem. Boys and girls—the first girls graduated in the early 1980s—dropped out if they didn't like the rules or the daily chore program, another foundational aspect of the school.

The Hershey School looked to rebrand the institution with the help of Wilmington-based Independent School Management—as a prep school. In 1988 the consulting firm submitted its 47-page blueprint for the future, "Market Plan for Milton Hershey School." It asserted that the Hershey School had to shed its "orphanage image" and market itself as a "year-round boarding school which offers full scholarships to qualified students. Acceptance to Milton Hershey School is an honor." Free tuition and board could be presented to the public as a $25,000 scholarship, according to author Rita Borden. "This will also help change the MHS image as a dumping ground for counselors' problem children."

The Hershey School's culture had to be modernized, and it couldn't treat students with parents, its new clientele, as if they were orphans, the report said. The staff had to smile. They had to be pleasant. Academic programs had to enrich student lives. "When what parents want intersects with what students want—and the school is not providing it—there is an almost irresistible push to leave the school. Example: 'lack of a caring atmosphere.'" It continued: "The middle class parents who are making up more and more of MHS's parent body are particular about everything that touches their children's lives. They are more demanding and hold the school accountable."

Students needed more personal time. Rules had to go. The farms had to close.

Student overcrowding in the group homes—a problem since the 1950s at the nation's richest orphanage, one that couldn't find sufficient kids to enroll in its program—had to ease. "If the goal is to promote a 'home' as well as a school, then create manageable family residences, perhaps eight maximum."

Houseparents should offer students positive reinforcement, not scolding. Burned-out houseparents should be retired. The institution should be more selective in hiring houseparents.

Many times, houseparents doted on their own children and treated the students as second-class citizens in their group home. The report was unflinching in its assessment: "Address the problem of differing standards for houseparents' children vs. MHS students."

Alumni should be recruited for presentations, videos filmed, brochures printed and parent letters personalized. Signs around the town of Hershey could be updated to point out the school and its amenities. The school should contact a national magazine to write a feature article. The report suggested a 5K or 10K run "through the campus. Objective is to show people cluster homes, school buildings, sports facilities, medical center, etc. End at Founder's Hall where runners and spectators be invited in for cold drinks, to pick up their T-shirt."

The report introduced the ideas being contemplated at the top levels of the charity. In February 1990, the Trust formally released its 21st Century Initiative, a radical transformation plan that involved stronger academics, reduced emphasis on vocational education, a centralized campus and racial diversity.

The plan noted that Jim Carney, the outside professional who had been hired to help search for a new head of school, had spent several days living at the school and meeting and interviewing staff members. Carney had come away with the sense that the biggest problem at the school was the perceived lack of direction. "People no longer were sure that the Milton Hershey School was moving in one direction and, to the contrary, felt it was moving in a lot of different and sometimes contradictory directions at the same time."

Top Trust officials, it continued, believed "the majority of our people will catch the excitement and enthusiastically join in our efforts to turn the dreams set forth in the enclosed documents into realities."

Three months after the release of the report, Hershey School president Bill Fisher, an alumnus, announced his retirement. The Trust hired the first outsider and first woman to head the school, Frances O'Connor, in July 1991. She resigned the following summer in August 1992. The Trust board hired Arthur Levine of the Harvard Graduate School of Education to replace O'Connor, but he quit without relocating to Hershey. McNees Wallace partner Rod Pera served as interim president while the Trust searched for a permanent president.

In September 1993, the Trust appointed William Lepley to head the Hershey School. Lepley was a former superintendent of the Council Bluffs School District in Iowa; he also headed the Iowa Department of Education under Governor Terry Branstad. The governor praised Lepley as "a visionary and energetic leader for Iowa's education system." Lepley had been a target for political and religious conservatives who said his educational standards "sought to impose a liberal social agenda." Six top Hershey School administrators were fired, sending shock waves through the campus. Teachers, houseparents and services employees unionized to protect their jobs.

7

"ORPHAN ARMY"

They Felt They Owed It to Mr. Hershey

DICK PURCELL and other Home Boy alumni didn't like the news they were hearing around Hershey in the late 1980s: farm closings, persistently low and sinking enrollment, a lack of accountability on the Trust board, and the sale of Trust land. Purcell, a 1961 Hershey School graduate, couldn't stomach the closing of Earle Markley's vocational education program. Seventy percent of the Home Boys, including him, had graduated with job-ready skills in printing, auto mechanics, machine shop, electricity, plumbing, sheet metal, electronics, food service, drafting, floriculture or poultry management over the decades of the program. Companies hired Home Boys right into apprenticeships or good-paying blue-collar jobs. Some boys graduated early if there was a job for them. The ethos of the place reflected a sense that Home Boys might not be the brightest stars in the sky; they might not come from the best families. But if they worked hard, the trades program could lift them out of poverty by fixing cars, framing homes, repairing pipes, machining steel or sweeping floors. Purcell built a two-car garage and opened a machine shop with brother Milt, also a Hershey alum. Dick Purcell, said his wife, "was determined to do everything he could to make sure the vocational trades did not go down the drain."

The concerned alumni organized a private brunch to talk with Trust leaders. No seems to recall the exact year, but was the late 1980s or early 1990s, around the time of the release of the 21st Century Initiative report, heralding a major shift in the school's direction. Alumnus James Harvey, class of '69, had opened a high-end restaurant on Chocolate Avenue, competing with Hotel Hershey and Rillo's. Condé Nast's *Gourmet* magazine featured some of Harvey's selections, giving it a real marketing boost. Patrons dined on stuffed shrimp wrapped in bacon, Norwegian salmon, seafood Louisiana, Australian lamb and steak in one of three dining rooms. They drank cocktails in a 45-seat lounge. A fire roared in the fireplace.

Harvey opened the restaurant on a Sunday for the private meeting between top Trust officials and alumni association members. He fired up the stove for a buffet of eggs, sausage, bacon, coffee and fruit juice. He had been exposed to preparing food and butchering animals as an orphan student, and believed the Hershey School's vocational program was one of the best in the nation. He felt strongly that the program shouldn't be closed—that it should continue as a valued part of the school. Those who attended the brunch included Trust insider Rod Pera, Ron Glosser, Bruce McKinney and John Rineman. Emotions ran as hot as the cooking stove during the brunch. "We said, 'You have got to get vocational education back,'" recalled William Schwanger, an alumni leader at the time. "They were totally blown away because it was the first time that a group of alumni challenged them....They were convinced we were a bunch of hooligans and we didn't know what we were talking about. We were taught in the school to be respectful, and we were trying to do this cleanly."

Schwanger was like Purcell. He felt indebted to Milton Hershey. His mother, Elsie, had died of a heart attack at age 46. He could have been raised by an older sibling, but his father, Jacob, thought he should go to Girard College or Hershey. Schwanger boarded at Fosterleigh and lived on the farms as a teenager. Bullying was rampant, but he and several younger boys jumped the juniors and seniors in a farm home one day. "We wanted to let them know we wouldn't take it anymore," Schwanger recalled. He played offensive and defensive tackle for the Spartans and graduated in 1964. Shippensburg University offered him a football scholarship, but he attended the more practical Hershey Junior College. "It was a fantastic experience. I did not, in my opinion, have a tough time going into the Home," he said. "I never related that my dad abandoned me, though he worried that I might."

Schwanger knew bullshit when he saw it. He knew bullshit when he heard it. He was seeing it and hearing it now from the Trust board members after the brunch. They weren't listening to the alumni concerns. Afterward, he and others agreed they had to do something more. They read the Deed, gathered information on Trust construction projects, land sales, Gil Nurick, and Deed modifications. They contacted a vocational education expert who said it was important to keep the program going. After more conversations, Schwanger said, "We sensed there would be a lot of gamesmanship and we needed more resources." The alumni retained a law firm and opened discussions with the Office of Attorney General Ernie Preate.

ERNIE PREATE was a consummate player of the Harrisburg political game as it existed then. He had come to the post of Attorney General for Pennsylvania in 1988, after serving as D.A. in Lackawanna County. What no one knew when the Hershey alumni contacted him was that his campaign funds had gotten a boost from video poker operators. Popular then in betting-crazed Pennsylvania, electronic video poker machines could be manufactured for $1,400 to $2,800 and produce illegal profits of $1,000 a week in bars and private clubs—a huge return on a capital investment for a businessman willing to take a risk on them. A shadowy network of manufacturers and distributors fed the outlawed industry. Preate, vulnerable due to leftover campaign debt from his earlier race for district attorney, made a deal: in exchange for the video poker operators' financial help, he would promise to go soft on prosecutions.

One poker operator introduced Preate to operators throughout Pennsylvania. Another operator was later quoted as saying, "I don't care if you pay the bills. Make sure Ernie gets his money." And the investment seemed to reap returns. In April 1988, the Scranton-area bar owners were warned of a pending bust of video poker operators. Some quickly pulled their video poker machines out of their taverns before the raid. Once elected attorney general, Preate didn't recuse himself from a statewide grand jury looking into video poker. Of the 25 individuals recommended for prosecution by the statewide grand jury on charges related to corrupt organizations, seven weren't arrested. The remaining 18 individuals were arrested in early 1990. Sixteen of those either had their arrest records expunged or had their charges withdrawn. Elmo Baldassari would boast from prison, "I made Ernie Preate attorney general."

Preate had higher political ambitions than attorney general: his eye was on the governorship. But as time went on, he couldn't shake the rumors of his connections to video poker operators, and he began cracking down on them. "We are not going to stand idly by and permit Pennsylvania to become a de facto gambling state," Preate told a news conference. "We're changing the risk-reward equation for bar owners and distributors....In the past they knew that if they were convicted of illegal gambling, the only punishment they were likely to get was a modest fine....Our goal is nothing less than driving every video poker machine out of Pennsylvania....And we're clamping down evenly on the entire industry, top to bottom."

The video poker operators felt betrayed. Political foes smelled blood.

Preate fought his political enemies in the corridors of power in Harrisburg. It was during the early 1990s that he got the request from Purcell and the other Hershey alumni to investigate possible mismanagement, and other breaches at the orphanage. In agreeing to do it, Preate set a precedent—he became the first Pennsylvania attorney general to take on the sacred Chocolate Trust.

It didn't seem like a difficult call once the staff at the Office of Attorney General blew the dust off Milton and Kitty's 1909 Deed and read it. It said of the education to be offered to orphan boys: *"Each and every scholar shall be required to learn, and be thoroughly instructed in some occupation or mechanical trade, so that when he leaves the School on the completion of the period for which he is to remain, he may be able to support himself."*

The Trust surrendered quickly. Ernie Preate's September 1993 Memorandum of Understanding didn't say the school had violated the Deed. But it seemed to be a close call. As part of its agreement with Preate, the Hershey School agreed "to provide job-specific vocational training to its students," hire certified teachers, publicize the program and counsel students on job skills.

Preate's memo seemed like a "big victory for us," said Joseph Berning, who now was one of the activist alumni, "because we thought that memorandums, agreements and board resolutions meant something. We were naïve."

THE ALUMNI had other gripes. They targeted Trust head Rod Pera, who succeeded Gil Nurick as the top McNees Wallace partner at the Trust. Alumni believed that Pera was behind the plan to transform the orphanage into a prep school and to shrink the 10,000-acre campus to a thousand acres so that the Trust could develop the school's bucolic land for tourist attractions. The Trust had elected Pera chairman of the board and then appointed him interim head of the Hershey School in the early 1990s, which allowed him to consolidate power over the school's financial assets, and the school's administration and culture.

The alumni didn't think Pera should be so powerful, and they didn't like him personally. He was raised in Hershey and historically Home Boys and townie boys didn't get along. They competed over sports, girls and jobs.

When he was alive, Milton Hershey had controlled the town and its economic resources: the land, the chocolate company and the diversified businesses (lumber company, hotel, department store, etc.). Townsfolk seemed to resent Hershey's decision to pledge the economic benefits of his estate to orphan boys, and the alumni believed that the town's residents constantly schemed to undermine the orphanage and take its land and money. Alumni discovered a memo from the 1930s in which a Trust official or consultant had suggested that Milton Hershey redirect some of his philanthropy to the community. He didn't do so, and in fact seemed to strengthen the Deed's provisions related to orphan boys.

Hershey had kept a lid on the town's discontent during his lifetime. He financed the Hershey Junior College, which was open to area students, and developed amenities that were available to everyone, including a first-class golf course, a sports arena and the community building with its rec room and pool. But after his death in 1945, it seemed to be a different story. J.O. Hershey, then a mid-level school administrator, felt compelled to circulate a memo on New Year's Eve 1946 to houseparents in the farm homes with this edict: "The movie privilege scheduled for tonight has been postponed indefinitely. This action has been necessary in view of the tension that is existing at this present time between the boys of the town and the boys of the Hershey Industrial School."

A tight circle of businessmen and other local insiders comprised the Trust board. They had ties to the community whose biggest economic resource was the chocolate-enriched trust fund for the orphanage, including its land. In the 1960s and '70s, Home Boys didn't feel welcome to stay in Hershey after graduation. Hershey children raised in the 1950s, '60s and '70s confirm that there was minimal interaction between the local residents and the orphan boys during this period. Home Boys themselves had one night of town privileges in Hershey. The streets seemed to empty as the boys wandered to hangouts or HersheyPark.

Now in the late 1980s and early 1990s, alumni thought Rod Pera would repurpose the school's economic resources for the community's benefit. They felt that he disrespected them. "He thought we were a bunch of farmers," commented one. One day, about 50 alumni picketed McNees, Gil Nurick's and Rod Pera's law offices in downtown Harrisburg.

THE ALUMNI APPEAL to the Office of Attorney General had gotten the state agency's attention. Now the OAG began asking questions that would start shining a light on the cozy back-room dealings that had characterized the Trust's modus operandi. Mary Beth O'Hara, senior deputy attorney general in the Office of Attorney General, sent the Trust a letter on November 10, 1993 asking about Rod Pera's compensation, and for board meeting minutes and paperwork relating to the sale of land to H.B. Alexander, a construction firm owned by a Trust board member, William Alexander. She requested any and all documents on construction projects greater than $10,000.

O'Hara also asked how much the Trust had paid to McNees, Wallace & Nurick for legal services for the Hershey School, Hershey Trust Company, Hershey Entertainment & Resort Company and Hershey Chocolate over the previous five years. Her inquiry included a request for details on why the Trust altered Milton Hershey's conflict-of-interest provision in 1970. Who prepared that change, and how did Trust board members vote? How much money from the orphans' fund had the Hershey Trust Company infused into the mismanaged Hershey Entertainment & Resort Company?

The Trust couldn't retain the McNees Wallace firm to defend itself with the Office of Attorney General: Rod Pera and McNees Wallace were part of the investigation. Instead the Trust retained the "special counsel" of Thomas Caldwell, Robert L. Freedman and George J. Hauptfuhrer Jr.

Caldwell and his family had deep political ties in Central Pennsylvania. Hauptfuhrer, a top Philadelphia lawyer, had been a first-round draft by the Boston Celtics in the late 1940s, but instead attended Penn Law School, joining Dechert, Price & Rhoads right out of that school. He made partner in eight years, and in time rose to head the firm. Hauptfuhrer chaired the Real Property, Probate and Trust Law Section of the American Bar Association, the Pennsylvania Bar Association and the Philadelphia Bar Association. He had excellent legal credentials and, perhaps as important, belonged to the best golf clubs: Pine Valley, the Honorable Company of Edinburgh Golfers, Huntingdon Valley, Johns Island and Roaring Gap. Robert Freedman also was an attorney with Dechert.

William Lepley, the new head of the Hershey School, wrote to Thomas Caldwell on December 20, 1993. "This letter is to confirm my understanding of how you are proceeding under your engagement by Milton Hershey School in connection with inquires which have been made by the Attorney General of Pennsylvania regarding School finances and regarding practices of the School's Board of Managers." Lepley added that it was "essential that these issues be resolved promptly, so Milton Hershey School can move on from preoccupation with past controversies to concentration on the care and education of young people, present and future, who are entrusted to our care."

The Trust's special counsel team, the attorneys Caldwell, Hauptfuhrer and Freedman, didn't find anything seriously wrong with its client's actions. Lepley then asked former Pennsylvania attorney general Fred Speaker for his imprimatur. Lepley didn't dance around the topic. "Mr. Caldwell of Caldwell & Kearns and Messrs. Hauptfuhrer and Freedman of Dechert, Price & Rhoads tell me that while representing the board in this matter they have been convinced there is no evidence of any violation of conflict of interest statutes or any other laws," Lepley wrote Speaker. "Of course, we value their opinion, but are conscious of the fact that it comes from legal counsel and paid as advocates."

The Trust presented Fred Speaker publicly as an independent fact-finder who would do his analysis *pro bono*. But the Harrisburg Republican insider had long ties—or at least a tangential connection—to the Trust. He had served as special assistant to former governor Scranton, who in the 1960s had agreed to divert $50 million in orphan funds to the medical center. Speaker also was the state's attorney general in late 1970 when Judge Swope modified Milton and Kitty's Deed, allowing for Trust land sales and the election of Gil Nurick to the Trust board.

Speaker responded to Lepley within weeks, with more than 40 pages of analysis. He too absolved the Trust of wrongdoing. Regarding the construction contract to the firm owned by William Alexander, Speaker noted: "Mr. Alexander was not a member of the Building Committee and he did not participate in its deliberations. In addition, when the recommendation of the Building Committee was presented to the entire Board, Mr. Alexander left the meeting and did not participate in either the discussion or the vote."

Speaker noted that Rod Pera, the head of the Trust, didn't participate in discussions or vote on his compensation. And Pera had paid the directors' fees from Hershey Entertainment and Hershey Foods back to the McNees Wallace firm.

Attorneys Gil Nurick and Jack Riggs had prepared the legal documents leading to the weakened conflicts provision in late 1970. Speaker observed that there didn't seem to be anything illegal about the modifications. Oddly, Fred Speaker would have been—or should have been—informed of them at the time in 1970 as attorney general. But he did not shed additional light on what transpired with the modifications, or on his involvement in them more than two decades earlier. Trust policies to avoid illegal conflicts met the standards of Pennsylvania law, Speaker concluded. But Speaker also cheered William Lepley's proposed reforms to cleanse the Trust of the scandal.

Lepley sold the findings to the public in an April 7, 1994 press release. "Armed with the independent finding of a former state attorney general as well as the opinion of its own legal counsel that its existing practices to control conflicts of interest were legally proper, the Milton Hershey School board of managers Wednesday night adopted tougher ethical standards and other procedures to change the way the school is governed," the Trust asserted in the first paragraph of the release.

The cleansing of the slate would involve a range of changes and reforms: William Alexander and Rod Pera would resign as Trust board members; board terms would be limited to 10 years, to bring new perspectives into the organization; and new board members would be appointed who would have skills that pertained to the school's child-care mission. The Trust also would adopt a new conflicts-of-interest policy.

When the dust of the news stories settled, though, Alexander didn't resign his Trust board seat. In a complex transaction, he sold his construction business to insiders and retained the position—without the construction business, he now complied with the new conflicts-of-interest policy. His former company retained construction contracts worth tens of millions of dollars with the Trust for many years. Pera resigned his Trust board seat, but retained his connection to the Trust through Trust-owned entities.

Where was Attorney General Ernie Preate in all this? As hard as Preate tried to extricate himself from the mushrooming video poker scandal, he couldn't do it. The FBI opened Operation Pokerhand, and in April 1994, the same month Fred Speaker released his report on the Trust, the Pennsylvania Crime Commission published the 204-page *Investigation Into the Conduct of Lackawanna County District Attorney/Attorney General Ernest Preate Jr.*

Fearful of the Preate scandal, the GOP supported moderate congressman Tom Ridge of Erie in the gubernatorial primary that spring. Preate lashed out that Ridge would be beholden to the Republican bosses and he doggedly campaigned along the thousands of miles of state roads. "Ernie Preate is a fighter and I'll be a fighter for you. People like the fact that Ernie Preate can take a punch and come off the floor. I'm like Rocky," he said on a campaign stop in Lancaster. Preate lost the May primary to Ridge, 342,913 votes to 285,220. Ridge won the general election in the fall.

The U.S. Attorney's Office sent Preate a target letter in early 1995. He resigned as attorney general and pleaded guilty to mail fraud. U.S. District Judge Sylvia Rambo sentenced him to 14 months in federal prison. Preate had spoken of his remorse in Judge Rambo's courtroom, but he later told John M. Baer of the *Philadelphia Daily News*, "I can do federal prison standing on my head. I'm a strong guy. I'm not afraid to do time. I did my time in hell in Vietnam." Governor Ridge chose top campaign aide Tom Corbett to fill Preate's unexpired term. Corbett agreed not to seek election as attorney general in 1996, but the interim appointment exposed him to statewide voters, helping him to achieve successful runs for attorney general in 2004 and 2008, as well as the governorship in 2010.

While Ernie Preate was undergoing his disgraceful fall, Trust advisors were making recommendations on how to modernize the Hershey School's vocational program. Delays dragged into months and years. The Trust restated its commitment to vocational education in a September 1996 non-binding board resolution. But it sounded like media spin.

"They were recruiting kids into the college path," alumnus Joe Berning noted, "but they weren't college material." Hershey School graduates dropped out of college and "had nothing to fall back on. By the mid-1990s, most of us were of the opinion that there had to be serious change, but there was a difference of [opinion on] how that would happen. There were constant meetings over and over again. We were jerked around for five years. They stalled us off all those years. Everybody thinks we were vigilantes and a bunch of yahoos. That wasn't so. The reason we couldn't accomplish anything was that we were too respectful."

FOLLOWING THE SHARP RECESSION in the early 1990s, parts of America were gripped in extreme poverty. Average family income fell and the nation's child poverty rates climbed. More than 10 million children lived miserably.

Meanwhile, the enrollment at the ultra-rich Hershey School fell to between 1,000 and 1,100 students—far short of the 1,600-student goal set by the Trust in its 1963 *cy-près* petition. The number only partly told the story of under-enrollment. Many days, the Hershey School lodged and educated fewer than 1,000 students because kids would drop out during the school year and wouldn't be immediately replaced with new students. Sometimes there could be as few as 800 to 900 students.

And not only was the number pathetically low, but the Trust seemed to be skimming the ranks of eligible poor kids for the best and brightest ones for admission.

Teachers and houseparents complained to activist alumni of students who enrolled with high IQs, had two parents and two cars—not the sort of needy kids the alumni believed the Trust should help. "Our big thing," said former alumni association president John Mardula, a Washington attorney, "was that they should be helping the 'most alone and the most needy' kids." When the alumni spoke with the school administration, they got vague answers.

As chocolate profits poured into Milton and Kitty's orphans' fund faster than the Trust could award new construction contracts to centralize the school's campus, the Hershey School's income account surplus swelled to more than $500 million. Eventually, the surplus would climb to *10 times* the school's annual operating budget. Trust officials began holding "stakeholder" meetings to talk about what to do with it. Alumni leaders, including some new ones, were skeptical. The Trust hadn't listened to them for years and seemed still to be doing pretty much what it wanted.

In early 1999, the Trust filed a new *cy-près* petition. As it had in 1963, the Trust sought again to divert orphans' funds into a new charitable purpose. Their argument was the same: that it had too many assets and there were too few impoverished kids in America to care for in Hershey—even though millions of children, boys and girls of all races, were now eligible for admission. This time, the Trust proposed diverting tens of millions of dollars—hundreds of millions of dollars over time—into a poverty research center for teachers. The Catherine Hershey Institute for Learning and Development, the Trust told the Orphans' Court, "will support the School's efforts to be a model of best practice in residential education, and it will be the mechanism through which the School serves those needy children who cannot be served directly as enrolled students of the School."

An executive director of the proposed institute would report to William Lepley. About a third of the Trust's operating budget—money that otherwise should directly fund a poor child's education and upbringing, based on the 1909 Deed—would fund the research center. Initially, this would be $20 million. Two-thirds of the Trust's operating budget would fund the legacy Hershey School, which would remain the charity's "polestar." Just as it had done back in 1963, the Trust planned to modernize the Hershey School campus with a flood of new construction—coming after about a decade of rapid construction to centralize the campus at an estimated cost of $300 million. What more could it possibly construct? The Trust said it would put an additional $227 million into new student homes, a middle school, an elementary school, a performance gym, a learning resource center and a visual arts center.

The new *cy-près* petition sought to establish an enrollment target of 1,500 kids at the Hershey School by 2007, insisting that this was the maximum number that could fit into Hershey's centralized campus. "The school, with its neighborhoods of student homes and surrogate families, school buildings, recreational facilities, and health and other support services, is a community where children from disadvantaged circumstances can be nurtured and educated," the Trust told the Orphans' Court. "Expansion beyond 1,500 students would undermine the School's traditional sense of community because it would require the construction of additional school and support buildings physically separated from the existing campus." In an interview with me more than a decade later, Lepley said that he also feared the rural town's reaction to enrolling more than 1,500 students, as many of the students now came from Philadelphia and other cities.

The centuries-old *cy-près* doctrine hadn't changed. A new charitable mission for the orphans' fund still had to be "as near as possible" to the charitable mission spelled out in Milton and Kitty's now-mangled 1909 Deed. The Trust had argued, and the court and attorney general had accepted in the early 1960s, the idea that there were too few white boy orphans in America to enroll at the Hershey School, and that financial assets had to be diverted into the medical center. The Trust modified the Deed in the mid-1970s to admit girls, black boys and poor kids of single or divorced parents, thus opening admission to many millions of kids. Still the Trust couldn't find enough of them to meet its targeted enrollment. In its 1999 filing, the Trust told the Orphans' Court that the research institute qualified under the *cy-près* doctrine because it was "consistent with Mr. Hershey's approach to business and to charity to not only attempt to create a school to aid needy children, but to also *apply innovative thinking....*" [Italics added.]

Alumni privately slammed the Catherine Hershey Institute as an ego-driven concept designed to boost William Lepley's national reputation with educators. They vowed to fight it every step of the way. The research institute seemed to be "another monument to people in power," said John Mardula, who was the president of the alumni association at the time. The alumni asked questions about it. They wanted to have a way to track the institute's performance. All the Trust would tell them was that it would be based in Derry Township, the one provision in Milton and Kitty's 1909

Deed that the Trust dogmatically clung to. "What [Lepley] proposed to do was a public function," Mardula said. "It was not the function of the Trust."

OVER TIME, a new generation of alumni association leaders replaced the early blue-collar activists, bringing sophistication and resources to the reform movement.

Chicago attorney and alumnus John Halbleib got an advance copy of the *cy-près* petition in early 1999 because he had just been elected to the alumni association board. Halbleib threw the unopened petition into his travel bag, and read it on the plane ride to Harrisburg. His first thought upon reading the document was that the new institute would "cannibalize the Trust. Once you have it, it's always there. If you add this to the Trust, it's only a matter of time and they tell the court there are not enough orphans or needy children or whatever." The orphanage would be totally transformed into a grant-making research institute with little direct contact with poor kids.

This was personal for Halbleib. His father had lost his Harrisburg fuel-delivery business during an economic downturn in the late 1950s, and it was pretty much downhill for the family after that. He packed himself and his young family for the stifling heat of Albuquerque, New Mexico, where he got a job as a motorcycle cop in the New Mexico sun and then ate, drank and smoked himself to death. He died in 1963, leaving a widow with eight children and a baby on the way. The Halbleib kids drifted back to Harrisburg, and five of them enrolled in the Hershey School: John, James, J. Michael, Robert and Dorothy. "There was no doubt you could be a child there and you were taught values and self-worth," said John, who enrolled in 1966. He lived in the Rolling Green and Canalview farms. He played football and ran track. "The fastest white guy I ever met," Joe Berning recalled. Halbleib graduated in 1971 and went to Lebanon Valley College as an undergraduate, and then on to Northwestern University in Illinois for MBA and law degrees. He had researched the Trust's 1963 *cy-près* petition as a law student and believed that Judge Swope's decision was flawed, but his law professors didn't seem to care.

John Halbleib hosted mini-reunions for Hershey alumni at his home south of Chicago. He invited William Lepley to attend, and they got along. Halbleib won an alumni board seat in late 1998; some believed that he might be a Lepley mole—a Trust plant in the alumni association. But Halbleib proposed to the *pro bono* committee at his Chicago firm, Mayer Brown, that he represent the alumni association to fight the *cy-près* petition. The partners agreed. For the first time, the Trust would face a sophisticated legal adversary with financial resources.

Halbleib consulted the firm's trust and charitable law attorneys. He requested information from the Office of Attorney General and from the Trust itself. He was shocked at what little information was available to him. One of the most reliable sources of information was Joseph Berning, who had been collecting books, going through court records and making contacts on campus. And Berning had a buddy named Craig Stark. Stark had been fascinated with the Hershey story since he was a boy, and had amassed a huge trove of information. Joe called Stark, with great admiration, "a groundhog in the courthouse."

Halbleib drove Joe Berning to Office Max to buy his first computer so that he could email information. He gave Berning stacks of FedEx slips and empty package containers. Berning packed documents, called FedEx to his rural home and shipped the packages off to Chicago. Clerks at Mayer Brown scanned the documents and books, and returned the packages via FedEx.

Halbleib also developed his own theories on the Trust. He came to believe that Milton and Kitty Hershey were creating a "family trust" and not a "public charitable trust" with the 1909 Deed. Indenturing the orphan boys was Milton Hershey's attempt to adopt them, Halbleib thought. Milton Hershey buried the indentured boys who died at the orphanage near his family plot in the Hershey Cemetery with Kitty and his parents Henry and Fanny. Halbleib believed the orphan boys buried there supported his view that Milton and Kitty considered the orphan boys as part of the Hershey family, their own sons. Halbleib had to learn more about those boys.

Berning walked through the cemetery, got the names and researched the circumstances of the orphan boys' deaths, storing the information in his computer in a file titled "Hershey RIP"—a forgotten history of the Hershey Industrial School. If anything, it seemed to confirm that the farms could be dangerous places. Charles H. Swartz died of influenza in December 1918. A school bus ran over Thomas S. Myric, age nine, in 1929. Raymond R. Zettlemoyer, age 12, died from complications from an appendectomy in 1931. Rheumatic fever took the life of 10-year-old Allan D. Tellet in February 1936. Several months later, tubercular meningitis got 11-year-old Frank J. Klein. Franklin Kurtz Neiswender, age 14, fell through a hay hole in July 1938. James E. Tranum drowned in the Swatara Creek in June 1949. Ten-year-old Leroy R.L. Wiest fell under the wheels of a farm wagon in August 1953. The Swatara Creek claimed its second victim in May 1958 when Benjamin Weaver drowned while crossing it to buy cigarettes. William F. Dayhoff, age nine, died of a heart illness in October 1958. Robert P. Curtiss, who had celebrated his nineteenth birthday three months earlier, died in November 1962 in a fatal car crash while attending Hershey Junior College.

DAUPHIN COUNTY Orphans' Court Judge Warren Morgan scheduled public testimony for the *cy-près* petition for June 3, 1999. Among those who testified was Peter Gurt, an alumnus who headed the Hershey School's admissions department. He told the judge that one of the nation's richest private charities for poor children, an institution that now had billions of dollars in assets, could be a difficult sell for poor parents. "We...refer to the Milton Hershey School as the best-kept secret in America," Gurt testified. "Oftentimes there is a shame from enrolling a child at Milton Hershey. Parents may feel they are less than adequate because they have been unable to provide the care that we can provide, and so it is a challenge for us to try and work with the families to eliminate that mindset and help them understand that we are providing an opportunity."

Gurt acknowledged that Hershey's child-care program diverged from the now-mainstream view that agencies and institutions should do all they could to keep families intact and not separate kids from parents. "Most folks," he told the judge, "are trained in a family-preservation model, meaning let's do what we can to keep families together. So, even in trying to network with other professionals, we need to help alleviate that perception that somehow Milton Hershey [School] is detrimental to a family-preservation model."

Peter Gurt offered no data to show that the Hershey School model produced more effective outcomes than other institutions, but he noted to Judge Morgan that the 13-person admissions department had approval to add seven new employees who would work to attain the planned-for 1,500 students—which meant it could more heavily market the institution to poor parents.

Kati Haycock, director of the Education Trust, testified to Judge Morgan that her Washington organization was doing what the Trust proposed to do with a research institute—only Hershey's would be on a grander scale because of its chocolate profits. "We are a very, very small organization," with a staff of about nineteen, Haycock stated. "Moreover, our research staff, if you can call it that, is one very productive data analyst, and at best one can only understand in rather simple and superficial ways things that we need to know much more clearly."

She continued: "What we are talking about, as I understand it, is not the kind of research that universities do, which is really mostly about professors researching the questions that are of interest to them and then reporting their findings in articles that educators are incapable of reading. It really takes the questions that teachers and principals have right now and tries to make a connection with the research that is out there, to bring the two together."

The proposed research institute wouldn't be a "university extension," William Lepley testified. "It is going to be getting into the hands of teachers and principals what are the best practices about curriculum, or [what] the best content strategy is telling us, the whole body of research unfolding how children learn…. We are going to take a very practical approach."

The Trust always seemed to win. It had the deepest pockets and the best lawyers. It had the best political connections. But times had changed. Attorney General Mike Fisher, when it came time to offer his official opinion, rejected the idea of diverting funds into a research institute. The Office of Attorney General's court filing, made after the public testimony and months of alumni protests, stated the Trust has "not sustained the burden of proving it is impossible or impractical to expand the School's enrollment and facilities to serve more students in the future."

On December 7, 1999, Judge Morgan also rejected Lepley's proposed research institute. He described the institute's planned functions as "conducting research on emerging trends…monitoring legislative activities and public policy at the federal level…in-service training programs…convening thought leaders…influencing government policies affecting disadvantaged children…designing new schools…developing programs…utilizing MHS funds as seed money."

The proposed institute, Morgan wrote, "does not come close to approximating the dominant intent of the Hersheys," adding, "any reading of the Deed of Trust must convince one that the Hersheys had in mind that theirs would be a direct gift to the child with observable results."

MORE ALUMNI now gravitated to the reform cause. One of the most passionate was F. Frederic "Ric" Fouad. Ric had no recollection of his father, whom he lost at the age of two. During a family visit to Baghdad in 1963, his father was picked up by the Iraqi police in the midst of a Baathist coup, then shot and killed. Ric and his sister lived with their mentally unstable mother in New York City, first in the Bronx and later in Greenwich Village. Authorities placed his sister in a long-term foster home. Ric bounced around. Alone for hours at a time, he went to school disheveled and dirty. His sister researched private schools and found the Hershey orphanage. She told their mother that Ric should go.

Ric enrolled as an 11-year-old in 1972. He lived in the Oakleigh group home with 15 other boys. During the first week, an older boy beat him when he didn't follow the house showering rules: older boys first and then younger boys. He feared his houseparents. Over the years, the Trust had recruited unemployed couples from the town of Vandergrift and other poor Pennsylvania coal and steel towns. "I watched a housefather take a kid in the bathroom and beat his head into the wall. We thought he would kill him," says Fouad. "It was a horrifying place staffed by people who could have been prison guards."

An eighth-grader taught Ric wrestling moves in the basement, and he tried out for the team in seventh grade. He was the last kid not cut. "I made the team and got a work-out uniform," Fouad recalled. "Making that team was the first time in my life I had experienced success." He ate, breathed and slept wrestling. He wrestled to an undefeated season as a freshman. He wrestled varsity as a sophomore with a wicked fireman's carry take-down. He would hold the school's take-down record for years.

The teenaged Ric met Joe Berning in those years. Berning had graduated in a few years earlier, and was hanging drywall on commercial projects around Hershey. He was also known for riding a chopper to football games. Berning, the former heavyweight wrestler, volunteered to help coach the Hershey School big guys. During one barn-burner of a match between Hershey and Lower Dauphin High, Fouad's opponent kept backing away from Ric to defend himself against the fireman's carry. Berning thought the referee was biased and was allowing the kid to stall. "I was screaming and I lost it and I called him a dick with ears," Berning remembered. The referee whistled Fouad's match dead and kicked Joe out of the gym. "I had to wait in the fucking bus," he recalled. Fouad talked about that wrestling match 30 years later in an interview in his Upper West Side apartment overlooking Columbus Circle and Central Park. Here was this big guy screaming at the ref. That was Joe. He was always there.

Fouad's confidence grew as he wrestled on the Hershey school team and started getting good grades. He complained about the chores, and especially about tending the cows. But so did the other boys. He learned how to overcome his fear of heights by climbing the silo ladder on the farm. He moved around to different farms: Bonniemead, Meadowbrook, Rosemont. Hershey School students believed they were second-class citizens in Hershey, "but we had swagger among ourselves," Ric noted. "It wasn't Choate-Rosemary Hall swagger. It was institutional pride."

Even in the late 1970s, Fouad believed, the Hershey School was drifting away from its mission of helping orphans and very needy children. "You smelled it. They were trying to change direction." The school didn't want to care for hardcore disadvantaged kids. Students elected him president for his senior year. He sat on a committee developing a new policy to expel students who failed academically. What kind of orphanage, Ric thought, expels orphans for bad grades? He opposed such a policy, and asked administrators if they would kick their children out of their homes if they got F's.

Fouad lobbied to allow students to go home to be with their families for Thanksgiving. Students then still had to stay at the Hershey School during the Thanksgiving weekend, as they had for decades. He also acted on a concern for the students' medical care. Even though the Trust had financed the Hershey Medical Center, the school did not provide specialized medical care for its students or athletes. Ric—who had lost only one match in his senior year and who some believed could be competitive for a state title in his weight class—dropped out of the tournament because of shoulder injuries, ending his high school wrestling career. But the school didn't send him to a specialist to check his shoulders. At a banquet in late spring, he met an orthopedic doctor who agreed to look at him for free. The physician told Ric that he had separated both shoulders and needed surgery. But ultra-rich Hershey School did not provide money for specialized surgery.

Fouad graduated in the last all-boy class in 1980. He attended Franklin and Marshall College for a year and finished at the University of Pennsylvania. He wrestled at Penn, but was never the same because of his shoulders. New York University Law School awarded him a merit scholarship. Ric learned to speak Japanese and practiced law in Japan. He had his own international law practice by the late 1990s, specializing in complex commercial litigation.

Through the years, Fouad followed developments at the Hershey School. In 1999, he met Joe Berning, John Halbleib and other alumni leaders at a Bob Evans restaurant near Hershey to talk about how he could help. Berning, an alumni board member, vividly recalled Ric as a tenacious wrestler. He believed Fouad could bring the same tough attitude to the reform movement. "I vouched for Ric," he recalled, "because I was really connected to the hometown crowd."

Fouad wasn't as concerned about vocational education as Joseph Berning and the other early reformers. He focused on child care. He told the alumni that the Hershey School was accepting students well above the federal poverty levels and that the Trust had to refocus on more needy children: foster-care kids, wards of the court, bona fide orphans and others. If it wasn't already, the Hershey School was being transformed into a prep school for only moderately disadvantaged kids. Fouad later obtained from a disgruntled employee the Independent School Management's marketing plan from the late 1980s, which confirmed his suspicions that the Hershey School was deliberately upscaling its image and admissions. As for those kids who enrolled and needed special services, the Hershey School didn't seem to know what it was doing. "When you took away the farms, you took away the best part of the program and you left the worst part, the group homes," he added.

Fouad rode Amtrak between New York and Harrisburg. He stayed overnight at the Hotel Hershey, or at the home of a retired administrator. Joe Berning would pick up Fouad at the train station. Ric Fouad brought an in-your-face activism and energy to the movement. At a Trust event during homecoming, Ric distributed flyers opposing the closing of Senior Hall. Milton Hershey had constructed Senior Hall on a hill outside Hershey in the 1930s. Generations of orphan boys had been educated there. Fouad called it "our Jerusalem." Now the Trust was talking about closing it. Alumni believed the Trust might demolish Senior Hall and convert the property into a water park for HersheyPark. Fouad recruited Berning to help him with the flyers. The New York international lawyer and the Pennsylvania auto mechanic placed hundreds of them on tables in the Senior Hall gymnasium. Alumni and Trust officials buzzed over it. "I thought it was time for a little vigilante activism," Berning declared. "I was glad it came."

Joe Berning and Ric Fouad attended a packed community meeting in the Hershey Department Store at which a consultant talked about redeveloping downtown Hershey with Trust land. Someone from the community spotted Berning, Fouad and other alumni there, and said the information didn't concern them or the school. Everyone laughed. Fouad stood up and told the crowd that it wasn't funny. The town believed Trust land was *their* land, Berning noted. But it wasn't *their* land. It was the school's land. Why wouldn't the alumni be part of the discussion as to what to do with the

Trust land? "It's like your neighbor coming into your basement and telling you how to renovate your house," Berning argued. "It's always been our view that we're part of the community. You can't separate the dirty orphans from the town."

JUST AS THE ALUMNI ASSOCIATION sought to press for deeper reforms after their apparent victory with Ernie Preate in 1993, the association now wanted to pursue structural reforms after Judge Morgan rejected the *cy-près* petition attempting to create a separate research institute on learning and development.

John Halbleib's firm, Mayer Brown, agreed to let him continue to represent the alumni *pro bono* after the alumni *cy-près* victory. In January 2000, Halbleib sent the Trust a 61-page document drafted in the form of a court petition. "There has been a consistent pattern of reduced benefits to the beneficiaries of the Orphans' Trust," he wrote, "a distancing from the alumni of the School, higher admission standards than are required by the Deed of Trust, and decisions that benefit the business interests of counsel to the Board and certain key members of the Board of Managers, rather than the orphan beneficiaries."

The Trust, realizing it faced a broader battle with the alumni association, retained the Pittsburgh law firm of Kirkpatrick & Lockhart to investigate the alumni claims, repeating its tactic from 1994 when it retained the special counsel of Thomas Caldwell, Robert Freedman and George Hauptfuhrer to cleanse itself of the alumni claims of Trust misbehavior. The Kirkpatrick & Lockhart attorneys spoke with 70 teachers, administrators and Trust leaders. They read thousands of pages of documents. No new information came out of the "Findings and Conclusions of the Special Counsel."

Ric Fouad authored most of the document in which the alumni flametorched the K&L report with a critical response, titled "Bias, Flaw & Avoidance." The Kirkpatrick & Lockhart attorneys considered only whether the actions of the Trust board were legal. The question pursued by the attorneys, the alumni document declared, should have been what would be best for at-risk children. The K&L report claimed to be an "Independent Evaluation of Fiduciary Compliance." But the alumni claimed that Dick Thornburgh, the former U.S. Attorney and two-time Pennsylvania governor whose name appeared on the K&L report, had a long-standing relationship with the Trust. Thornburgh had held a gubernatorial inaugural party at

Founder's Hall. The party's inclusion of alcoholic beverages went against the school's strict prohibition of "the presence of alcohol anywhere on the school's campus under any circumstances—a rule so sacrosanct that even alumni banquets are alcohol-free, as are homecoming tailgate parties. So well understood is this rule by the school's children that one boy called on to perform the task asked whether they might get in trouble for serving alcohol even under direct instructions," the alumni wrote. The boy was immediately dismissed and sent back to his student home for having dared to mention the topic, according to "Bias, Flaw & Avoidance."

People magazine profiled John Halbleib and what the magazine dubbed "the Orphan Army" in January 2001. A few months later, alumni criticized William Lepley during a ribbon cutting for his centralized campus, usually considered among his crowning achievements. Joseph Berning and the alumni also publicized instances of child-on-child sexual abuse in the school's group homes. Alumni believed that the policy of housing children with significant age differences resulted in the older boys sexually abusing younger or weaker boys. Lepley responded by distributing a memo to school employees and asking for a review by outside experts and the school's staff.

In October 2001, the parents of a 10-year-old boy from Schuylkill County filed a lawsuit claiming abuse and negligence. The boy lived in the Harris student home. While there, according to the lawsuit, "beginning in September 1999 and extending into February 2001," another boy in the Harris student home "forcibly and without consent sexually assaulted [the plaintiff] in the shower...during bathing time."

The suit claimed the Hershey School had relocated the alleged abuser to the Harris home after misconduct in a prior student home. The school, the suit further claimed, had failed to have in place, implement or practice "procedures for housing and supervising children with a history of misconduct."

David Barash, a former U.S. Attorney for the Middle District of Pennsylvania, participated in a "Blue Ribbon Task Force" that offered safety recommendations. Some of the same observations made by social service experts in the independent review from the late 1950s appeared in the new report. Among the new report's recommendations: The Hershey School should professionalize its admissions department. It should collect more information on students. New students should visit the campus for more than one day. A counselor or psychologist should be assigned to each new student, and there should be more communication between parents and the Hershey staff. Overcrowding had to be reduced. Group homes should have no more than eight children, and children in a home should be no more than three years apart in age.

In December 2001, about 30 alumni met with officials from the Office of Attorney General at Strawberry Square. Mark Pacella, the OAG official who headed the charitable section, told them to expect broad, sweeping reforms. But they needed to be patient. Months later, in July, Attorney General Mike Fisher—now running for governor—announced a sweeping agreement to reform the Trust by breaking apart its interconnected complex of boards for Hershey Chocolate, the Hershey Trust Company and Hershey Entertainment & Resort Company.

Fisher's agreement also attempted to refocus the Hershey School's mission on finding and helping more needy kids. The agreement dictated maximum household income for new Hershey School students at no more than 150 percent of the federal poverty level. In 2002, that was $22,530 for a single parent with two children. The cutoff had been 250 percent of the poverty level. The Hershey School also had to consider for admission children with a minimum IQ of 80—the previous IQ cut-off had been 90. The institution had to admit children who had fallen behind in their classes. The Hershey School also had to use the Blue Ribbon Task Force recommendations as a safety blueprint. The reforms were to officially take effect on June 30, 2003.

WILLIAM LEPLEY, now locked in a long-running war with the alumni, agreed to Mike Fisher's reforms, but then dropped a bombshell: in order to diversify the charity's assets, the Trust was negotiating to sell Hershey Chocolate. Fisher's reform agreement would sever the board linkage between the Hershey entities—Hershey Chocolate and Hershey Entertainment and even the M.S. Hershey Foundation—and the Trust could now be run more like a normal child-care educational charity without the tacit economic-development mission.

Mainstream charities rarely concentrated their assets in one company or industry because of the dangers of an overweighted portfolio. Economic problems in an overweighted company or industry could lead to a decline in the portfolio's value and spending power, depriving potential beneficiaries of charitable services. Trust law experts recommended a diversified, or balanced, portfolio. Hershey Foods would have to be sold.

Lepley's decision grabbed headlines in the globalizing candy industry. Hershey Foods controlled more than 40 percent of the U.S. chocolate market share. Competitors jumped to bid. A joint Nestlé/Cadbury Schweppes offer valued the company at $10.5 billion, and a William Wrigley Jr. Company bid valued it at $12.5 billion.

A sale would be a windfall for the Trust and the Hershey School. But the proposed sale stunned the community's residents, who feared that a buyer would slash Pennsylvania jobs and hollow out the Hershey Foods headquarters. "We knew it would be difficult and perhaps a bloodbath with the white-collar employees," said former Hershey Chocolate CEO Richard Zimmerman. "Nestlé did not need the Hershey technical center; Wrigley had its sales force." Civic boosters asked: What would Hershey be without Hershey Chocolate? Residents planted "Derail the Sale" signs in their front yards. The TV networks came to Hershey to tell the story.

The alumni association joined forces with the community leaders in opposing the sale of Hershey Foods, believing that a political alliance with the community would ultimately help them reform the Hershey School itself. Television news stations captured images of residents with protest signs on their lawns, and assembled for protest gatherings. Mike Fisher's campaign was hurt politically in this Republican bastion by Lepley's timing on the sale of the chocolate company. Fisher sought to block the Hershey Foods sale through the Dauphin County Orphans' Court, an extraordinary intervention by an attorney general into the day-to-day affairs of the Trust. Seeing the public's outrage through almost daily stories on TV or the local newspapers, Judge Warren Morgan agreed with Fisher. "The Attorney General has sufficiently carried his burden proving the potential harm that he seeks to prevent, namely, the adverse economic and social impact against the public interest if a sale of Hershey Foods Corporation takes place, particularly in its effect on employees of the Corporation and the community of Derry Township," Morgan wrote in his September 10, 2002 adjudication that began the process of halting the sale.

The Orphans' Court had done nothing for decades as the Hershey School failed to heed its 1963 cy-près agreement and enroll 1,600 kids, or efficiently spend the orphanage assets on poor kids. Now it proactively protected the town's economic jewel, owned by the orphanage. Judge Morgan acknowledged that Milton and Kitty's 1909 Deed gave the Trust board the power to sell Hershey Foods. However, the rule, Morgan chided the Trust, "is a general rule, not an absolute."

Child care and the concerns of the school got pushed to the back burner as the community lashed out at the Trust over jobs. "The memorials of a good and generous man have not been well served by events surrounding this litigation," Morgan said in his adjudication of October 16, 2002. "In this mid-state area, Hershey is everybody's town; there is shared pride in identifying with that community, its industry and the School, all founded by Milton Hershey. Respect for Milton Hershey demands reconciliation among those interests as essential to effectively carrying out his philanthropic scheme."

State lawmakers drafted legislation protecting Hershey Foods against a hostile takeover or surprise sale. The proposed law would require the Trust to give notice to the attorney general at least 60 days before a sale—sufficient time to block it. "The ultimate beneficiary of a charitable trust in Pennsylvania is the public," Fisher, the official protector of the Trust's named beneficiaries—orphans and poor kids—told the Associated Press on October 23rd. "This legislation will ensure that a charitable trust which is considering selling a business as part of its fiduciary duties will consider how a sale will affect the workers at the business and the surrounding community."

Philadelphia charitable law attorney Donald W. Kramer warned, "This is bad legislation that appears to be quickly proposed to deal with a single transaction without considering the impact on the rest of the world. It would be unfortunate to pass broad general legislation without public hearings."

State lawmakers did it anyway. The measure passed in the Senate, 48-1. The House also passed it, and Governor Mark Schweiker signed it.

MIKE FISHER CARRIED rock-ribbed-Republican Dauphin County in the November election, but Ed Rendell, the populist former mayor of Philadelphia, trounced him statewide, 53.4 percent to 44.4 percent. With the election over, Fisher and Morgan dealt harshly with Lepley and the recalcitrant Trust board over the attempted chocolate company sale. Fisher announced on November 14th that 10 of 17 board members who had voted to sell Hershey Foods would not remain. He added that the board changes would end the uncertainty at the Trust "without the delay that is inherent with litigation."

Many viewed it as a Republican takeover of the multi-billion-dollar private Trust. The Dauphin County Courts were controlled by Republicans, and Fisher was a Republican. LeRoy Zimmerman, one of the state's top Republican power brokers and a former two-term attorney general, joined the Trust board controlling Hershey Foods, Hershey Entertainment, thousands of acres of land, and hundreds of millions of dollars in surplus orphan funds.

Other politically connected civic boosters also joined the Trust board: former *Patriot-News* publisher Raymond L. Gover, Hershey Chocolate CEO Richard H. Lenny, and Pennsylvania-American Water Company attorney Velma Redmond. None of them—not Zimmerman, Gover, Lenny or Redmond—was a state or national expert on education, poverty, child care or foster care, although they had near-total power over the Hershey School as members of the Board of Managers. There were no alumni activists appointed to the board.

The new Trust board designated alumnus Anthony Colistra as chairman. A 1959 graduate, Colistra had a doctorate in education from Temple University; he had served as president of the alumni association, and had retired as superintendent of a Harrisburg-area suburban school district. Lepley had tapped him for the Trust board in the mid-1990s. Activist alumni had taken to calling him "phony Tony."

The reconstituted Trust board hired alumnus John O'Brien as interim president, replacing Lepley. O'Brien had no experience as an educator, or running a school. He was the first Home Boy admitted to Princeton, and now a corporate consultant who specialized in "organizational change leadership," according to his résumé. He had been a keynote speaker, seminar leader and performance coach for managers and executives.

Other good-paying and influential school jobs went to alumni as William Lepley's educators and administrators quit or retired—a form of alumni patronage aimed at neutralizing alumni critics. Peter Gurt had been director of admissions, but left under Lepley. O'Brien rehired him as vice president of administration. Gurt, a popular guy with alumni, graduated from the Hershey School in 1985. The school hired Nick Nissley, 1984 graduate, as chief learning officer and director of organizational effectiveness. The institution hired Robert Fehrs as head of the middle school. He'd graduated in 1963. Ralph Carfagno, a 1973 graduate, became director of graduate services. Mike Weller, a 1966 graduate, became director of special projects and later head of the high school, or Senior Division. Weller had been the executive director of the alumni association during its most confrontational times with the Trust.

Mike Fisher and other officials at the Office of Attorney General met with the activists in the spring of 2003. Fisher asked Ric Fouad how many kids he thought could be educated at the Hershey School. Fouad remembers offering him a figure of 5,000 or 6,000. Fisher's response, according to Fouad, was that the community wouldn't allow the school to grow that large.

Joseph Berning asked Fisher about the reform agreement that had been signed in the summer of 2002 and would be implemented in the summer of 2003. Fisher responded that it was an agreement between the Trust and the Office of Attorney General. As such, it always could be changed. "I knew then we were screwed," Berning admitted.

On the Friday before Mike Fisher's sweeping reform package was to be implemented, he replaced it with a watered-down version. The Trust boards would remain interconnected and the new Trust board would have largely the same powers of the Trust boards through prior decades. There was no talk of the Blue Ribbon Task Force child safety recommendations.

"The newly reconstituted board," the attorney general said in a statement on June 27, 2003, "has assured us that it is committed to fulfilling the vision of Milton and Catherine Hershey that poor children receive a home, the education and upbringing that will allow them to succeed in life."

Fisher resigned as attorney general in 2003 and was confirmed as a federal appeals court judge in Philadelphia. He explained in a brief phone conversation with me about a decade later that he believed that the harsh reforms of the 2002 package were unnecessary with Zimmerman and other local individuals on the Trust board.

THE ACTIVIST ALUMNI felt betrayed by Mike Fisher. They now viewed the previous decade as mostly wasted efforts—there were no structural reforms at the charity, only new faces on the Trust board.

Unwilling to surrender, the alumni association sued in Orphans' Court to reinstate Fisher's original reform. "We fought for years to get some type of real structural improvement. Then the Office of Attorney General just let the new Trust board shred the reform agreement," John Rice, the new alumni association board president, said in announcing the legal action. "The Attorney General has made it clear that he wants this $5.5 billion trust to continue to function like an asset of the general public. His new agreement is basically a blueprint for selling off Trust land, and for perpetuating the view of the Trust as an economic engine for Central Pennsylvania."

Judge Morgan heard the alumni association's lawsuit. The case turned on an arcane but critical legal point for the Trust: Did the alumni association have the "legal standing" to sue the Trust? With Milton and Kitty's Trust, legal standing to sue was restricted to the Office of Attorney General and Trust board members. But the alumni association believed both groups were compromised as it regarded protecting potential beneficiaries of Milton and Kitty's trust fund.

On November 10, 2003, deputy attorney general Heather J. Vance-Rittman testified to Judge Morgan that the alumni association was not qualified to bring the suit, and that the attorney general sufficiently regulated the Trust and looked out for the impoverished kids who were the Trust's beneficiaries.

"There is nothing," Vance-Rittman said in court, "to stop the attorney general from acting. If the school were to revert back to the way it was before, there's nothing to prevent the attorney general from bringing action and correcting the situation." She continued, "The only course available to the alumni is to complain to the attorney general. The attorney general has been very receptive and open to their comments. We welcome their input."

Fouad testified that the Office of Attorney General had failed to protect poor kids, and would likely fail again. "At every turn," he told the judge, "we have been before the attorney general on these issues. Our work contributed to getting this reform agreement. If the reforms fail, all of our resources that we expended will have been for naught, and we'll be here in seven years or we'll be at the attorney general for another seven years, for another 10 years."

Judge Morgan ruled against the alumni association on November 19, 2003, saying, "We reject out of hand the implication that the school and the attorney general have subordinated to other interests the interests of the children who now or later may attend the school."

The alumni, unified, now split into two factions. John O'Brien, the new school president, headed a group seeking a truce with the Trust and the Office of Attorney General. They wanted to dial down the anger and confrontation and give the new Trust board time to implement reforms. O'Brien circulated a 20-page memo written by alumni-relations expert Dan White, proposing friendlier relations between school administrators, the Trust board and the alumni association. The Trust should consider designating a vice president to manage external relations and creating an alumni center on campus "as a sacred space."

O'Brien described his transition plan in a letter to alumni. The plan included sections titled, "Find and Serve the Children Who Need Our School the Most," "Be Obsessed with Graduate Success," "Focus on Character and Leadership Development" and "The Milton Hershey Way." There was talk of a huge construction program, and exceeding the enrollment goal of 1,600 students on the campus in Hershey. The Trust could renovate Senior Hall. A North Campus would be added for middle school students. The Hershey School held a gala in September 2003 for O'Brien's inauguration as Home Boy president. Color-guard students came down the center aisle of the packed auditorium in Founder's Hall to the tune of "Johnny Comes Marching Home."

Ric Fouad was concerned that the reconstituted Trust could revert to the ways of former Trust boards, and he was concerned as well with the influx of alumni administrators. During Homecoming, he spoke to alumni in the same auditorium where John O'Brien's inauguration had been celebrated, comparing the alumni activists to the desperate Nez Perce tribe that in 1877 fled the U.S. Army on horseback across Oregon, Washington, Idaho, Wyoming and Montana, looking for political asylum. They surrendered only miles from the Canadian border and safety. Fouad implored the alumni to keep fighting, "We're 15 miles from the border."

O'Brien tightened the screws on the alumni activists when he mailed a letter to alumni, printed on Milton Hershey School letterhead, in June 2004. The letter said they had "worn out their welcome with the Office of Attorney General, burned their bridge to the Orphans' Court and alienated most past [alumni association] presidents and leaders. It is time for a change." He evicted them from the Homestead. The alumni board rented conference space in the Holiday Inn.

The alumni association appealed Judge Morgan's ruling to the next higher court level, Commonwealth Court. A judges' panel heard the arguments on December 8, 2004. That court issued a decision on January 31, giving a surprising victory to the alumni. "At bottom," Commonwealth Court Judge Dan Pellegrini wrote, "the MHSAA [Milton Hershey School Alumni Association], whose membership consists exclusively of past beneficiaries of the Hershey Trust, is the only other party with a sufficient relationship to the Trust that would have any interest in assuring that its charitable purpose is achieved." Legal standing for the alumni association, Pellegrini added, "will serve the public interest in assuring that the Trust is operating efficiently and effectively to serve its beneficiaries." His opinion would be cited in trust law textbooks.

The deep-pocketed Trust appealed the Commonwealth Court decision to the state Supreme Court, the highest state court. The Trust and the alumni association argued their sides on May 9, 2006. Representing the alumni association were Ric Fouad and John Schmehl, a partner in the Philadelphia law firm of Dilworth Paxson. Schmehl's father, William, had graduated from the Milton Hershey Industrial School in 1939. "He was always grateful to the school," John said of his father. William Schmehl went on to teach political science and history at Hershey Junior College. After it closed in the 1960s, he taught at Harrisburg Area Community College. He helped to raise funds for the iconic statue of Milton Hershey with a young boy in Founder's Hall, and kept accounts as treasurer of the alumni association. The elder Schmehl died in 1981, and John's mother, Mary, purchased a cemetery plot so he could be buried near Milton in the Hershey Cemetery. "She probably paid more than she should have. She knew how much it meant to him," John Schmehl reflected.

John G. Knorr 3d argued for the Attorney General's office, and Barbara Mather of Pepper Hamilton represented the Hershey Trust. "You could tell from the moment that [Judge] Cappy spoke, we were dead," Schmehl noted. Cappy warned, "We don't want emotions to rule the day." Schmehl thought the justices asked "some decent questions but a lot of them did not look very interested and that was not good for us." Attorney General Tom Corbett and LeRoy Zimmerman, the Republican power broker and now head of the Trust, sat near the front of the courtroom.

Also attending the Supreme Court hearing was Hershey alumnus Bobby Chalmers. He came to Hershey in 1954 from a Philadelphia row house crowded with seven kids after his dad, Walter, died at age 42 of a brain hemorrhage. His mom had talked to Girard College about enrolling sons Bobby, Jerry and Harry. But there was no room, so Girard referred her to Hershey. "I was young and I really didn't know what was going on," said Bobby, who began as a kindergartner in 1954. His brother Jerry didn't stay. "Here's a kid who had a little freedom and then he had none. He told me later he thought he was in prison."

Bobby remembers playing fort with the other boys and mowing the lawn with a push-mower down by the cherry tree orchard in Hershey. Once a week they would be bused into town for a night out. The boys would gravitate to their favorite places to smoke. Bobby was at the all-school assembly when J.O. Hershey announced the plans for the medical center. J.O. really pumped it up, he recalled, telling them that Home Boys could go to medical school and be doctors. But most of the Home Boys were training for blue-collar trades. Bobby learned carpentry. He did his farm chores. He milked cows in the barn. He thought he was part of the chocolate factory.

"What do dairy cows make?" Chalmers asked me as we talked over coffee in Philadelphia's Reading Terminal Market. He made motions like he was milking a cow. "Milk. What do you put in a milk chocolate bar? Milk. Those who don't think that that thought didn't go through Milton Hershey's mind are in denial."

Bobby Chalmers graduated in 1966, and stayed connected to the Hershey School. He heard in the 1990s that the school had closed its vocational education shops. That didn't sound right to him. He heard about the activists. He thought he'd like to help. One of the Home Boys in the alumni association drove to King of Prussia, where he lived, and gave Bobby the addresses of the alumni living in the Philadelphia area. He mailed letters out to them—his wife helped him with the labels—and launched a Philadelphia alumni chapter. They met in a church on Aramingo Street, where another Home Boy worked as a maintenance man. Chalmers arranged for Fouad to speak to the Philadelphia chapter. It was electrifying. "At that moment," he said, "the alumni association was very unified."

Chalmers supported the alumni's court case seeking the right to sue the Trust, and Joe Berning asked him to go to the Supreme Court hearing. There were about 40 people there. He saw Attorney General Corbett and Trust head Zimmerman, who would eventually earn about two million dollars in Trust-related directors' fees, sitting near the front of the courtroom.

"I had a lot of faith in the Supreme Court," Chalmers reflected. But as he sat listening to the judges, he felt the alumni weren't getting a fair shake. The questions to the alumni lawyers were pointed and challenging. One justice kept glancing over at Corbett and Zimmerman with, it seemed, a knowing look. "You could tell that this was fixed. I thought, we lost."

The Supreme Court's December 28, 2006 decision crushed Chalmers, Fouad, Berning and the rest of the alumni activists. "We find the Association did not have a special interest sufficient to vest it with standing," the decision read. "Nothing in this litigation would affect the Association itself; it loses nothing and gains nothing….The Association's intensity of concern is real and commendable, but it is not a substitute for an actual interest. Standing is not created through the Association's advocacy or its members' past close relationship with the School as former individual recipients of the Trust's benefits. The Trust did not contemplate the Association, or anyone else, to be a 'shadow board' of graduates with standing to challenge actions the Board takes."

There were no other appeals. Millions of dollars and thousands of hours of volunteerism over 15 years had gone into trying to reform the Trust.

Between 1999 and 2003, John Halbleib estimated that he spent about 8,000 hours on the Trust business, valued at $3.5 million in legal fees. He stored a terabyte of information on his computers in the Chicago area. Ric Fouad practically suspended his legal career for the alumni cause. Those efforts and financial resources swirled down the drain that day, defeated by Harrisburg politics, the courts and the Trust lawyers.

Ric Fouad booked a flight to Tokyo the day after the Supreme Court decision, and took a job as an in-house counsel at a Japanese financial advisory firm. He created the non-profit Protect the Hershey's Children as a clearinghouse for information on the Hershey School and a place for students and parents to complain. Activist alumni gravitated to it, while the Hershey School administration ostracized him and blocked his emails. "I've been living up in the hills and trying to keep alive," he said wryly in the New York interview. "The public officials are the bad guys. [The alumni] were the only agent of change."

8

RECURRING PROBLEM—
THE CHOCOLATE PROFITS

How Should the Trust Spend Its Billions on Poor Kids?

*"There is accumulating evidence that if you keep kids
at home there seems to be long-term benefits as opposed
to institutionalizing them."*
> —Former Hershey School vice president
> Ron Thompson

O VER THE DECADES, the Trust had constructed more rural student homes, more classrooms, more gymnasiums and more administrative buildings in Hershey with the trust fund surpluses that had been built up from burgeoning chocolate profits. Now, following Judge Warren Morgan's 1999 rejection of his proposed research institute, William Lepley cast about for what to do with the hundreds of millions of dollars that Morgan said had to be spent directly on poor children.

The former Iowa education bureaucrat asked his staff the obvious question: Was an all-in-Hershey expansion of the school's services the best option going forward for the nation's poor kids? Should the Trust try something new? Should the Hershey School stay bottled up in rural Hershey with so much poverty in cities? How effective was the super-rich Hershey School, still based on Milton Hershey's outmoded model, in improving the lives of poor children?

The public looked at the Trust's massive wealth emanating from the chocolate company, and at the school's gorgeous campus, and thought the Hershey School must be doing great things for poor kids to lift them out of poverty. The institution's PR machine continued to crank out stories of poor kids graduating from high school on an upward trajectory, painting the institution as a ticket to college and the middle class.

Insiders knew differently. Few kids enrolled as kindergartners or first graders because parents were reluctant to send their young children away from home. Many Hershey School students entered in eighth, ninth or tenth grades, giving the institution only a few years to develop them academically and socially for college.

Teenage students were rebelling against the strict rules. Attrition had been a problem since the 1970s even though the institution now practically threw money at poor boys and girls, at least according to its IRS filings. The Trust spent annually about $100,000 per student—a whopping amount when compared with the value of tuition and boarding fees at elite private schools and the other specialized residential child-care institutions. Because it was so expensive to operate, and costs were not offset by any tuition fees as they would be at most boarding schools, a student who attended the Hershey School for two years and then dropped out cost Milton and Kitty's trust fund $200,000 with minimal charitable return on those funds. A child attending there for five, six or 10 years could drop out or be expelled. Those kids cost Milton and Kitty's trust fund between $500,000 and one million dollars. Students and their parents viewed the Hershey School as a college-prep boarding school—an idea promoted by the institution with its academic-based curriculum, centralized and compact campus and college-aid scholarship program. But most MHS graduates who went on to college dropped out before earning a degree.

Since the late 1950s, the Trust or its consultants had told the Orphans' Court and the attorney general that the Hershey School should enroll 1,500 or 1,600 orphans or poor students in Hershey. But that could easily be changed without a huge legal battle. Judge Morgan had included a footnote in his decree rejecting the 1999 *cy-près* petition, indicating that the Trust could consider locations outside of Hershey to expand school operations with its surplus because, he wrote, of the "doctrine of deviations is the available remedy; location is merely a detail of trust administration."

This perhaps could be the opening. Lepley himself had reservations about expanding the school in Hershey: he believed that the "larger the school got, the higher the potential there was for problems with the town." He began considering satellite schools. Lepley hired Ronald Thompson of Boys Town in Nebraska to oversee an independent research project which would evaluate the Hershey School and its programs—the first independent evaluation by experts since the late 1950s. Morgan had ordered the Hershey School to expend its surplus directly on poor kids. Lepley would find the best way to do it, using the best standards of research.

Hershey School could be a powerful force for good in helping the nation's poor children, Thompson believed. But he came to the project with knowledge built of years of research, and he didn't think an all-in-Hershey approach was the best option. "There is accumulating evidence," Thompson said in a phone interview, "that if you keep kids at home there seems to be long-term benefits as opposed to institutionalizing them." Having the Hershey School expand in Hershey, Thompson continued, meant that "you got one solution to child poverty in America and that was to convince parents to send their children to Hershey."

Thompson had a budget of several million dollars—one estimate was five million—for a sophisticated and comprehensive analysis of the Hershey School's programs. With this much money, work could proceed at the highest professional level. Thompson engaged some of the leading British and American researchers as advisors, including Sir Michael Rutter, "the father of child psychology" and author of the classic *Maternal Deprivation Reassessed*; the University of Maryland's Richard Barth; Penn State's Mark Greenberg; Michael Little, from the Research Unit at Dartington, and the University of Chicago's Harold Richman. This advisory board met at the Hotel Hershey and toured the campus.

Thompson retained Chapin Hall, a policy research center at the University of Chicago, to crunch the numbers and assemble research. According to its website, Chapin Hall's "impact derives largely from a distinctive marriage of the most rigorous academic research and innovative partnerships with public systems, institutions, organizations, and programs that are in a position to deploy that research." Chapin Hall's areas of specialty were child welfare and foster care, community change, economic supports for the family, home visitation and abuse prevention, schools, workforce development and crime. Its researchers chose tough topics: why more blacks than whites seemed to be placed in foster care, the transition of foster children into adulthood, and underperforming poor schools.

Michael Little of Dartington coordinated the Hershey project. The British had more experience with boarding schools, and it was only logical that they were more advanced in their analysis of them. Dartington's Social Research Unit had been "key in bringing about the closure of residential centers for delinquent youth, limits on the number of children placed in secure settings, and the provision for more contact between looked-after children and their parents," according to its organizational history. "We have also been an important voice in the national debate about more pre-vention and early intervention in children's services."

Data collectors knocked on doors and interviewed parents in poor neighborhoods in Philadelphia and other Pennsylvania cities, asking them what they thought of sending their children away to a boarding-type school with world-class educational facilities and college-prep academic track. High-income parents saw boarding school as a rite of passage for their children. But this wasn't the view in impoverished, jobless brick row house neighborhoods. Mothers and fathers there feared county social workers tak-ing children out of their home for neglect and placing them in foster homes. "Parents in lower socioeconomic levels have even stronger bonds than fam-ilies who send their children to private boarding schools," said Thompson. "They hate to have their kids placed out of their home."

Researchers also were troubled with how the Hershey School interacted with parents. Contemporary research showed that a poor child in a resi-dential school had to maintain close relations with their mother, father and other family members. These were people with whom they'd have relation-ships that lasted the rest of their lives. The Hershey School still operated as if the kids had been orphaned without family. It restricted visits home by the students and didn't regularly update parents on their child's performance in Hershey.

WHAT EXCITED top-level British and American researchers the most about the Hershey project was the potential to answer the bet-the-farm question: How did poor students who attended the Hershey School, the world's richest boarding school for impoverished children, compare with poor students who applied but didn't enroll there and perhaps were educated in public or private school near their homes?

Put more simply: Using objective comparisons, did the Hershey School improve the lives of kids who went there and who benefited from the $100,000 a year from Milton and Kitty's trust fund, when they were objec-tively compared with the students of the same socioeconomic background who did not attend the Hershey School?

Like proud parents, administrators told stories of students who achieved college or professional success after MHS. Each year, the school still handed out a distinguished alumni award. But those were anecdotes in newspaper stories and public relations and marketing brochures, not the result of vet-ted research. Those same administrators neglected to tell the sad stories of students who dropped out of MHS, or flunked out of college. There seemed to be at least as many, perhaps more, of those students as successful ones.

Skeptical researchers also asked whether the high-achieving MHS student would have succeeded without MHS. Was it the institution or the individual? When one tallied up the successes and failures, were there more of one than the other? "There are exceptional stories of people from Hershey," said one of the dream team researchers. "But we can't tell if they would have done as well if they had not gone to Hershey."

The British and American researchers structured the project like a random drug trial. In such a drug trial, one patient group takes an experimental drug while a second group doesn't—that's the control group. At the trial's end, over weeks, months or years, researchers compare the health outcomes of the two groups. If the experimental drug improved the health of the group whose members took it while health of the group whose members did not take the medication didn't improve, the drug could be considered effective and safe to be sold to the public. And vice versa.

The researchers believed they could compare the lives of poor kids who attended the Hershey School with the lives of those who applied for admission and were rejected. They could look at current students and recent graduates, and they could look retrospectively by analyzing historic data in the admissions department. With Lepley supporting the project, the researchers could access student and admissions data—names, ages, race and household income. The project's results would look at the broad performance of the Hershey School with poor students. It also could look at other factors, such as differentiations based on race.

The Hershey School had adjusted its admissions criteria over the years to maintain a 50-50 racial balance of African-American and white students. The Hershey School had the hardest time recruiting poor white kids from rural Pennsylvania, while it easily found applicants among African-American populations—most likely because of the dangerous and poorly run public schools in Pennsylvania's larger cities. Philadelphia schools were careening from one financial crisis to the next over funding. At this point, if the Hershey School were to enroll only the most qualified students who applied on a color-blind basis, most students who attended the Hershey School would be African-American, according to a former top school official. Because African-American children came from homes that were generally poorer than poor white students, the Hershey School might be most useful raising the living standards of African-American students, some believed. But such a research conclusion seemed to cause discomfort in Trust board members who were determined to maintain a 50-50 student racial balance.

In the midst of this multi-million-dollar research project, Judge Morgan and Attorney General Mike Fisher ousted William Lepley and his allies on the Trust board over the proposed sale of Hershey Chocolate. Replacing them were the politically powerful LeRoy Zimmerman, former newspaper publisher Raymond Gover, and other civic boosters. Alumni remained a powerful voting bloc on the Trust board. The new Trust board said it wanted to continue to cooperate with the researchers. But now, data wasn't forthcoming. The new school president, John O'Brien, balked at participating in some areas of the project, believing it required the institution to deliberately reject some students who would qualify so they could be tracked.

The new Trust board also seemed to be leaning toward expanding the school's operations in Hershey—keeping Milton and Kitty's orphans' funds local instead of financing school facilities and operations in other parts of Pennsylvania or the nation. In late 2003, the Trust board finalized plans to boost the enrollment to 1,800 students, a project that would cost hundreds of millions of dollars in construction. Later the Trust board raised the bar even higher, with a goal of 2,000 students by 2013 in Hershey—400 students more than the target in the 1963 *cy-près* petition and 500 more than the 1999 *cy-près* petition. The Trust moved to expand in Hershey without the results of the research project, which very likely would have showed that an all-in-Hershey expansion wasn't the best option for poor students. "It was clear," said one of the advisory board members, "that this wasn't like a [National Institutes of Health] grant in which the government gave you money and went away so you could research."

The Trust's tax filings with the Internal Revenue Service in 2002 and 2003 eventually were the only public evidence that the research project existed at all. Those 990's referenced $1,117,410 spent on "educational researchers," paid to Chapin Hall in 2002, and an additional $996,791 in 2003. The Trust listed the amounts in the section for compensation paid to independent contractors. In 2002, Chapin Hall was the Hershey School's highest-paid independent contractor, and in 2003 it was the second highest. There were no references in the IRS documents to Chapin Hall after the 2003 filing.

Richard Barth, the dean of the School of Social Work at the University of Maryland and an advisory board member, commented on the project's termination: "There seemed not to be a great seriousness or compunction on their part to see whether what they were doing was making a difference, or whether they could improve." A second advisory board member said he believed that local and state politics overrode child-care concerns. Ron Thompson, the vice president recruited for the project, quit and returned to Boys Town in Nebraska. The project "kind of never got off the ground in the two years I was there," he said. "I felt like we were not on first base. It was moving at a snail's pace. They were not interested in the answers."

The Chapin Hall researchers never published a report for public consumption on the Hershey School. But Thompson, Michael Little and Amelia Kohm placed an article in the *International Journal of Social Welfare* in 2005, blandly titled, "The impact of residential placement on child development: research and policy implications." Thompson forwarded the article in an email to me. The journal article did not name the Hershey School, but addressed residential-education issues consistent with those at the institution.

"Very little is known about the impact of separation on the functioning of the separated adult and its impact on the separated child," the authors wrote. "Where information on the success of residential interventions exists, it usually indicates that some children do well, meaning others do not improve (and, as we have hypothesized, that some may actually be worse off as a result of the experience)."

The authors bemoaned the guessing. They thought bullying could be a problem, but they didn't know the extent. There were few more "intrusive interventions" in a child's life than placing them in a residential facility, and the "potential positive or negative impact alone justifies the cost of rigorous evaluation."

The authors concluded: "Without significant changes, the future of residential provision for children looks bleak. Certain sectors, such as the elite boarding schools, will, of course, remain, although it seems reasonable to assume they will continue to decline in terms of numbers of children served....

"Is there an alternative scenario? We do not know which children will benefit...or why interventions work when they do. But we have evidence that there are positive outcomes for some children in some domains, and we should try to build upon this knowledge."

THE HERSHEY SCHOOL was now an institution based on the concept of residential education that not only lacked scientific underpinnings and broad support, but was an outlier in terms of the conventional educational system in the United States. But it had advocates in Washington. Community activist Heidi Goldsmith established the Coalition for Residential Education to lobby and advocate in Washington for the residential education concept in the 1990s. The group went by the acronym CORE. Its membership today consists of about 35 institutions: repurposed orphanages and current or former homes for delinquent, homeless, abused or troubled children. They include the Ben Richey Boys Ranch; Florida Sheriffs' Youth Ranches; Girard College; Methodist Children's Home; Oklahoma Baptist Homes for Children; the SEED Schools and the Tupelo Children's Mansion.

Their history is as colorful and varied and daring as Americans themselves. The Reverend James A. Scott and his wife Theodocia opened an orphanage in Oklahoma City in 1903, seven years before Milton and Kitty. The Baptist minister explained in his 1936 manuscript: "Now this institution was born in the heart of Mrs. J.A. Scott. While I was at the Seminary at Louisville, we frequently visited the Louisville Baptist Orphanage and Masonic Orphans' Home. It was often expressed that if we ever were to go to Oklahoma, if others had not, we wanted to start a Baptist orphanage. The way did not open in our first coming to Oklahoma, but when we took the work at Washington Avenue in Oklahoma City, the Lord opened the way and three children were put in our hands."

The mother of the first child "was living in a one room house on the alley of Chickasaw Street. The mother and child seemed hopeless and ready to die," Scott wrote. "The next baby, Annabelle [Hunt], was a foundling left in a wagon at Paul's Valley, then Indian Territory. She was brought by Mrs. Scott's suggestion to the Home. Mrs. Turner found her when she heard a baby cry at one o'clock in the morning."

The Oklahoma and Indian Territory Orphans' Home shortened its name to the Oklahoma Baptist Orphans' Home in 1917. There were other name changes, new buildings and new services. A crisis pregnancy center opened. In the early 1990s, in the face of smaller enrollment, the former orphanage closed eight cottages and cut its staff.

In Texas, the Abilene city commissioner, Ben Richey, noticed "how boys in the area who were without Christian role models fell into the same rut." The charity's literature says the "Ben Richey Boys Ranch, opened in 1947, will provide a clean, comfortable and safe home for each boy at the ranch. Through nurturing and guidance of home parents and staff, each boy will develop confidence and learn to take responsibility for his actions." It shelters 20 to 25 homeless boys for about a million dollars a year.

The Reverend T.C. Montgomery drove the back roads of Mississippi with a Bible, collecting $322 to found the Tupelo Children's Mansion. In 1952, it was recognized by the United Pentecostal Church, and the state granted it non-profit status the same year. Its first four children, ages four through 12, arrived by train the next year.

In the 1970s, the group's campus expanded to 26 buildings from seven. In 2004, the charity opened a home for troubled teenage girls with special needs. The Tupelo Children's Mansion says in its IRS filing that it spent $2.8 million in 2010.

Nicholette Smith-Bligen, CORE's executive director, says residential education is a "boarding school model" for disadvantaged children. "They are all residential and their programs are centered on education," she said. The "primary focus is on the academics and not the mental health," while acknowledging "the kids we target may come from difficult circumstances and may need additional support."

Though anecdotal evidence shows that residential education helps children, Smith-Bligen acknowledged that more research needed to be done on residential education. She added, "Boarding schools have been around forever, but they have not been talked about in impoverished communities. It's a viable option for all youth, not just youth in the wealthy community."

MILTON AND KITTY HERSHEY had initially launched an orphanage. With that institutional model discredited, the modernized Hershey School with its centralized campus directed peoples' attention to college-prep boarding schools as its model. The glory years for U.S. boarding schools came between 1890 and 1910—America's Gilded Age. Even one of their biggest advocates today, Peter Upham, executive director of the Association of Boarding Schools, acknowledges "there is certainly not growth in the number of North American students going to a boarding school. It's what they'd call a mature market." Choate-Rosemary Hall, Deerfield, the Gunnery, Lawrenceville, Groton and other private boarding schools enroll 35,000 children of upper-middle-class and well-to-do parents in the United States or Canada. Another 15,000 foreign students attend the institutions, bringing the total boarding school population to about 50,000 kids.

Upham described boarding schools as "pretty counter-culture" and said that only one in 500 American students enroll in one. "You are kind of an oddball if you go to a boarding school." Parents are only willing to pay boarding school tuition, which averages around $40,000 a year but could be significantly higher at the most elite institutions, because of the so-called boarding-school effect. Children who attend boarding schools do more homework, watch less TV and interact more with teachers, Upham contended. "There is a mountain of evidence on a battery of measures that boarding schools make a big difference. Parents wouldn't pay the money we charge if they did not think their kids would be able to compete for slots at the most select [colleges]."

The Association of Boarding Schools, or TABS, keeps a database on its members that can be sorted and searched on the Internet. The Hershey School is now ranked in the TABS database as the nation's largest boarding school by wealth and enrollment, accounting for about 5 percent of the U.S. boarding school population. Upham welcomed Milton Hershey's former no-frills orphanage and trade school as a peer in the association of the nation's elite boarding schools because the Hershey School "shares our criteria. It is a residential school and it is college preparatory in mission and practice." But could the benefits of a boarding school for rich kids be transferred to poor kids? "I'd like to think so, but I don't know either way," Upham said. "I haven't thought a great deal about this but I don't see any reason a boarding school…couldn't work with a population Milton Hershey serves."

ALUMNUS JOHN O'BRIEN, taking over as the new president of the Hershey School in 2003, inherited a confused and traumatized institution. O'Brien's base of support, the alumni association, had fought the school's administration most of the prior decade. They believed the outsider William Lepley, didn't know what he was doing and neglected to emphasize teaching discipline, respect and good behavior. O'Brien and his new alumni school administrators would restore these traditions to the Hershey School with busy kids and a culture of "more gratitude, less attitude."

Alumni administrators formalized a system of merits and demerits that had existed on the Hershey School campus for decades, with behavior ratings and a point-based discipline scheme. At the same time, O'Brien attempted to lower attrition rates—kids dropping out of the Hershey School before graduation. He and others viewed the school's failure with attrition as particularly troubling. To them, a kid who walked out of the Hershey School was the same as a kid walking away from their family home. Many of them thought of the institution as the "Home." No one thought that was OK.

O'Brien developed the idea of welcoming Springboard Academy: an experimental stand-alone educational facility on the Hershey School campus for middle school children. The Trust approved the concept and agreed to spend $36 million on its construction. It was to ease kids into the rigors of the Hershey School with its regimented daily life. At Springboard, though, kids slept in dorms, not group student homes. There was one for girls and one for boys. They didn't even attend traditional classes. An embarrassing failure, the Trust closed it after a few years because it didn't measurably boost attrition and because of safety concerns with so many kids sleeping together in a dorm.

The trade school as it had existed in the 1950s wasn't coming back. The Trust had invested heavily into the boarding school model and centralized campus. It recruited students with the promise of Trust-funded college scholarships accruing with each year of high school attendance. O'Brien and Trust leaders realized that by the early 2000s this was a big problem. Most MHS graduates weren't earning college degrees. They didn't have the so-called persistence to get through four years of college and dropped out or failed out. For those who read Milton and Kitty's 1909 Deed, this pointed to charitable failure. The Deed stated that the institution's purpose was to educate orphans, now poor kids, to lead "productive" lives as middle-class American citizens. Milton Hershey's solution had been to graduate "employable products" with trade skills in plumbing, electrical work, carpentry and other blue-collar jobs. Now the institution graduated kids with high school diplomas and sent them to college with the belief they'd matriculate. Few Americans believed in the early 2000s that a high school education—even a very expensive chocolate-funded high school education—was the ticket to a middle-class life.

Part of the problem with college persistence seemed to be a legacy of the institution's history as an orphanage. The Hershey School rigorously structured student lives down to the minute. Students had little independence. They were told what to do and what to talk about and where to go and what to do with their time. There were limits on their use of social media and mobile phones and even visits home. When MHS students graduated, they were unprepared to shop, budget, find medical care, study, make good friends and work on their own. O'Brien and the new alumni leaders developed apartment-style "transitional living" units for high school seniors to experience some freedoms. This was a good start. But it didn't seem to go far enough, and it didn't solve another problem for impoverished kids: a lack of family support when they entered college. Milton Hershey believed that poor boys had to quickly enter the workforce and earn a paycheck because they couldn't count on family to help them through college. Times hadn't changed all that much for poor kids between 1920 and 2013. One 2005 MHS graduate observed in an interview, "It was difficult for some of the kids during the summer. They didn't have a place to live. There were a lot of students who were homeless in the summer and then there were some students who weren't smart with their money. Hershey expects you to be an adult when you get out, and a lot of kids are not at that maturity level."

MHS students tended to aim for select colleges. This was part of the allure of the gorgeous campus and the prep school model. But MHS students struggled very hard at whatever college they attended. Beginning with O'Brien, the Hershey School tried to calibrate student expectations and to link scholarship aid to high school performance. Students were evaluated through a matrix of grades, SAT scores and state proficiency scores, limiting their options. Based on the matrix, many would only qualify for community colleges.

Financial aid administrators also thought that if impoverished students had loans—as opposed to aid—they'd have an incentive to graduate from college because they'd have to pay off the loans. The multi-billion-dollar Hershey School told students they had to borrow $2,500 a year from the federal Stafford loan program for college. The amount could be repaid with Hershey School college scholarship aid if they graduated from college. If they didn't graduate, they'd be on the hook for thousands of federal student dollars themselves. One top school official, an alumnus, called it "skin in the game." But the policy also shifted the financial burden of paying for college from the Hershey School's chocolate-funded endowment to its impoverished graduates.

The Hershey School marketed the $80,000 in college aid as a recruitment tool to bring in good students. But in many cases, top academic achievers at the Hershey School didn't even need the Hershey School's scholarship program that had seemed so attractive to them and their parents back in seventh or eighth grade. With good grades and low household income, these students independently qualified for grants and non-Trust college aid programs based on financial need.

One girl dropped out of the Hershey School months before graduation when a college of her choice near her home town offered her a full ride.

She lived hours from Hershey and missed her family. She was a very intelligent and motivated student—well above the average MHS student. "No one wants to be here, and I feel the administration uses the $80,000 like a carrot on a stick. We have to keep chasing it even if it makes us miserable," she told me.

There was also the problem of SAT scores. They remained a pervasive factor in college admissions, though studies consistently indicated that the scores were strongly affected by household income. The Hershey School had transformed itself into a boarding school to prepare poor students for college, yet the historic SAT scores of poor students who attended the Hershey School strongly suggested that MHS graduates would struggle to get through college—unless the Hershey School could develop an innovative program to substantially boost its SATs.

It hadn't. In 2011, the Hershey School's average SAT scores ranked 515th out of 648 among Pennsylvania public and charter schools, lower than some Pennsylvania public schools with high percentages of poor students, according to the Hershey's "Annual Student Life Report Card," released in 2012, and Pennsylvania Department of Education data.

Trends showed that average SAT scores at the Hershey School weren't heading higher, but lower. Female student SAT scores fell—from an average of 1352 for math, reading and writing in 2009 to 1304 in 2012. The Hershey School succeeded with one student population over this time, though: African-Americans. The average SAT scores for African-American students were slightly better than the state average.

With average SAT scores at the lower end of the state's spectrum, choices and the likelihood for success at college narrowed sharply for Hershey School students. Hershey School showed that top destinations for MHS graduates were community colleges and fairly nonselective state universities, including Harrisburg Area Community College, Pennsylvania Institute of Technology, Kutztown University, Northampton Community College and the Community College of Philadelphia. Many of the MHS graduates were dropping out of these post-secondary institutions as well.

A January 27, 2012 Hershey School internal school memo told a sobering story about college persistence a decade after Mike Fisher and Warren Morgan reconfigured the Trust board, and the John O'Brien-led administration attempted to tighten discipline and boost college success. The memo listed recent college grads by student name and post-secondary institution they were attending after graduation.

Twenty-seven percent of the Hershey School's graduating class of 2010, significantly less than one-third, were enrolled in community or four-year colleges and earning a 2.5 grade point average or higher after three semesters in college.

In the Class of 2011, 30 percent of MHS graduates earned a 2.5 grade point average or higher after their first semester in a community or four-year college.

Many MHS graduates were simply not making it at college after the Trust had spent hundreds of millions of dollars, perhaps a billion, over two decades to transform the former vocational school into a prep school for poor kids.

JUNE 10, 2012 broke gloriously in the Lebanon Valley for the pageantry and jubilation of the Hershey School graduation in Founder's Hall. The parking lots around Founder's Hall filled to capacity. Men and women, grandmothers and grandfathers, walked into the building dressed in their Sunday best. There was an overflow area inside the cafeteria with giant-screen TVs showing the ceremony for the several hundred attendees who didn't have tickets.

The somber strains of Bach's Toccata and Fugue in D Minor opened the ceremony. The members of the Board of Managers took their places on the stage with the top two school administrators, president Tony Colistra and chief operating officer Peter Gurt, both alumni.

At this moment, it was hard not to set aside concerns about the school and student achievement, and just feel the pride in the students that reverberated through the room. Houseparents and teachers sat in the seats in the front rows. There were sobs and hugs with houseparents as the seniors, dressed in brown and gold gowns, streamed down the auditorium's long aisles and toward the stage.

Ariana Neely of Baltimore, who had enrolled nine years earlier in the elementary school, and who hoped to be a pediatric oncologist, gave the "Welcome Speech" to the crowd. It was an uplifting speech like so many of the comments that day—including those by school administrators—and it touched on the difficulty of leaving home and parents for Hershey. The consistent theme was overcoming hardship.

"Milton Hershey seemed like the perfect getaway for an adventurous little girl who needed to be away from the family turmoil," Neely said on the stage to the crowd. "Although I wanted to be here, every day for that first month I cried and cried over the absence of my family. I remember my houseparents telling me to stop crying and be a big girl. I thought they were being insensitive. However as time went on, I realized they were teaching me to be strong."

She told a story. During her first days at Milton Hershey, her housemother asked her to use "elbow grease" to clean the kitchen. She hadn't heard of elbow grease and didn't know what that was. Maybe it was a cleaning solvent? She looked through the cabinets for the "elbow grease." Of course she couldn't find it and she learned that it was hard physical scrubbing that the housemother expected of her. *Put some elbow grease into it.* Elbow grease was her metaphor for her experience at Hershey, and she connected the dots to Milton Hershey himself and thanked him.

"Mr. Hershey put his elbow grease into making the perfect chocolate bar," Neely said. "When Mr. Hershey finally experienced mass success he did not spend his fortune selfishly. Rather he listened to Catherine's suggestion and built this school. He wanted us to know that in order to have our own success we would have to learn how to use our elbow grease. We are eternally thankful to the Hersheys for the opportunities they have given us and the lessons they have taught us."

She thanked the staff. "Houseparents, you have been forced to use a lot of elbow grease while working with us," Neely said. "Through my time here I could see the stress written on your faces when we pin things such as unlikable rules and policies on you. It was obvious that you were struggling not to take your frustration out on the student. Through those hard times… you always found a way to teach us life lessons."

Neely told of her housefather who taught her to manage her time. "Many times we thought he was just being cruel. We did not realize that he was giving us the tools and skills we would need for college and beyond," she said. She alluded to the hardship on her family. "Perhaps the people who used the most elbow grease were our family members. You made the biggest sacrifice. You sent your children away. You struggled to let us go. But you did it. There were so many times that we ran to you crying that it was too hard here," Neely said. "We did not want to be here anymore. We wanted to be normal teenagers. Fortunately though, you have stood strong, said 'No,' and sent us right back."

Neely looked ahead toward a future of elbow grease. "Class of 2012, as we begin our final hours at MHS, I encourage you to remember all the good times you have had, but more importantly I encourage you to remember the struggles. Those hard times that we faced taught us important lessons for life. By remembering those times we will remember the lessons we need to know. As we move on with our lives we will face difficulties and hard times. Just remember, with a little elbow grease we can get through anything."

Students in the senior choir ensemble sang Katy Perry's "Fireworks," and chief operating officer Gurt, an '85 graduate, told the crowd that of the 192 graduating seniors, 41 students had attended the school since the elementary grades. Gurt said that 54 percent of the graduating students intended to enter a four-year college, and 33 percent a two-year institution. The remaining students would enter the workforce or the military.

Now the moment the students had been waiting for came. Senior boys strutted and chest-thumped as they walked to accept diplomas. Family members and friends hooted with joy. Senior girls playfully waltzed on the stage. Sesay Bayoh, a Reading girl, had enrolled in 2004, and hoped to be a nurse practitioner. She gave the farewell speech, comparing her trek through the Hershey School as a triathlon—a grueling running, swimming and biking race. "I have crossed the finish line with my head held high and with all that is left of me." She spoke of homesickness on her first days at Hershey, and how she didn't know what to expect—she thought she would be going home and not staying there.

"My mother looked at me, kissed me goodbye, and walked away with tears in her eyes. I did not understand what was happening. I just did what I was told and stayed. The next morning I was ready for my mother to come and get me. I was in the mudroom with my bags packed looking out the window. When my housemother woke up and noticed me, she told me that my mother was not coming back today; that was when I realized that this was permanent. I felt, as we have all felt, as if I was pushed into the water and treading to keep my head above the waves."

Over the last Christmas break, Sesay told the crowd, her mother had been admitted to the hospital, and died on January 18, 2012. "I was at my weakest point. The future was blurry and seemed hopeless. However, I still had strength to make it up the mountain. With the help of teachers, house-parents, staff, counselors, teammates, coaches, friends and family, I was able to make it over the mountain. I never felt more love and support from the school than during my time of hardship. They pushed me over the mountain even though my tires were running out of air."

She quickly brought her speech around to Milton Hershey. "Obstacles," she said, "may come our way, and it is okay to get tired in a race; however, it is how you finish that makes all the difference. Milton Hershey portrayed that countless times by persevering through his failures to create a chocolate bar."

After the 90-minute ceremony, the students and their families gathered in the rotunda of Founder's Hall. This could be the last time they saw each other as they took their next steps, scattering to different parts of Pennsylvania and the nation.

Martayla Poellinitz had come to the Hershey School when she was eight years old. She was one of six children of a single mother in Harrisburg. Five of the six children in the family ended up attending the Hershey School—she was the second youngest. "The hardest part was adjusting to the rules and the houseparents," she said. She said she had wanted to quit in her middle school years but stuck it out. She planned to enroll in the fall in Duquesne University. Hopeful of success, she said, "I learned so many things here there is no way I could fail unless I don't try."

Monazia Joseph-Ward, 18, of Lebanon, Pennsylvania had attended the school for four years. She hadn't wanted to come, but her mother, Chaka Ward, "would not budge," the girl said. She described with a laugh the most important lesson of the school: "One thing, I know how to clean very good." She added, seriously, "I know how to associate with other people." She intended to attend cosmetology school.

Monazia's mother said the school had done what she had hoped. "Look at her," she said, referring to her daughter. "If she was in Lebanon she would have been cutting school and running about the streets."

Dereck Perez, a handsome 18-year-old from Harrisburg, had enrolled in Hershey at four years old. His mother was jailed, and his aunt and grandmother were raising him. "They said it was better for me," he said. "They said I would come to appreciate it." He intended to attend Shippensburg University and study journalism.

Alusine Barry, 18, of southwest Philadelphia commented, "They taught me that if you have your head on straight, you'll be okay." Barry had enrolled in the seventh grade at his mother's insistence. "This was a better option. The only option," he amended, noting that two of his best friends from first grade in Philadelphia were serving prison sentences. He planned to attend Central Penn College for fashion design in the fall. "I think I'm ready."

9

KOONS

Danger on Campus; a Serial Pedophile

"My gut feeling is that they were trying to protect Milton Hershey [School] and hope it would just go away. You know Hershey is Hershey and they have to protect the Hershey name."

—THE MOTHER OF A BOY MOLESTED BY SERIAL PEDOPHILE
CHARLES KOONS 2D

HE GRAYING former Hershey School hockey coach was now 48 years old, and his accuser was 24. They had met years earlier when he was a younger man, and his accuser was a young boy in the coach's car, his apartment, a Hershey School locker room and supply center. They engaged in touching, oral sex and watching X-rated movies. The molestations continued even after the school dismissed the coach.

The older man denied the 27 felony and misdemeanor counts, but in a preliminary hearing on February 20, 2014, District Justice Dominic Pelino ordered him held for trial. The Hershey School had no comment in the *Patriot-News* on the day of Pelino's decision, though Trust spokeswoman Lisa Scullin downplayed the incident when police first disclosed it in 2013. "It is deeply upsetting," she told the newspaper, "to learn of allegations that *one* of our students was abused while in our care."

Actually, it was the most recent *one*.

Over the years, sexual incidents between staff members and impoverished students living hours away from home have been a systemic problem at the chocolate-funded Hershey School, which advertises itself on the Internet and mailings as a compassionate safe haven for vulnerable boys and girls. The school has publicly admitted that it can't prevent its students from having sex on its sprawling campus of over several thousand acres and more than 150 buildings and homes. But it hasn't publicly acknowledged the far more insidious problem of staffers preying on students. This can only be pieced together through court filings and police reports. Longtime observers of the Trust believe the documents give only a partial accounting of sex abuse at the institution. Some of the sex abuse also is of the student-on-student kind prosecuted in juvenile court. According to multiple police departments and court documents:

In 1995 and 1996, a Hershey School housefather downloaded pornography onto a school-owned computer and showed it to eight girls under his care. He was "convicted of indecent assault on two of the girls for touching one 12-year-old girl's breasts and another 14-year-old girl's buttocks," a federal government sentencing memorandum for the housefather disclosed in 2013. By the time of his sentencing, he was a repeat sexual offender. His first offense had been abusing animals.

In 2001, the Derry police prosecuted a married nurse at the school for engaging in an affair with a female student.

In early 2002, the Derry Township police arrested a Hershey School housefather for having sex with a female student in his home. He was 54 years old and she was 17.

In 2006, a 30-year-old female English teacher pleaded no contest to a charge of corrupting a minor after engaging in a sexual relationship with a 17-year-old male student. A Dauphin County judge sentenced her later that year to two years of probation and a $500 fine, according to court records.

In 2007, a part-time drum instructor at the Hershey School admitted to having consensual sex with an underage female student during a trip to her home in New Hampshire in 2007. The two stayed overnight in a Days Inn in Windsor, New York. Court records in New York showed the instructor was charged with disorderly conduct, sexual misconduct and endangering the welfare of a child; he was fined $250.

Dauphin County's most prolific pedophile of the modern era, Charles Koons 2d, preyed on young boys as he accompanied his mother, a substitute houseparent, on weekends to the Hershey School. The details of Koons' molestations and eventual capture point to the dangers of parents sending their child to a residential facility, and reveal the incompetence of Hershey School officials and local police. Specifically, officials and police failed to respond to an April 2, 1998 sworn statement by a grief-stricken mother who said her son had been molested as a 10-year-old boy by Koons.

"During this conversation we were both crying," the mother wrote the police and the school in the notarized statement when disclosing the alleged abuse. "[My son] asked that I stop crying and I told him that I was crying because of this sort of thing happening to him. I asked why he never told me that this was happening to him. His response was that he didn't want me to feel guilty about sending him there in the first place."

The boy had attended the Hershey School for only a few months in the late 1980s. Other boys in the home went camping for the weekend, leaving him behind with a part-time housemother and her son, Chuck. "While he was in bed sleeping, Chuck Koon [sic] came into his room and woke him up and had him go with Chuck to the back room where they keep raincoats," the mother wrote. "Chuck Koons pulled down his pants, exposing himself....As this was going on, Koons reached down and grabbed [her son's] penis.

"They were disturbed by Mom Koons, who was walking by this room. Chuck Koons at this time placed his hand over [her son's] mouth and made a sound like the sound of the letters S and H together, so that Mom Koons wouldn't hear them. When she passed this area, Chuck told [her son] to go back to his room, which he did and went back to sleep." The mother named a second boy whom Koons may have molested, as well as the full-time house parents at the cottage.

Police had a name and a specific incident in a specific group home, and they had a victim and an upset mother. Derry police assigned Detective Leslie Meals to investigate, and the Hershey School appointed a top administrator as a liaison to help the police obtain information. The Hershey School administrator reassigned the task to a lower-level staffer because of a family emergency. Nothing happened with the Koons investigation between April 1998, when the mother sent the notarized letter, and November 1998.

In December, the boy's attorney called the police department to ask about it. "I searched the case," a Derry Township sergeant wrote on December 16th. "Despite the fact that I had several discussions with Detective Meals on this case, and advised her on what action to take, no action or supplementation was taken to date."

The sergeant assigned a new detective, Steven P. Coulter, to the case. Coulter spoke with the boy's mother. "She was extremely upset that nothing has been done, and asked where the notarized statement she had sent up here [was]. I told her I had no idea, and would check with Records," Coulter wrote on December 21st.

Coulter spoke in early January 1999 with Beth Shaw, the Hershey School staffer and liaison. On January 5th, "Coulter met Dr. Beth Shaw at MHS Kinderhaus to discuss this incident. Shaw advised [that] Detective Meals had never spoken to her in person regarding this incident, and in fact Shaw had in her notes that Meals contacted her by phone approximately October 10, 1998."

Shaw informed Detective Coulter that "she was under the impression that Mr. and Mrs. Koons had been house parents at one time, and that Mrs. Dorothy Koons was still serving as a substitute house parent. She looked up the address for Mrs. Koons, and it was the same as we had for Charles Koons."

The school released confidential information to the police about the boy who claimed he had been molested—information that seemed to cast doubt on his character. There was an incident of sexual behavior toward his sister, and bullying. In May 1995, the boy told his mother he would "do anything" to get out of the Milton Hershey School, the school told police. The mother had withdrawn him.

Coulter contacted the boy's attorney and told him he needed a separate sworn statement. The boy responded on February 4, 1999. "One night I was asleep," the boy wrote. "Some of the kids were on a camping trip including my roommate. That night Chuck Koens [sic] came in my room, woke me up, and told me to come with him. I thought he was going to let me stay up to watch TV, but we went to the raincoat room. He dropped his pants and took my pants down. He had me place my hands and mouth on his penis as he rubbed mine. I remember being scared at the time, but also ashamed. It happened for about five to 10 minutes and then he heard his mother and got scared and he had me pull up my pants and pulled up his. He sent me back to my room. I couldn't tell my parents because I was ashamed of what happened. But I finally did. I hope this is enough imformation [sic]."

On February 23rd, the boy's mother called Detective Coulter to ask about the investigation. She told Coulter that her son had a new attorney. On March 11th, Coulter reported that Shaw "was getting all the information I needed...and was going to call me when she had the stuff ready." On April 5th, Coulter wrote that Shaw told him she had the information, but that "she would be out of town until 041299. I will be calling her and setting up a meeting for 041299 or 041399."

That was it, the last reference to the investigation in police files. The internal Derry police narrative of the investigation ends there with the plans of a local detective and a Hershey School staffer to meet to discuss a sexual molestation claim at the nation's richest residential facility for poor kids, which had occurred over a decade earlier.

INFORMATION on the Koons' investigation gathered dust in the Derry Township police files for years. In 2007, a second mother brought Charles Koons to the attention of police. She told a patrol officer in nearby Middletown Borough Police Department about a gangster-pose photo of her son that Koons posted on his MySpace page. She thought it weird. It made her uncomfortable. The patrol officer passed the information to Detective David Sweitzer, who specialized in sex-crimes investigations in the small working-class borough near Hershey and Harrisburg.

Sweitzer looked at the MySpace page, and thought it could be that of a molester. But he had no criminal case based on a social media posting. He told the mother to wait. Months later, a different boy disclosed to the Dauphin County children's services agency that a man—an uncle—had molested him years earlier in Middletown Borough. Sweitzer connected the dots of the two stories. Police arrested Charles Koons at his factory job in August 2008 and searched the apartment he shared with his parents, seizing 12,000 pornographic images. Many of the images were contained on computer storage devices. Once in custody, Koons confessed to molesting not just two boys, but eight. One of them, he told the police, had fatally overdosed.

Sweitzer had Koons in custody and a confession. But the detective believed there were more victims, potentially many more. He learned that Koons networked through family and people in his apartment complex to meet young boys. He came off as a happy buddy with a car. He'd drive the young boys around in his Buick and shoot off fireworks. He molested them in his car, in a hotel, in a park and under a bridge.

Some of the boys were as young as four or five years old. Sweitzer found enough victims to fill a classroom. But he believed he was missing some. Among Koons' possessions were a list of boys' names in his wallet and boxes of faded snapshots. One of the boys had on a Batman costume. A very young Koons had his arm draped around another boy. There was a photo of a boy's private parts. Who were these boys? Where were the photos taken? They didn't seem like any of his recent victims.

Sweitzer and a fellow detective kept coming back to the faded photos—where were they taken? Finally, his partner remembered. He handled a canine unit that had swept Hershey School's group homes with dogs for a training exercise. He recalled the bathroom tile work; the same tile work was visible in one of Koons' faded snapshots. Sweitzer contacted the Hershey School to arrange for teachers to look at the photos. Teachers put some names with faces. One of the boys they identified had overdosed—as Koons had said. Sweitzer tracked down former students in Indiana, Ohio, Florida and Pennsylvania for interviews, but none of the students told Sweitzer they'd been molested by Koons.

One night almost a year after Koons' arrest, and two years after the mother first complained about the MySpace page, a Maryland man called Sweitzer's office and left a voice message. It was June 2009. The man sounded drunk. He had read about the Koons arrest on the Internet. He said he had information. He'd been a former Hershey School student, living in the Revere student home in 1989. His mother told the Derry Township Police that Koons had molested him. With this tip, Sweitzer approached the Derry Township police. The department produced the incomplete file on the investigation from 1998 and 1999.

The Dauphin County District Attorney eventually prosecuted Koons for 17 molestations of local boys, some of them from the apartment complex where Koons lived with his parents, and one Hershey student. The statute of limitations had run out on the other Hershey School students who came forward as having been molested by Koons. But the Hershey School itself faced potential civil litigation from those other students. Eventually, the school paid three million dollars to settle five claims. School spokeswoman Connie McNamara said the institution was "brokenhearted by what happened here." The school was trying to make it right with the financial settlements. "We believed what the individuals were alleging," she said. "We found it to be true."

While the Hershey School students obtained on average $600,000 each, the local boys who were molested by Koons after Derry police let the investigation lapse had no one to sue. The school couldn't be sued for bad police work, and the police department couldn't be held liable. The mother of one of those uncompensated victims spoke to me more than a year after the ordeal, over lunch in a restaurant in Central Pennsylvania. She blamed herself for being naïve about Koons. She cooked dinner with him. She believed him when he told her he was a pro football scout. She hadn't suspected anything was wrong until she saw the TV news on the day of his arrest. She cried when she heard that he hadn't been prosecuted in the late 1990s over the alleged Hershey School molestation. She wanted to speak out. But other mothers didn't want to bring attention on themselves or their boys. Shame was part of it. Mothers of the child victims hoped the nightmare would end and their boys wouldn't have permanent psychological damage. Plus, they feared battling the powerful Hershey Trust and its PR machine.

"All I could think about was that all this didn't have to happen," the mother said. "My gut feeling is that they were trying to protect Milton Hershey [School] and hope it would just go away. You know Hershey is Hershey and they have to protect the Hershey name."

THE TRUST settled the Koons case in early 2010, and hoped the sex scandal would fade. But another one was brewing. The Internet service provider AOL had flagged emailed child-porn images in late 2009 in the Hershey area, and informed the National Center for Missing and Exploited Children. Experts identified the images as the "Trevor" series and the "Dalmatian" series.

"One of the images is a nude prepubescent boy sitting on top of an adult male, who is also nude," read a court document. "The adult male is touching his own penis and the penis of the boy....One image is of a nude prepubescent boy bent over. There is a closeup of his genitals and bottom....Three images contain a prepubescent boy with an adult male putting his penis on the boy's mouth."

The flagged email banter between two individuals was more disturbing. FBI agents located one of the emailers in the Hershey area, and they raided the Trust-owned home of William Charney in February 2010. He lived on Meadow Lane near Founder's Hall. Law-enforcement officials seized almost 700 child-porn images and about 40 videos along with computers, iPods and storage devices. Charney lived with his wife, Mollie, and two children.

One obvious concern for investigators as they pursued the case: Had Charney done more than look at child-porn videos and photos on a campus of about 1,000 impoverished children? He had lived and worked there for almost 10 years, first as a houseparent and then as a housing administrator. The school promoted Charney and presented him as a model employee. With online child-porn becoming a national political issue, researchers were making a connection between child-porn viewers and child molesters. One widely referenced online article on the topic had appeared in the *Journal of Family Violence* in December 2008. Michael Bourke, chief psychologist with the U.S. Marshal's Service and one of the article's researchers, devoted years to evaluating and treating sex offenders in federal prisons. Reliable information on child-sex offenders and their victims has been difficult to gather, but Bourke said that living with the offenders and gaining their trust allowed him to develop relationships with offenders, and gave him insight into their thinking. "How many people who have collected 10,000 baseball cards have never gone to a baseball game, or played baseball, or thought about playing baseball?" Bourke asked me in a phone conversation. "People collect that which they are interested in." For molesters to find a "perfect victim," they need "to be around many of them," he added. Bourke had no knowledge of the Charney case and was speaking generally.

The U.S. Attorney in Harrisburg formally charged William Charney in February 2011 with one count of receiving and distributing child pornography. A press release disclosed the charge, identifying Charney by name and disclosing his living in Hershey. The Hershey School confirmed he was an employee and said that none of the images had been of Hershey School students. But neither the school nor federal prosecutors disclosed publicly that he lived on the Hershey School campus amidst the students. The Hershey School also did not inform students' parents, many of whom lived hours away. These parents did not have access to Harrisburg-area newspapers or TV stations that would have allowed them to learn of the presence of a child pornographer on the school's campus.

On October 20, 2011, Charney walked into the Harrisburg federal courthouse on Walnut Street, about three blocks from the Susquehanna River. Forty-three years old and a retired Navy officer, he was dressed in a blue blazer, khaki pants, docker-style shoes, white shirt and tie, and seemed in good spirits on that crisp morning despite his appointment with a federal judge for sentencing. He had pleaded guilty in April. Charney looked rested but older than when he appeared in a Hershey School yearbook photo with other top administrators. Family and friends accompanied him through the metal detectors and to the elevator taking them to the eighth-floor courtroom of the grandmotherly Judge Sylvia Rambo, who had sentenced former attorney general Ernie Preate years earlier. Charney leaned against the courtroom door, waiting for an employee to unlock it. There were no TV cameras and no representatives from the Hershey School in attendance. The only person there, other than Charney's family and friends, the prosecutor, Charney's attorney, court employees and the judge, was me.

Judge Rambo began the sentencing hearing promptly at 11 a.m. The U.S. government was represented by Daryl Bloom, an assistant U.S. Attorney; Charney's lawyer was Dennis Boyle of Camp Hill. The school had been concerned that Charney might have molested students, and had asked him to submit to a lie-detector test, Boyle told the judge. Boyle said in court documents and at the sentencing that Charney passed the test. Connie McNamara, the school spokeswoman, said in an email that Charney volunteered for the lie-detector test and the school accepted his offer. "It's a difficult case because Mr. Charney is truly a good man," Boyle told Judge Rambo. Charney had a compulsion; he downloaded the images and then deleted them. The compulsion began with homosexual pornography and progressed to child porn. He had two children and an intact marriage. He was a decorated military officer. Charney included letters of support from his mother and sister, a cousin, and a minister in his sentencing memo on file with the court. He cited child abuse as a mitigating factor. Rambo told him there were factors that could contribute to leniency, but she was troubled by a check that Charney wrote in order to meet a teenage boy. Boyle said that the meeting never took place. Charney expressed remorse, saying, "The shame was overwhelming and I didn't know what to do about it....I apologize for my actions. I wish there was more I could do."

The judge sentenced William Charney to more than seven years in federal prison. The Trust issued a statement afterward, and confirmed that Charney had lived on campus for years. "Milton Hershey School is a safe place for children," the school's statement read. "No school is without isolated instances of problems and they are heartbreaking when they occur. We do everything humanly possible to prevent them and we learn from them if they do occur. But these isolated instances are not the story of the Milton Hershey School. The story of the Milton Hershey School is the story of a safe environment for children to learn and grow."

10

SORRY KID, NO HIV IN HERSHEY

Justice Department Investigates; the Trust Settles for $700,000

"Despite our best efforts, some of our students will engage in sexual activity with one another. Given our residential setting, when they do, they will be doing so on our watch."

—HERSHEY SCHOOL STATEMENT POSTED ON WEBSITE IN 2011

N A RUNDOWN BLOCK in Center City Philadelphia, the offices of the AIDS Law Project of Pennsylvania could be found in early 2012, along with a boarded-up Chinese restaurant, a Sprint phone store and a state-run liquor store. One unseasonably warm day in late January, with reggae music playing outside the EZ Bargain discount store, pedestrians hurried past panhandlers toward City Hall in one direction, or the Thomas Jefferson Hospital complex in the other. Ronda Goldfein, the AIDS Law Project's executive director, welcomed me into the agency's modest offices. "We are grateful for a landlord who doesn't always expect his payment right on time," she said. Goldfein and I sat down in her office with a second lawyer, Sarah R. Schalman-Bergen, and they told me the story that led to their little organization taking on the wealthy and politically connected Hershey Trust.

The story began with a 13-year-old boy with HIV who lived with his single mother in one of Philadelphia's older suburbs. The boy controlled his HIV himself by taking five pills and a vitamin a day. He had A's in school and played sports, and he did not want HIV to ruin his life. After researching private schools, he had selected the Hershey School because it was free, a boarding institution, and offered a path to college through its scholarship program that awarded as much as $80,000 to kids with good grades and behavior.

The boy's mother didn't think it was a good idea. He was sick, and she was afraid a rejection could crush his hopes. She realized that even a multi-billion-dollar child-care institution that advertised itself on its Web site and in brochures as compassionate and nurturing could react negatively to the idea of enrolling a boy with HIV.

But the boy told his mother he had the law on his side. This was 2011, not 1981. His mother consented, and asked her son's healthcare case manager at the Children's Hospital of Philadelphia to look into it. Layla de Luria contacted the Hershey School. A Hershey School official seemed to cut her off quickly, telling her the institution "didn't take kids like that." De Luria contacted Hershey School medical staffer Helen Burkabyle and admissions director Danny Warner. Burkabyle told de Luria to send the boy's medical records, and de Luria faxed them on March 3, 2011. The boy's mother completed Hershey's enrollment application in April. The school formally rejected the application in late June.

Ronda Goldfein fell into HIV/AIDS advocacy after leaving a lucrative legal career defending doctors in malpractice cases and insurance companies against asbestos claims. She quit her brother's firm in 1992, hoping to find something more fulfilling. Around this time, she learned of issues related to HIV/AIDS through the experiences of two friends. A childhood friend had learned that she and her baby had AIDS. The friend thought she contracted the disease from a rape. A second friend received an HIV diagnosis as the result of a routine blood test. Goldfein read that the Philadelphia Bar Association offered free legal aid to people who were discriminated against because they had HIV/AIDS; the project was looking for volunteer attorneys. Goldfein had found her calling.

HIV/AIDS activism was big in Philadelphia in the early 1990s. Hollywood released the movie *Philadelphia*, with stars Tom Hanks and Denzel Washington, in 1993. The movie told the story of a Philadelphia lawyer who sued his law firm for wrongful firing in one of the nation's first AIDS discrimination cases. The film's treatment of issues of homosexuality and homophobia was unprecedentedly direct for the time. Crews shot the court scenes in City Hall, two blocks away from Goldfein's office. In the movie's Hollywood-style ending, the Philadelphia lawyer won the court case against his former law firm. Movie viewers came out of the film feeling good, though the Hollywood story seemed ahead of then-prevalent attitudes in its understanding and treatment of individuals with HIV/AIDS.

On a regional level, the AIDS Law Project and other organizations came into existence to help those who faced discrimination because of the disease. Society's perceptions of the disease began to change and fears eased as medical researchers developed medications, so-called cocktails, to control the disease. The Supreme Court, meanwhile, expanded the Americans with Disabilities Act of 1990 to include people with HIV/AIDS. But discrimination persisted for years. In 2008, the project filed a complaint with the Pennsylvania Human Relations Commission against a state-licensed Medicaid-financed personal-care home when it expelled a 36-year-old woman who was schizophrenic and incontinent. The woman's HIV was discovered when the medical staff asked about her medications, and she revealed that the shingles, for which she had medication, was a side effect of having HIV. Shamed by the way they had treated her, the woman left, and entered a homeless shelter. Social service officials later transferred her to the lockdown unit of a psychiatric ward. In September 2010, Pennsylvania Human Relations Commission ordered the care home's owner to pay $50,000 in compensatory damages for humiliating her.

In the summer of 2011, the mother of the boy who had been rejected by the Hershey School phoned the law project's hotline. She told them of her son's story. Law project staffers quickly concluded that if all the facts the mother was telling were true, there seemed to be very little doubt that the Hershey School's actions were illegal. "The law is clear that there is no risk from congregate living. We couldn't quite believe it was happening," Goldfein told me.

The mostly volunteer group chose its legal battles carefully; now Ronda Goldfein considered what to do. Strategically, the project needed wins to rally supporters who could contribute funds or time. Even a cursory check of newspaper clips revealed the wealth of the Hershey School, which controlled the chocolate company and managed a huge investment portfolio. The powerful and politically connected LeRoy Zimmerman, the former two-term attorney general, headed the Trust board. Goldfein also wanted to be sure about the boy: "I'm a firm believer that if we didn't get a good vibe from the client, no one else would either." She arranged a face-to-face meeting at their offices. Goldfein got the vibe. She contacted the Hershey School, and told them that the boy wanted to attend in the fall. Why couldn't he? Conversations dragged into September and then October. Goldfein got impatient. The boy could be attending classes. She wanted a yes or no answer. The attorney for the Hershey School told her that the institution believed the boy posed a threat to the other students.

On October 20th, the AIDS Law Project filed a charge with the Pennsylvania Human Relations Commission. The next action—if it got there—

would be a federal lawsuit. Goldfein realized this suit could go the distance. She also knew she'd have to win over the media. She believed the boy would be viewed sympathetically by TV news stations, newspapers and wire services if she could focus press attention on his story. The one complication was that the boy's name wasn't to be disclosed. Goldfein scanned the calendar for a date to file a federal lawsuit. December 1st, World AIDS Day, caught her eye. The AIDS Law Project attorneys drafted a lawsuit and sent it to the Hershey School's attorney. "They deal with poor people," she said, "and I don't think they were prepared for the pushback."

The AIDS Law Project filed the lawsuit on November 30th in Philadelphia federal court, blandly titled, *Mother Smith, on behalf of herself as a Parent and Natural Guardian, on behalf of Abraham Smith v. Milton Hershey School.* The 13-year-old boy now at least had a name—though not his real one—to which he could be referred: Abraham. The suit quoted the Centers for Disease Control and Prevention as finding no documented cases of HIV being transmitted through casual contact and no cases of it being transmitted through participation in sports. The National Association of State Boards of Education could find no reason to exclude an HIV-positive youth from recess or gym. The Associated Press picked up the story out of the Philadelphia federal courts, the *New York Times* ran a story, and the cable-TV news networks ran with it.

Connie McNamara, the Trust's spokeswoman, responded as if it had been politically attacked. In legally coded language, she told reporters that the institution had to protect its other children. "In order to protect our children in this unique environment, we cannot accommodate the needs of students with chronic communicable diseases that pose a direct threat to the health and safety of others," McNamara told Reuters. "The reason is simple. We are serving children, and no child can be assumed to always make responsible decisions that protect the well-being of others."

Direct threat was a term contained in the Americans with Disabilities Act. This concept offered institutions an out, or a means to ignore parts of the Disabilities Act without legal consequence. The specific direct threat, school officials said, was the potential for the 13-year-old boy to engage in unprotected sex on campus after puberty. He could then spread the HIV to other students. The Hershey School said it had been considering asking a federal judge in Harrisburg for an opinion on its legal position when the AIDS Law Project "took the adversarial action of filing a lawsuit" in Philadelphia. The Hershey School posted a statement on the home page of its website:

Unlike public schools, the Milton Hershey School is not required to accept every student. We can lawfully exclude students who do not meet our eligibility criteria or where we cannot meet the needs of the student in our unique environment. Under the ADA, we are not required to admit any student who would pose a direct threat to the health and safety of others that cannot be avoided by reasonable modifications of the School's policies and procedures. This is the same legal standard that applies to students with active communicable diseases in public schools; the difference is our unique environment.

During the admissions process, the School gives careful consideration to any issues that can affect the ability of our children to learn, would require accommodations beyond the scope of our programs and services, or could impact the health and safety of our student body. When medical issues are identified, they are given careful review. We understand the law and we follow it.

The School decided that it could not admit the student who uses the pseudonym Abraham Smith due to factors relating to his HIV-positive status. This decision was not made based on bias or ignorance. We considered a number of factors relating to the risks posed to the health and safety of others, and our ability to reduce those risks and maintain confidentiality in our unique residential environment.

We know that HIV is not transmitted through casual contact and, thankfully, that universal precautions can address the concerns of transmission in a typical school environment. Our unique environment, however, also poses unique concerns. A significant concern is that HIV can be transmitted through sexual contact. We systematically encourage abstinence, and we educate our children on sexual health issues. But, as special as they are, our teenagers are the same as teens all across the country. Despite our best efforts, some of our students will engage in sexual activity with one another. Given our residential setting, when they do, they will be doing so on our watch.

The statement effectively presented the boy to the public as an HIV-ridden menace on campus. Public comment forums in the local newspaper in central Pennsylvania lit up with readers supporting the Trust's position. But as media reports on the case continued, independent legal experts thought the Trust was skating on very thin ice. In 1998, the U.S. Supreme Court had ruled in *Randon Bragdon v. Sidney Abbott* that individuals with HIV were disabled and qualified under the Americans with Disabilities Act. Abbott, a woman infected with HIV, had been denied treatment in a Maine dental office for a cavity.

Other cases were coming to the federal courts, too. One of them seemed to offer a guidepost: *Jane Doe, as Parent and Natural Guardian, on behalf of Adam Doe v. Deer Mountain Day Camp Inc.; Deer Mountain Basketball Academy* in the Southern District of New York. The camp had denied admission to a 10-year-old boy because of his HIV, in the belief that he would transmit the HIV through bloody urine or stools to other campers. The camp used the "direct threat" defense.

Judge Donald C. Pogue rejected the camp's claims, saying a direct threat defense couldn't be based on HIV stereotypes. "The court," Pogue wrote in January 2010, "agrees that Defendants were obligated to protect other campers from a serious, life-threatening viral infection. But this obligation does not excuse the Defendants' actions when based on unsubstantiated fears."

Abraham Smith's rejection also caught the attention of AIDS activists in Hollywood and New York, who compared him with Ryan White, the Kokomo, Indiana, boy who wasn't allowed to attend public schools in the hysterical early days of the AIDS crisis. A hemophiliac, White had contracted HIV/AIDS through contaminated blood. (It was not disclosed in court documents how Abraham Smith contracted HIV; Goldfein declined to answer the question.) The Ryan White case was eventually settled in the Indiana courts in White's favor. An AIDS movement celebrity and icon, White died in 1990.

CNN's Anderson Cooper aired a "Keeping Them Honest" segment on the Hershey School case in early December. Dr. Kimberly Manning of the Emory University School of Medicine told Cooper, "This was a decision rooted in fear and not public health concerns." Abraham Smith told Anderson in writing that he wished that the Hershey School would "stop making out like I'm this vermin that's out to get the student body at Milton Hershey." McNamara, Hershey's spokesperson, told Anderson that the school "had to balance the risk to those other 2,000 students in our home." Ronda Goldfein wryly noted that the Hershey School apparently thought her client was a danger to every student there, even first and second graders.

Early actions by the Hershey School complicated its defense. Plaintiffs suing over HIV/AIDS discrimination have to prove in court that the defendant knew of their HIV/AIDS infection, and the defendant used that information to deny them a job, housing, medical care, education or other services. It's a high and many times insurmountable legal bar. Defendants can deny they knew the person had HIV/AIDS or can claim they denied them services for other reasons. The Hershey School relinquished those defenses when it said repeatedly and publicly that it didn't admit Abraham Smith precisely because he had HIV/AIDS. Officials even posted the rejection and the reason on its official website, in the process publicly humiliating the boy.

The Trust now had only the "direct threat" defense to fall back on. But even here, the Hershey School had a problem. For Abraham to be a "direct threat" to other students as the institution claimed, the Hershey School had to individually assess him. The AIDS Law Project contended that there hadn't been an individual assessment of the boy. The school rejected him after receiving the fax that disclosed his HIV.

The Pennsylvania AIDS Law Project and Abraham Smith won the opening media battle. But now came the court fight. In its first legal action, the Trust filed to litigate the HIV/AIDS case on its home turf in Central Pennsylvania. Liberal Philadelphia had a vibrant and politically powerful gay community. Trust lawyers wanted to pry the case loose from there and relocate it to solidly Republican country in Harrisburg; they argued two points for the new venue. A federal judge would have to visit the Hershey School and see for himself the inner workings of the institution to fully understand why the school rejected Abraham. "The decision not to continue the enrollment process for this potential student is based in large part on the unique, residential and home-like setting of the Milton Hershey School—a setting so unique that a true understanding of it and its significance in the decision made here, will require a site visit by the ultimate fact-finder," the Trust wrote in its legal documents.

The Trust's second point was that litigating in Philadelphia would be inconvenient for school employees. "These people need to be at the school, or, as near the school as possible, essentially 24/7," it wrote the court. "This is virtually impossible when the School can be anywhere from two to any number of hours from the federal courthouse in Philadelphia, depending on the traffic. By contrast, the School is 20 minutes from the federal courthouse in Harrisburg."

Seeking a new court venue also sent the run-on-a-shoestring AIDS Law Project and its impoverished teen client a message: Prepare for a bruising and costly fight with a politically powerful child-care charity represented by the prestigious Philadelphia law firm Saul Ewing, with its eleven offices, including those in Boston, New York, Washington and Harrisburg.

Ronda Goldfein and her legal team wouldn't be cowed. The project filed as evidence the Trust's 990 tax-filing with the Internal Revenue Service that described its billions of dollars in assets, and number of employees. "MHS's request would simply shift the inconvenience of a two-hour commute from the School to Abraham and his mother, a low-income family represented by a nonprofit public interest law firm. In contrast, MHS has close to eight billion dollars in assets and approximately two thousand employees and volunteers."

Frustration crept into the AIDS Law Project's court document. "MHS hides behind the laudatory banner of protecting its children as a blanket excuse for its continued insensitive and unlawful treatment of Abraham— whether in denying him admission to its school or seeking to move the case several hours from his home," it wrote.

Some 40 gay activists protested in Hershey on February 8, 2012. One dressed in a Hershey's Kiss costume. Four or five police cars with officers watched the protest, with an empty paddy wagon. The police warned that if they stepped on Trust property, they would be arrested. As they were protesting, people drove past yelling, "This is a private school. They can do what they want."

The activists also protested at the Hershey store in Times Square. In May, about 20 activists flew to Chicago for the annual candy industry expo. They dressed in business suits to enter the exhibit space, and once inside unfurled pillow cases that said "Boycott Hershey" and "No Kisses for Hershey." Security escorted them out and arrested one. "Of all the protests," said one of the activists, "I think the candy expo was the most effective because it really pissed them off."

The Trust had other problems. Justice Department had sent civil rights investigators to Hershey to look into its handling of Abraham Smith's enrollment application, looking for possible violations of the Americans with Disabilities Act and the Fair Housing Act.

THE TRUST BOARD—whose members were earning a minimum of $100,000 a year in part-time directors' fees—were woefully unprepared to respond to modern issues related to admitting a boy or girl with HIV/AIDS to the school. And the controversy was quickly snowballing into a national scandal. The board included no national experts on residential education, poverty or child psychology who could offer sage advice. The organization seemed to be relying on its lawyers, who billed by the hour for their advice.

At the same time, the Trust board was facing an investigation by the Office of Attorney General over its business decisions and internal dramas. Powerful board chairman LeRoy Zimmerman retired in late 2011 in the midst of the OAG investigation and internal board conflicts. Meanwhile, alumnus and Trust board member Joe Senser was entangled in a sensational media story back at home in Minnesota.

On the night of August 23, 2011, Senser's wife was involved in a fatal hit-and-run accident. She had struck and killed a popular local chef while driving the family's Mercedes-Benz ML350 SUV on an exit ramp off Interstate 94, and then sped off. Anousone Phanthavong's car had run out of gas on the darkened road and he was refilling his gas tank. Police photographed him after the accident: face down, arms splayed, shoes knocked off his feet, his liver lacerated, nine broken ribs.

The next day the family's attorney turned the SUV in to police with a broken headlight and blood on the car body. Amy and Joe, meanwhile, took their two daughters on an unplanned overnight trip. As it became apparent that the Mercedes-Benz SUV was involved in the fatal accident, the Senser family didn't disclose who had been driving the SUV on the night of the fatal accident.

Joe Senser graduated from the Hershey School in 1974 and played tight end for the NFL's Vikings. A local celebrity in Minneapolis-St. Paul, he operated local sports bars and did a radio show. Without the name of the driver, suspicion fell on one of Joe Senser's daughters from his first marriage. Texts released publicly many months later showed Brittani Senser texting her dad on September 2nd: "I'm so sorry this is happening. But dad u need [to] clear your name. The news is talking about how much of a stand up guy u are and that ur a charitable and loving human being. It's not ur job to protect someone who prob wouldn't protect u if the shoes were on the other feet." In an expletive-filled text on the same day, Brittani said to her stepmother: "Amy everyone thinks its me. That is so [messed] up that by you guys not fessing im getting thrown under the bus. Take responsibility 4 ur actions. Go online watch the news that is so [messed] up Amy."

Brittani Senser later told ABC's Robin Roberts, "I believe that the defense's strategy was that if they couldn't figure out who was driving that no one could be convicted."

Ten days after the accident, Amy Senser finally told police in a fax that she was the driver. Phanthavong's family wasn't satisfied; on September 6, 2011, they filed a civil lawsuit against Amy Senser because of what the victim's family perceived as police stonewalling.

"The Senser family has really put a lid on this," said the Phanthavong family's attorney. "There is a lot of frustration in the community with people thinking the rich and powerful don't have to answer for what they've done." A big question was when Joe Senser knew of the accident and what he did the night of it.

At the criminal trial in April 2012, Amy Senser testified that she'd first met Joe while working in one of his restaurants. On the night of the accident, she drank part of a glass of wine at a restaurant and scalped a ticket to the Katy Perry concert that her daughters were watching. During the concert, she didn't feel well and left to go home. She had second thoughts—believing it was "pretty ridiculous to drive all the way home," she decided to return to the concert arena and wait outside for her daughters. Exiting the highway at Riverside, she struck Phanthavong. "I'd never been in an accident, so I didn't know if I'd hit a pothole or a construction sign." She assumed it was an orange barricade barrel. Because of the construction, Amy got lost before finding her way home.

The jury returned a guilty verdict on two counts of vehicular homicide. Afterward, reporter Abby Simmons of the *Star Tribune* interviewed juror Jay Larson. He noted inconsistencies in some of the testimony. Joe Senser explained that an eight-minute phone call between him and his wife on the night of the accident was the result of his keeping the cellular line open while he was picking up his daughters and their friends at the concert. "I don't think any of us bought that," Larson told Simmons.

Amy Senser was sentenced to three and a half years in prison. Hennepin County District Judge Daniel Mabley said he didn't "entirely trust" Amy Senser's account of what happened on the night of the accident but he believed she was remorseful that a man died. After the trial, Joe Senser lashed out at the media and apologized for the unwanted publicity the case brought on the Vikings football organization. "We are good and decent, hardworking people and I don't apologize for hard work. They tried to paint Amy Senser as this rich, white Edina housewife, and nothing could be further from the truth."

Senser's troubles were unreported by the media in Pennsylvania. Through the months of the accident investigation and criminal court case in

Minneapolis—the period that coincided with the Trust's rejection of Abraham Smith and the Justice Department's investigation into discrimination at the Hershey School—Senser remained an active participant on the Trust board that controlled one of the nation's richest private child-care charities. The organization later gave him additional responsibilities that doubled his directors' fee compensation, naming him to the Hershey Entertainment board.

PHILADELPHIA JUDGE C. DARNELL JONES II issued his decision on where the "Smiths'" case would be heard on June 1st. It was a sharp defeat for the Trust. The case would stay in Philly. Litigating in Philadelphia wouldn't disrupt school operations, Jones said. "The court cannot fathom how a long-standing institution of the Defendant's size and stature would be unable to function merely because a few of its numerous employees might have to appear—one at a time—to provide testimony and possibly testify at a trial."

Amtrak ran between Philadelphia and Harrisburg in an hour and 35 minutes, and Jones noted he'd be flexible with travel times and scheduling testimony. "If ultimately deemed necessary, this court would be more than willing to accommodate commuting witnesses by allowing presentation of their testimony to begin after 10 a.m. and to conclude early enough to return to Harrisburg at a convenient time towards the end of the workday." The school's venue-change request "fails to identify the specific witnesses who will be inconvenienced, fails to provide the nature of the intended testimony...," the judge noted.

Jones didn't view the controversy as a local one. "The issue involved in this case is not uniquely or necessarily tied to MHS or the Middle District of Pennsylvania but instead is relevant to the lives of over one million people nationwide, many of whom are currently living in congregate-living settings, and are not creating a direct threat to others."

A month later, Hershey School president Anthony Colistra sent a letter to Abraham Smith's mother, saying the institution had rescinded its rejection and would admit her son. Negotiations continued between the Trust, the AIDS Law Project and the Justice Department. On September 12th, the Trust settled the case with the boy for $700,000. Colistra apologized in a statement posted on the Hershey School website's home page for what it had put the boy through: "We had hoped that the student known as Abraham Smith would attend the Milton Hershey School this fall and experience the life-changing opportunities this unique environment provides. He and his mother have decided that Abraham will not attend, and we respect their decision. I am sorry for the impact of our initial decision on Abraham and his mother." The statement remained on the website for months as part of the settlement.

The Trust also settled with the Justice Department's Disability Rights Section on September 12th. "The United States, having considered all information gathered in the course of its investigation, has determined that while the School states that it did not act with malice or animus toward Abraham Smith or children with HIV, the School cannot show that enrolling Abraham Smith or other children with HIV would pose a 'direct threat' to the health or safety of others," the settlement stated.

The government concluded that the school violated the Americans with Disabilities Act and discriminated against "Mother Smith." The school agreed to pay a civil fine of $15,000, and to draft within 15 days a non-discrimination and equal opportunity statement. This EO Policy was to state, in part, that children with HIV "may not be a factor on which applicants, or current students, may be denied admission to or disenrolled from the School." The EO Policy, based on the signed agreement, was to continue with a second, even broader assertion on inclusiveness at the Hershey School: *"The School does not discriminate against applicants or students on the basis of disability."*

The Hershey School had to post the EO policy on its website and distribute it to employees. Through 2016, the government could monitor the Hershey School's training of staff and students on HIV, and the use of universal precautions to prevent the transmission of HIV, hepatitis B virus, and other blood-borne pathogens. According to the agreement, the Hershey School also would instruct students on "the importance of treating individuals with disabilities in a respectful and courteous way" and of "the School's refusal to tolerate harassment or bullying on the basis of disability."

Ronda Goldfein considered the government oversight and financial settlement a huge win. But Abraham "did not feel welcome," she said. "It was hard for a 14-year-old to put behind him what they said about him."

11

ABBIE'S DEATH

A Revolving Door for Poor Kids Leads to Tragedy

*"I wouldn't even consider sending my child there again. And I
wouldn't recommend it to anyone else either. I'm so disgusted...."*

—THE MOTHER OF AN EXPELLED MHS STUDENT

ABBIE BARTELS, an eighth-grader at Milton Hershey School, seemed to
be doing fine. She wrote in her diary on September 28, 2012, "I made
Gold in my student home this week. So, after school, the Gold and
Spartans went to the movies to watch *Paranorman*." She liked *The Vampire
Diaries*, Selena Gomez, kayaking, roller coasters, cats and painting.

By the following April, though, things were not going well for her. Abbie
worried about her dad's drinking, and she had a dispute with a girl in her
student home. She seemed to be more upset about everything than she
should be. Her mother, Julie Bartels, attributed Abbie's surprisingly worked-
up behavior to "teenage angst." She asked the school if Abbie could take a
temporary leave and cool out on a visit to her grandmother in Arizona. Julie
didn't think this should be a problem. But a school official told Julie that if
she pulled Abbie out of classes for two months, her daughter could lose her
enrollment. Abbie would have to reapply for admission. And there was no
guarantee she would be readmitted.

Abbie had enrolled at the Hershey School in 2004 when she was four
years old. Julie was laid off at the time, and Fred, Abbie's father, was out of
work. They later divorced. The school's admissions department evaluated
Abbie before accepting her into the program, and she'd been an exemplary
student. "The children," Abbie's mom said, "really have to be perfect to go
through there. They only take perfect children."

Abbie didn't want to take the risk of leaving the school. She had grown up at the Hershey School. She had friends there; she liked her houseparents. She felt safe in its rigidly structured environment, and even found ways to have fun. You couldn't do wild things with your hair on campus, as teenage girls sometimes like to do. When Abbie dyed her hair with Kool-Aid, it was on summer break. "She wanted to be there," Julie said. "That's where she wanted to go to school. She was a Milt. That's what she wanted to be. That's why I jumped through all these hoops."

Abbie's mental state seemed to career out of control through the spring of 2013. On May 15th, Abbie wrote in her red notebook, "I keep thinking about killing myself. I have tried many times before. My only problem's I believe and have faith in God, but if I killed myself wouldn't that mean I'd go to hell?"

The Hershey School told Julie in late May that Abbie's moods had been swinging wildly, and they had sent her to Philhaven Hospital for a week of treatment for depression and suicidal thoughts. On May 30th, Abbie wrote in her diary: "This fucking sucks. It's a mental institution! If this place asks me to do one more weird thing I am going to flip out. I hate this! I may be crazy, but not that crazy. Knowing I'm in a mental institution isn't going to make me happier, what do they expect!" Several days later, she seemed to have turned a corner: "I'm leaving this place! Yeah!" Philhaven discharged her on June 5th with the recommendation that Abbie "receive aftercare in the supportive environment of… the Milton Hershey School." Abbie returned to campus but did not attend regular classes. School officials watched her.

A teenage girl with suicidal thoughts shouldn't have come as a surprise to a private residential school that recruits impoverished children as students. Karen Fitzpatrick, the longtime girlfriend of Abbie's father, had watched Abbie grow up. She said, "All the kids who go there come from some abnormal family life." National health statistics, moreover, pointed to a disturbing rise in the rate of suicides among young Americans. More teenagers and young adults died in 1996 of suicide than the combined deaths from cancer, heart disease, AIDS, birth defects, stroke, pneumonia and influenza, and chronic lung disease, according to statistics from the National Alliance on Mental Illness. Though the suicide rate had declined modestly in the 1990s, the suicide rate among teenagers and young adults had tripled between 1965 and 1987. It was the third-leading cause of death for young Americans between 15 and 24 years old, and the fourth-leading cause for those 10 to 14 years old. Between the early 1980s and the mid-

1990s, the suicide rate for black male teens and young adults more than doubled.

Support groups and suicide-prevention organizations offered advice, and health-care professionals viewed youth suicides as treatable. "Bringing up the question of suicide and discussing it without showing shock or disapproval is the one of the most helpful things you can do. This openness shows that you are taking the individual seriously responding to the severity of his or her distress," the National Alliance on Mental Illness counseled on its website. "Even the most severely depressed person has mixed feelings about death, wavering until the last moment between wanting to live and wanting to die. Most suicidal people do not want death; they want the pain to stop. The impulse to end it all, though, no matter how overpowering, does not last forever."

Katherine Dahlsgaard, a psychologist at the Children's Hospital of Philadelphia, told the author, "Suicide is absolutely preventable by noticing the signs and treating it very seriously." Scott Poland, a psychology professor at Nova Southeastern University in Florida, who authored the 1989 book *Suicide Intervention in the Schools*, added that the "vast majority of individuals with suicidal thoughts, particularly adolescent girls, are not a threat to others."

Abbie couldn't get away from the suicidal thoughts. She mentioned something to another girl on campus. The Hershey School told Julie that Abbie needed more treatment, and arranged for her to be admitted to the Pennsylvania Psychiatric Institute in Harrisburg. "She had a complete breakdown at PPI because she did not want to go there," Julie said. "She was crying. She was throwing a fit on the floor."

Instead of drawing up a mental-health care plan with Abbie's doctors to help her get better, the "compassionate" Hershey School now began reviewing Abbie's enrollment status—the first step toward expelling her. Abbie knew about this development. Showing her sarcastic streak, she wrote in her diary on June 14th, "People are having a whole meeting about me! I feel so special."

Pennsylvania Psychiatric Institute's treatment focused on rebuilding Abbie's self-worth. She wrote of 50 positive things about herself. "My eyes are pretty." "I have a good smile." "My hair is thick." "I'm pretty." "I am creepy (oops)." She listed her discharge goals as "to get out of here" and eighth-grade graduation. The institute discharged her on June 19th, listing her diagnosis as "major depressive disorder, recurrent, without psychotic episodes." Doctors prescribed Zoloft.

Abbie thought she could go to her eighth-grade graduation two days after her release. She had a grade point average of 91, and had completed all her coursework. But the school said she couldn't visit campus for the June 21st graduation because it didn't consider her a current student. Julie couldn't believe it. "She was excelling in the program and she wanted to be there. She earned that eighth grade graduation. She's a child."

Julie believed the school was washing their hands of her mentally vulnerable daughter at a time that it needed to be most supportive of Abbie. "She was a liability to them at that point," Julie said. "She did not fit their corporate structure."

Karen Fitzpatrick pleaded with the Hershey School to let Abbie attend a post-graduation barbecue party at her student home. She didn't understand how the school could ban her from campus, especially since the institution hadn't yet officially terminated her enrollment. "We knew," Karen said, "that in our lives that was the best place for her because she was doing well until the spring of 2013." They couldn't seem to get anybody to listen to them other than Abbie's school psychologist, who seemed powerless to affect the decision on her enrollment.

Karen and Julie had agreed upon Abbie's discharge from the Pennsylvania Psychiatric Institute to follow the requirements laid out by the Hershey School for her possible re-enrollment following a year off campus. These included Abbie seeing a therapist that the family paid for, continuing her Zoloft and attending Al-Anon meetings. "When she was discharged everything was on our plate," Karen said. Karen and Julie promised to school officials that one of them would be there at both the graduation and the barbecue to watch Abbie. The school still said no—she couldn't attend either event. Karen waited until the day of the graduation to tell Abbie she couldn't go.

Abbie seemed okay on the outside, but Julie and Karen suspected otherwise. Julie worked with Abbie's houseparents at the Hershey School to hold a private graduation ceremony in Julie's brick house, with its little backyard, in Steelton. Abbie wore her best dress. Julie and Karen couldn't do anything about the barbecue, though. Karen later found handwritten cards hidden in Abbie's bedroom that she'd intended to hand out to friends. The girls were like her sisters. Abbie's card to one girl, Jame-James says, "I miss you! Sorry I 'abandoned' you. I might be able to come back in 10th grade. Keep going to Facebook so we can keep in touch." Another one, addressed to Lil Sissy, reads, "I hope to see you again. I might be able to come back in the 10th grade.… I'm sorry I had to leave early, I miss and love you!"

This Indenture made the _3rd_ day of _September_, in the year of our Lord,
One Thousand Nine Hundred and _Ten_

Witnesseth, That _Mary H. Wagner_, of the
Borough
City of _East Donegal_, in the County of _Lancaster_, State of _Pennsylvania_
Township

the Guardian
Mother of _Nelson A. Wagner_, by these presents does release and relin-
next-friend
quish to the Managers of The Hershey Industrial School at Hershey, Derry Township, Dauphin County, Pennsylvania,
Managers under the deed of Milton S. Hershey and Catharine S. Hershey founding and endowing said school, and their
successors, appointed to maintain, direct and manage said school, the custody and control of the said
Nelson A. Wagner, he to dwell with and serve the said Managers and to be under their exclusive
custody and control from the day of the date hereof until the said _Nelson A. Wagner_ arrives
at the age of eighteen years, that is until the _28_ day of _April_, 19_22_,
unless the period of this release is earlier terminated or further extended as hereinafter provided for; during which time
the said _Nelson A. Wagner_ shall faithfully, honestly, and obediently serve the said
Managers and conform to all their rules and regulations with reference to residence, studies, work and duty, and all other
rules and regulations established by the Managers, their executive officers, or others by them appointed; the intent of this
release being to enable the Managers to enforce in relation to the said _Nelson A. Wagner_
every proper restraint, and to prevent relatives, friends, or others from interfering with or withdrawing the said
Nelson A. Wagner from the school.
The Managers of The Hershey Industrial School, for themselves and their successors, undertake that they will
teach and instruct, or cause to be taught or instructed, the said _Nelson A. Wagner_ as set
forth in the deed founding and endowing the school, and will keep and maintain the said _Nelson A._
Wagner during the period aforesaid: Provided, however, that if at any time during the period
aforesaid shall be determined, in the opinion of the Managers (which shall be final and conclusive, and from which there
shall be no appeal), that the said _Nelson A. Wagner_ should be or become incompetent to
learn or master a trade, or that from physical ailments it would be inexpedient for him to continue his studies and training, or should become insubordinate, or be guilty of vice or crime, or become an unfit companion for others in the school,
or has so conducted himself as not to be worthy of future and continued support and education, or is so competent to work
at his chosen trade that he is qualified to be self-supporting, or for any other reason good and sufficient in the judgment of
the Managers, they shall have the right (notwithstanding this release and undertaking) to remove or expel him from the
school and cancel this release and undertaking and dismiss him from their care, and upon so doing it is specially cove-
nanted and agreed that all responsibility on their part to the said _Nelson A. Wagner_, or the
said _Mary H. Wagner_, or any other person or persons, shall absolutely cease and
determine anything herein contained to the contrary notwithstanding, and the said _Mary H. Wagner_
thereupon agrees to immediately assume the charge and care of the said _Nelson A. Wagner_:
Provided further, however, the Managers may in their discretion, before or after the arrival of the said
Nelson A. Wagner at the age of eighteen years, provide for his further education at some
other school, college or university, in which event the period of time hereinabove named for which this release is executed
shall be extended for such additional period as the Managers may determine, not extending beyond the arrival of the said
Nelson A. Wagner at the age of twenty-one years.
The home provided for the said _Nelson A. Wagner_ by the Managers is situated at
Hershey, Dauphin County, Pennsylvania, and that will be his residence unless in the judgment of the Managers it shall be
expedient to maintain him elsewhere, in which event it shall be the right of the Managers to make the necessary change.

In Witness Whereof the parties to these presents have hereunto set their hands and seals the day and
year above written

WITNESS PRESENT:

W. S. Risser, M.D.

Mary H. Wagner [SEAL]

M. S. Hershey [SEAL]
Chairman of the Managers of The Hershey Industrial School

Mary Wagner signed this September 1910 indenture for her son, Nelson A. Wagner, as stipulated in the Deed. The mothers of fatherless boys had to sign indentures, which historically were labor contracts. Milton Hershey signed the documents and said that the indentures allowed him to raise, educate and train the boys without family interference. As part of his program, the fatherless boys milked cows and worked on his farms. The indenturing practice ended in the early 1950s.

Milton Hershey purchased the Homestead in the late 1890s. He lived there with Kitty until the High Point mansion opened in 1908. Now a scenic stop on Hershey sightseeing bus tours, the Homestead housed the first orphan boys and is still owned by the Trust.

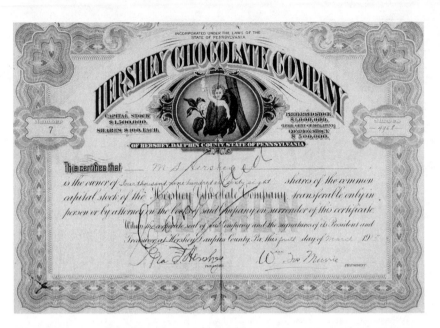

In November 1918, Milton Hershey pledged his fast-growing chocolate company and his other business assets to the Hershey Industrial School. He did it with a stroke of a pen on the back of this stock certificate. At the time, Hershey was borrowing heavily to create a vast sugar plantation in Cuba.

A February 22, 1919 letter from George Copenhaver, superintendent of the Hershey Industrial School, to S.J. Frehn, superintendent of the Cumberland County Poorhouse. (*Source: Cumberland County Archives*)

Milton Hershey died in October 1945. He is interred with his wife Kitty and his parents Fanny and Henry in the Hershey Cemetery. The orphan boys who died are buried to the left of the monument.

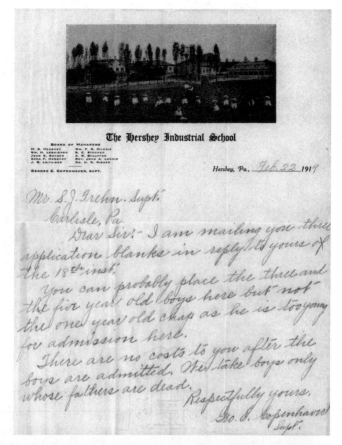

The Hershey Industrial School

BOARD OF MANAGERS

Hershey, Pa., *Feb. 22* 1919

Mr. S.J. Frehn, Supt.
Carlisle, Pa.

Dear Sir:- I am mailing you three application blanks in reply to yours of the 18th inst.
You can probably place the three and the five year old boys here but not the one year old chap as he is too young for admission here.
There are no costs to you after the boys are admitted. We take boys only whose fathers are dead.

Respectfully yours,
Geo. E. Copenhaver
Supt.

The students of the Evergreen home, circa 1951. They are standing on the steps outside the home with their houseparents.

Students assembled in front of the Hershey School on November 12, 1923. *(Special Collections Research Center, Temple University Libraries, Philadelphia, PA)*

Hershey School graduate F. Frederic "Ric" Fouad, a New York attorney, brought new energy and militancy to the alumni activism in the late 1990s. He continues to bring attention to the school's child-care policies.

Hershey School graduate Joseph Berning has sought governance reforms since the early 1990s. He is shown in the basement of his home near Harrisburg with a framed picture of the Milton Hershey postage stamp and a map of the Trust-owned farms.

The Trust constructed the Scottish-themed, five-million-dollar Highlands Grill with school funds on the Wren Dale course, which it renamed Hershey Links. The Trust closed the golf course and Highlands Grill in 2013. The Trust did not say how it would redevelop Highlands Grill, which includes high-tech beer taps, for the use of poor students.

Posing in front of "Zimm's Palace," or the Hotel Hershey, are Hershey Trust board members James Mead, Joseph Senser, Bob Cavanaugh, LeRoy Zimmerman, Velma Redmond and James Nevels. The Trust-owned hotel underwent $70 million in upgrades and modernizations. A court petition later said the costs couldn't be justified.

Police mugshot of Charles Koons. The serial pedophile visited the Hershey School campus for years, accompanying his mother, who was a part-time houseparent. *(Photo: Middletown Borough Police Department)*

Ronda Goldfein, executive director of the AIDS Law Project of Pennsylvania, sued the Hershey School over its rejection of a 13-year-old boy with HIV. The school settled with the boy for $700,000. She was photographed in the lobby of her nonprofit advocacy group in Philadelphia.

Abbie Bartels holds a family cat at her grandmother's house in the summer of 2012. *(Photo: Julie Bartels)*

Milton Hershey's trust for orphans and impoverished youth still controls the chocolate company that manufactures and markets some of the biggest candy brands in the nation. Each year, tens of millions of dollars from Hershey candy sales, in the form of stock dividends, flow back to the troubled Milton Hershey School—making many everyday Americans financial supporters of Milton Hershey's charity.

The Hershey School mailed a letter to Julie and to Karen formalizing the break with the institution. It seemed to place the blame on Abbie, even though it was the Hershey School that had insisted on her mental-health treatment, which forced her to miss classes. "In light of Abbie's absence from the Milton Hershey School, it is important to share with you the recommendations of the service providers who have been working with her," the letter began. It told how Julie or Karen could obtain Abbie's academic records and described necessary follow-up dental care. Hershey School dentists had put braces on Abbie's teeth. With her departure, the institution would not be responsible for taking them off. As for the leave of absence that could allow Abbie to return, Heather Teter, the coordinator of student health services, said there had been no final decision. The institution had virtually no contact with Abbie or the family at that point, Karen said.

With Abbie living back at home in Steelton in late June, Julie gave her daughter space, not wanting to breathe down her neck. Afterward Julie thought Abbie looked haunted, and she remembered little things her daughter had said. When Julie asked Abbie about her knitting, Abbie responded, "I won't need my knitting anymore."

Abbie went to be with her father. He lived with Karen and Karen's father, Tom Fitzpatrick, in Newport, a small town in Perry County. Their house is located across from a Dollar General store. Karen shopped for school clothes with Abbie—this would be her first year in a public school.

On June 29th, Abbie rode her bike around the neighborhood and cleaned out the cat litter box when she got home. The grandfatherly Tom told Abbie around 11 a.m. that they would have noodle soup and grilled cheese sandwiches for lunch. About an hour later, Tom called Abbie for lunch, but she didn't respond. He climbed the stairs to her second-floor bedroom and through the open door saw her foot sticking out of the clothing closet. She had hanged herself with a bathrobe sash on the clothing bar. The devastated Fitzpatrick said to the lifeless girl, "Oh Abbie, what did you do?"

Now that Abbie was gone, the Hershey School was ready to help in any way it could, Julie said. The school paid to bury Abbie in the Hershey Cemetery. There is a marker there with Abbie's name, along with the names of the indentured orphan boys who died from disease or farm accidents. Top school officials attended the funeral along with Abbie's extended family.

That fall, Hershey School spokeswoman Lisa Scullin said that the school could not comment on Abbie's case or even confirm her name. As policy, Scullin she said in an email, "Ongoing repeated behavior of an unsafe nature that includes harm to self or others forces us to make some tough decisions. We must ensure safety first, but we work very hard to make sure children have every opportunity to thrive here." She said that the emailed questions "suggested an incomplete story," and that the Hershey School provides families with support to obtain treatment and medications in their home communities.

CNN would later do a segment on Abbie's death. Fred was still in shock months after Abbie's suicide. "It basically seems to me," he said on the deck in the Newport home where Abbie hanged herself, "that they gave up on her after she had been there so long."

ABBIE BARTELS' SUICIDE, when considered alongside a decade of internal Hershey School statistics, raises questions as to whether the multi-billion-dollar child-care institution fails many impoverished and vulnerable children—fails more students, in fact, than it helps—despite recruiting them to Hershey with claims of "unbelievable opportunities for children in need."

Over the last decade, 2,034 students dropped out or were kicked out of the fabulously wealthy and free school, while only 1,439 graduated. On average, in recent years, one child a day departed voluntarily or involuntarily. Kids who dropped out walked away from a free prep school education valued at more than $100,000: an indication that either the Hershey School wasn't delivering charitable services to those kids, the kids didn't think that being in Hershey was worth it, or the institution didn't make it easy for them to stay. Kids who were kicked out had no say in their departure and couldn't appeal.

This revolving door for impoverished children has gone unreported for years. The Milton Hershey School hasn't posted attrition figures on its web site. It also doesn't report them to a state agency that would make them public. Parents who are considering enrolling their children in the Hershey School have no idea about these figures.

The institution initially refused to disclose the year-by-year dropouts and expulsions to me, and instead provided an average attrition rate and range over 10 years—which really said nothing. My initial request for information had been prompted by conversations with students and their parents, and predated Bartels' suicide by eight or nine months.

The Hershey School, which was then under an Office of Attorney General investigation for its business decisions, eventually agreed to give the information under the condition that I drive the 90 miles from Philadelphia to Hershey to get it. "We are not a public school, and while we are not required to share this information with you, we are willing to do so," Hershey spokeswoman Lisa Scullin wrote to me. "Our only request is that you come here to get it and talk with our experts while you are here, in order to understand the numbers and what they mean. That is our only condition—and it is to make sure that you give the necessary attention to the facts and the larger context. We have ample historical reason to believe that will not be the case unless we insist."

I asked to see the data in advance, so I could be prepared for the conversation. Scullin refused; I would get the data and talk at the same time. On the morning of January 18, 2013, Scullin handed over a manila folder with the data. It showed that the Hershey School has struggled with retaining students since the early 1970s. The best year in the chart was the first, in 1968-69, when the school, then an all-boy orphanage, retained 94.1 percent of students.

After the mid-1970s when the Hershey School opened admission to girls and non-orphans, the school's retention fell to a low of 84.3 percent in 1986-87 and rose to a high of 91.4 percent in 1997-98. The rate was 87.1 percent in 1972-73, and 86.1 percent in 2011-12, no change over about 40 years.

The Hershey School's target, officials said in the meeting, was to retain 100 percent of students. But missing it didn't really matter because the Hershey's School student retention rate compared favorably with the nation's college prep boarding schools for privileged children. The average retention rate for the nation's boarding schools in 2011-12 was 90.3 percent.

This seemed like a preposterous justification. The Hershey School recruited kids from households with an average income of about $15,000 a year, according to its statistics. They may have been exposed to sexual abuse, or alcoholism, according to the school's own description of its student body. A parent or both parents could be in jail. The children could live in violent or near-bankrupt school districts. When they departed the Hershey School for whatever reason, they returned to those same homes and those same terrible school districts. Kids at traditional boarding schools who drop out return to a comfortable life or another elite boarding school. How could these two populations be considered remotely similar or comparable? When asked, Hershey officials acknowledged differences between poor kids and rich kids.

Participating in the conversation were Dr. Beth Shaw, the executive director of student support services; Dr. Erica Weiler-Timmins, director of psychological services; Dr. Jennifer Wallace, the school's chief physician; Cindy Kelly, health coordinator of student health services; Christopher Rich, coordinator of student health services, who headed homesickness initiatives; Mark Seymour, senior director of enrollment management; and Dr. Bob Fehrs, an alumnus and head of the middle school. Shaw explained that Hershey's "standards of care are reflective of the best practices" and that the services were "incredibly integrated, with health professionals talking with one another." A child's individual health assessment begins at admission and the school was committed to "total and complete services delivery." Thirty-five mental-health professionals were available to provide care for students. About half of students utilize services that include grief counseling, group therapy for students with family issues, instruction on social and organizational skills, and anger management. The school looked at a child "holistically," Weiler-Timmins noted.

Parents sometimes pulled their children out of Hershey because they missed them and wanted them home. In other cases, homesick students dropped out—a problem for decades at the rural institution. "No matter what the home is and no matter what the deal is," Seymour conceded, "being away from home is difficult."

OVER THE PRIOR MONTHS, well before Abbie's suicide, students and parents repeatedly told me of a very different reality: a Big Brother-like campus in which kids many times felt unwelcome, and school programs seemed designed to stamp out well-behaved kids with the efficiency and conformity of Hershey chocolate bars or Reese's peanut butter cups. If the kids didn't do what they were told and follow the institution's rules, or fell short of expectations, they would be disciplined.

Houseparents rated student behavior weekly in one of four categories: Spartan, the highest; Gold, Brown and Novice. Low-rated students scrubbed floors and pulled weeds. High-rated students got to go to recreation night or shopping at Wal-Mart.

Students also were subject to a detailed, five-level point-based discipline scheme—a disciplinary debit card that maxed out at 100 points. Under this system, violations ranged from Level I, the lowest, to Level V. Level I violations were disobeying a houseparent or staff member, and failing to follow rules on what clothes to wear. The first offense results in a verbal reprimand, no TV and extra house chores; a student would have no points assessed against them. Level II violations could be repeated Level 1 infractions, defiance, insubordination or cheating. A student was assessed five points. Level III's were destroying property and making threats to teachers, staff members or students. The consequences on this level were detentions of 10 to 15 days, the potential loss of sports and other co-curricular activities, and campus work assignments. A student was assessed 15 points. Level IV's were serious misconduct or repeated behaviors for which prior disciplines failed to correct. The consequences were penalties similar to Level I through Level III, along with the potential loss of college scholarship funds and 20 days of detentions. They cost 25 points. Level V violations lead to expulsion. These include selling or dealing drugs, possession or use of a weapon, arson, sexual assault or fighting.

Hershey School officials intervened at the 20-, 30- and 50-point level so that students knew they were racking up points. A student's enrollment status was reviewed at 100 points, at which time they could be terminated. In that review, four administrators "and those who work mostly closely with the child" consider the child's status. If previous interventions failed, the group could recommend expulsion. An expulsion is then reviewed by additional administrators.

Misbehaving students also might have to sign "behavior agreements." Drawn up like formal legal documents, they describe a student's improper behavior. If the student violated the agreement by repeating the behavior or violating the school's behavior code in other ways, they would be expelled.

"Once a child is on a Behavior Agreement, and the child violates terms of the agreement by engaging in another infraction, the School must move forward toward expulsion. If that does not happen, the Behavior Agreements and the behavior standards which exist will lose meaning and effectiveness," the school said.

One upset teen girl whom I interviewed had been cutting herself. As punishment, she had to sign a behavior agreement instead of undergoing counseling. This was what it said:

"I understand and accept that the Behavioral Agreement is necessary because of past behaviors;

"I understand and accept that this Behavior Agreement can be modified as necessary;

"I understand and agree to meet with my houseparents and Home Life administrator on a monthly basis to review my compliance of the conditions of the agreement;

"I understand and agree to follow all instructions that are given to me by my houseparents or any other adults at the Milton Hershey School;

"I understand and agree that I will not engage in self-harm/injury behaviors which are a safety concern. Also, should I witness any of my peers engaging in such behaviors I will report it to an adult immediately;

"I understand that I have control over my behavior and am working to understand what triggers my emotions. I have developed a coping plan and will use that plan when I start to feel dysregulated. I will also make realistic modifications to that plan, as necessary....

"I understand and agree that I will maintain appropriate boundaries with others including in person, through the use of technology, and in any other way so that others will not feel uncomfortable;

"I understand and agree that as a student at Milton Hershey School, it is an expectation for me to live by the Sacred Values—Integrity, Commitment, Mutual Respect and Positive Spirit—and further understand that I will be held accountable when I fail to follow these values;

"I understand that any future Level III or IV infractions of the School's Discipline Policy or any further incidents of self-harm/injury will result in a review of my enrollment at Milton Hershey School."

The girl was expelled a month later for violating another Hershey School rule.

JOHN O'BRIEN, a corporate consultant, had been appointed the school's new president after the Office of Attorney General and the Orphans' Court reconstituted the Trust board in 2002. He and other alumni administrators then embarked on a "back to the future" plan to restore discipline and spirit to the Hershey School.

Expulsions soared in the subsequent decade.

The institute terminated the enrollment of 1.1 percent of its students, or 15 of 1,315 children, in the 2002-03 academic year. The rate rose to 4.9 percent by 2007-08, with 83 of 1,703 students being expelled. The rate then retreated to 3.3 percent, or 62 of 1,866 students, in 2011-12.

Shaw, the Hershey School's executive director of student support services, said the school's research into factors that could lead to student expulsions was inconclusive. The research looked only at factors in play before the student entered the Hershey School.

Pennsylvania Department of Education data indicate that the expulsion rate in the state's public schools was about 0.1 percent. Hershey School officials say it's unfair to compare the private institution's expulsion rate to public schools because public schools don't look after children in their homes. Bad behavior in the student homes were the cause of most expulsions or terminations, explained Bob Fehrs, the alumnus and head of the middle school. However, public schools also have to accept all students who live within their district, while the Hershey School rigorously screens its applicants and accepts only those children it believes will benefit from its well-funded, decades-old program. Fehrs told of how when he was a student at the Hershey orphanage he wanted to return home, but his mother told him he had to stay. "Sometimes," he said of today's children, "kids like to be kicked out so they can go home."

An official with the Association of Boarding Schools says few students at private boarding schools, the post-orphanage model for the Hershey School, are expelled; school administrators are motivated in part to do all they can to keep students on campus because each expelled student means the loss of a $40,000 to $100,000 yearly tuition fee. Funded independently by the chocolate company and a multi-billion-dollar investment portfolio, the Hershey School doesn't have this economic incentive to keep students on campus.

EVEN AS Hershey School administrators vigorously clamped down on discipline and student behavior after 2002, the institution failed to modernize its bureaucracy or policies to protect students against wrongful expulsions or punishment. School administrators might not like a student and try to kick them out. Houseparents could blame a student for something to have them moved from a group home.

Since the U.S. Supreme Court's decision in the *Goss v. Lopez* case in the mid-1970s, the nation's public schools recognized that students had due process rights. Because of Goss, public schools today hold highly formalized court-like expulsion proceedings. Facts are presented to a school board. Parents or a lawyer can advocate for a child, and there is an official record of the proceedings.

According to its website, expelling a student in the Philadelphia public schools entails this sequence of events:

1. A parent will be notified of the charges against the student in writing by certified mail.
2. Parents and students have three days' notice of the time and place of the hearing and they are to be told they have a right to be represented by a lawyer.
3. The hearing will be private but it can be public at the request of the parent or student.
4. The names of witnesses against the student will be disclosed to the student and parents and copies of their statements or affidavits will be given to them.
5. Parents and students can request that witnesses appear in the hearings to be cross-examined.
6. The student has the right to present witnesses or make an argument in their defense.
7. A written transcript or audio recording of the hearing shall be kept and a copy made available, at the student's expense, to the student.
8. Students will be told they have the right to appeal a decision when they are informed of an expulsion.

At the Hershey School, no formal hearing is scheduled with the student, parent or advocate when a student is being considered for expulsion. The charges and evidence are not formally presented to the parent or the child. The parent isn't told formally in writing of the infraction. A parent also can't attend an expulsion hearing because they don't know when and where it is. For many of these parents, just getting to Hershey by car is a financial hardship.

During the expulsion process, the student is kept isolated in the medical center for several days to a week and does not attend classes. Students say they can call teachers or other staffers and ask them to advocate for them in the secret expulsion hearings. Staffers may informally do this but the students don't know what they said about them.

When I asked the Hershey School professionals whether parents could attend the expulsion hearings, they said they could not. Bob Fehrs, the middle school head, said parents could call them. Legal due process rights accrue to public school students because of real estate taxes that finance districts. The Hershey School says it's a private institution, with its own source of funding, and can make its own rules independent of public school standards.

After a termination, the Hershey School sends the student's parent a tersely worded form expulsion letter. The letter states that the child could not be educated by the Hershey School. They have no right to appeal. The student isn't allowed back on campus unless granted special permission. I reviewed several of these letters. In one, the Hershey School misspelled the name of the mother and the terminated child.

The student's expulsion letter then becomes part of the child's official academic record. A Pittsburgh-area mother said the Hershey School expelled her middle-school daughter for kissing a boy on campus and other public displays of affection. Because of the expulsion letter, the woman had to enroll her daughter in a school with at-risk and problem children, which led to other behavior problems for her daughter.

Because the Hershey School takes total control of a child's life, including medical care, parents of an expelled student have to find new medical care for their son or daughter. Most times, these low-income parents participate in state-funded medical care and have limited access to family doctors, psychiatrists, specialists and prescription drugs.

The expelled Hershey School student also loses all accrued college scholarship aid worth up to tens of thousands of dollars, even though the Hershey School tells the student they're "earning" the scholarship with good behavior while they're enrolled as a student.

The only recourse for many parents is to call the Office of Attorney General and beg for help. The state agency will then inform them that they need to hire a private attorney, though these poor parents don't have a prayer of obtaining thousands of dollars to retain a private attorney.

Expelled Hershey School students typically disappear into the rural poverty or the urban row house neighborhoods from which they came, leaving no paper trail, with the administrators at the Hershey School saying the child did not meet their "high expectations." But some have spoken out in recent years. Here are some individual stories.

READING IS ONE of the poorest cities in America, and it was in that Pennsylvania town that the famed Hershey School promoted its programs with full-color brochures and free lunches. Cesar Escudero-Aviles lived in one of the poorer sections of Reading with his single mother, Sylvia, who was anxious and excitable. She was desperate to keep her son out of the city's public schools, particularly its industrial-sized and violent high school. "He was about to start ninth grade and we were terrified of Reading High because of the violence," said Sylvia. "I thought Milton Hershey would be the perfect place for him.... It was the type of education I dreamed of for my son." As for the Hershey School, it would get an extremely bright and accomplished kid. The *Reading Eagle* had published a feature on Cesar, whose IQ tested at 142, and who ranked 50th among chess players in the state. The headline read, "Master in the Making Likes to Beat Adults."

Cesar enrolled in ninth grade at the Hershey School, playing hockey, baseball and football. His grades were good. He traveled to Mexico to participate in a volunteer building project for poor Mexicans. He earned high scores in job-skill certification classes in computers, and his academic evaluations contained mentions of exceptional test scores, working well in class, self-motivation, exemplary behavior, accepting responsibility, and cooperative and courteous behavior. He visited Lehigh University as a prospect.

Cesar had problems outside of the classroom, though. His housefather called him a "wetback." A grudge among the kids led to his being jumped in the bathroom of the high school by two boys, with a third boy looking out for guards. In March 2009, an older boy grabbed Cesar's girlfriend at the high school and hugged her. The action was intended to provoke Cesar. He walked to his next class. The boy followed Cesar and taunted him in front of the class after the class bell rang. The teacher watched. With other students there, Cesar agreed to step outside for a fight.

A high school administrator gave him detentions. When he missed a detention because of a driving test, he was declared a runaway. Cesar protested that he had told a secretary about the driving instruction in advance, and had permission to do it. Still, the incident led to an "enrollment review," and to his expulsion in the spring of 2009. Those who represented him in the review procedure were among those who didn't like him, Cesar said. His mother couldn't defend him. He absolutely disputed that he should have been expelled. He believed he had done everything he could to stay. Cesar wasn't allowed to return to his student home after his termination to collect his clothing and awards. His housefather dumped the awards and certificates into the trash, Cesar told me.

On October 7, 2011, and with what he viewed as his statute of limitations running out, Cesar himself filed a federal lawsuit against the Hershey School in federal court in Harrisburg over his expulsion—the first of its kind.

The suit claimed that Hershey had discriminated against him and violated his civil rights, his due process rights and his right to a good education. Cesar scribbled by hand the damages he was seeking: "three million dollars [scholarship and damages to mother and son] and four billion dollars to any foundation the judge [may] consider for benefit of some [present] and future Hershey students providing the right education with the right people." He was seeking to strip the Trust of its financial resources, believing the organization wasn't using those resources to help poor kids like himself.

Cesar represented himself in the lawsuit because neither he nor his mother could afford a lawyer. A lawyer they approached said they would have to pay a $5,000 retainer fee—an amount far beyond their means. The *Patriot-News* published a story on Cesar's lawsuit. On October 17, 2011, Hershey School president Anthony Colistra responded by attacking Cesar and the boy's only advocate, the former head of the alumni association, Ric Fouad. Fouad had discussed Cesar's case with the Trust board. Colistra pointed to a public statement that Fouad had made asserting that the school "systemically hurt" children.

"Those statements are simply not true, and they are a glaring insult to the men and women who have dedicated their lives to providing a supportive home and nurturing community to thousands of boys and girls. I cannot stay silent while our staff is maligned," Colistra stated. At the same time, he added, "Let me be very clear. While an overwhelming majority of students who leave do so voluntarily, some students are expelled. We have high standards and high expectations for our young men and women."

The Hershey School, he noted, does "not hesitate to make tough decisions necessary to make sure all of our students can enjoy a safe and constructive campus environment. Sometimes this requires terminating the enrollment of a student. That is not a decision made lightly."

Eventually a federal judge threw out Cesar's lawsuit on procedural grounds. But others read of Cesar's lawsuit online, and sympathized with the highly intelligent boy, who later worked in a chocolate factory and a pretzel factory to make ends meet. When he entered the Hershey School, he'd dreamed of attending an Ivy League college; he even had one in mind: Columbia University. Instead he attended Reading Community College.

Cesar and his mother walked with me to my car after our interview in their cramped but tidy row house. It was quiet and dark and felt dangerous in the neighborhood of government-subsidized housing. "It was like a waste," Cesar said of his Hershey School experience. "I was depressed about it and I probably still am because I gained weight." He thought a moment and then mentioned some of what he had missed: "no prom, no football, no senior year. I lost a bunch."

The Hershey School had recruited Cesar from this risky place, offering an opportunity to lift him out of poverty and help him fulfill his potential. Then it booted him right back to where he came from.

ON FEBRUARY 15, 2012, the teenage girls in the Silverbrook student home woke to find writing covering the walls. The lines, written in black marker in the hallways, bathroom and common areas of the Silverbrook student home, included sexual references directed at the housefather.

Graffiti in the bathroom sink referred to a part of the housefather's anatomy. On the bathroom mirror, the writing said the housefather "puts 12 of us in a van, is that safe?" The girls walked around the house wide-eyed. They dressed for school. Before going to class, they gave handwriting samples to Hershey School housing officials.

Over the course of that school day, school officials pulled girls out of class, individually or in groups, to interview them about the previous night and the writing. At one point, school officials told the girls everyone would be punished if they didn't find who did it. By the end of the day, Hershey officials concluded that a Philadelphia girl, Meleisha, and two other girls wrote on the walls. They had matched two letters in Meleisha's handwriting sample to letters in the bathroom.

Because Meleisha had fought with a girl several months earlier over a Facebook post, she could be expelled. Meleisha called her mother for the first time at 6:30 that evening, about 12 hours after the writing had first been discovered and after she'd been interviewed by school officials. She was crying. Her mother, Vivian, wrote of her recollection of what Meleisha told her: "I didn't do it, Mom, I didn't do it. Please help me, I didn't do it. They are trying to blame me; they want me to confess to something I didn't do."

If she had written on the walls, Vivian told her daughter, she should be punished. But after thinking about it overnight, Vivian didn't believe Meleisha would vandalize the student home or make those sexual references. It didn't sound like her daughter. Meleisha was a good girl who dressed stylishly and stayed out of trouble. Her family lived in North Philadelphia, and Meleisha had attended Hershey partly because it offered a safe refuge from the dangers of her troubled and violent Philadelphia neighborhood. Vivian told a story about how one day, when she learned that Meleisha could be jumped by other girls on the way home from school, she had called ahead for the school to keep her daughter so that she could pick her up. Vivian also had been concerned about Meleisha taking public transportation to school.

Vivian began asking questions of the Hershey School officials. Why hadn't she been called before Hershey School officials interviewed her daughter for hours? "This girl is not an orphan," she told them.

Vivian wanted to know who was qualified to say that Meleisha's handwriting matched the handwriting in the Silverbrook bathroom. Did the school employ a handwriting expert? Were they trained? The school told her it had not hired an expert and that its staff analyzed the handwriting.

Vivian asked over the phone to meet with the home-life administrator investigating the incident. The woman "said she was busy and could not meet with me and had a busy schedule the entire day. I then told her she had time to conduct an investigation while making accusations against my daughter, but she couldn't find time to meet with me."

Vivian drove to Hershey and took her daughter home to Philadelphia over the weekend. The following week, the two drove back to the Hershey School to resolve the matter. But again Vivian couldn't arrange a meeting with the school officials who were deciding Meleisha's status. While the two brown-skinned Philadelphia women waited on a bench on campus, Meleisha pointed out one woman who was investigating the graffiti incident. Vivian said the woman briskly walked the other way when she saw them. She took her daughter home again. Sensing that the door was closing on her daughter, Vivian offered over the phone to voluntarily withdraw her daughter. But the school expelled the girl.

The form expulsion letter stated that Meleisha's actions "made it impossible for the Milton Hershey School to meet its goal of nurturing and educating [her]." The decision couldn't be appealed. The last paragraph of the letter continued: "Students whose enrollments have been terminated are not permitted to return to the Milton Hershey School campus or attend Milton Hershey School sponsored activities until after their class has graduated. Any exceptions to this must be approved in writing by the Head of School."

This letter from a multi-billion-dollar educational institution that advertises its compassionate care and broad suite of health and mental services made it sound as if Meleisha had exhibited behavior so toxic that she shouldn't even be around other kids. Vivian received no other explanation for her daughter's expulsion. Meleisha would have to present the letter to future school officials to explain her history.

During several interviews with me, Meleisha said she hadn't vandalized the house walls and that she'd had no problems with the houseparents. "My grades were high and I was making Gold"—the behavior rating that the houseparents assigned to her. Her mother complained to the Department of Education, the governor's office and the Office of Attorney General. She wanted the expulsion cleared from her daughter's school file because she would be applying to colleges. Vivian believed a college could ask if her daughter was ever expelled from a school. "I don't want to lie," said the mother. She got no help from the state agencies.

Five months later, on August 9, 2012, the Hershey fire department was called to Silverbrook at 4:46 in the morning because of an incident. There were eight girls and two adults in the house who escaped without injury. Fire investigators determined that one of girls, a 15-year-old, had put a pot of oil on the stove during the night and turned up the burner. The girl was charged with two counts of arson, causing or risking a catastrophe, institutional vandalism, and recklessly endangering another person, according to Lieutenant Tim Roche of the Derry Township Police Department. Vivian believed this raised the strong possibility that another girl had vandalized the house, not Meleisha. "We were right all along, and my daughter was set up," Vivian said after hearing of the fire.

In late 2012, Meleisha was attending a Philadelphia charter school. Vivian wanted nothing to do with the Hershey School—other than having the expulsion letter withdrawn. "I wouldn't even consider sending my child there again," she stated. "And I wouldn't recommend it to anyone else either. I'm so disgusted in this school. It's horrific."

SEVERAL DAYS after the discovery of the graffiti in Silverbrook, 16-year-old Kayla heard other girls gossiping about the incident. The sexual references had taken on a life of their own. Talking with other girls in their student home at the dinner table, Kayla mentioned the gossip that she'd heard. Her housemother reported the dinner-table conversation to Hershey School home-life administrators—the residential-life cops. At first, Kayla's conversation chat didn't seem like a big deal. But a few days later, it was. A school staffer asked Kayla where she heard the comments and from whom. It seemed to Kayla as if the school wanted her to snitch on other students. She wouldn't give the staffer information on the other girls. The school placed Kayla under an "enrollment review."

Sarah, Kayla's mother, pleaded on the phone with the Hershey School to keep her daughter. Kayla had been an athlete, an exceptional student, and a cheerleader, and had acted in the school play. The school's position seemed to be that her daughter "was so bad they couldn't handle her, but she was OK to go home and go to a public school," Sarah recalled.

Sarah, 33 years old and a single mother, had enrolled Kayla in the Hershey School so her daughter would have access to a good education at a boarding school, participate in sports without worrying about extra fees, and be safe. Kayla's father was not part of the girl's life. During part of her childhood, Kayla had lived with a grandparent. Sarah waited tables at a Lancaster diner, earning $600 to $1,000 a month as a server on the overnight shift. She had been particularly excited about the Hershey School's college aid program: paying for college would be impossible on her diner wages and tips. A thin woman with blond hair and an anxious manner, she qualified for food stamps and participated in a Medicaid healthcare program for poor families; she drove a 1997 Saturn with more than 200,000 miles on it.

In a conversation with a Hershey School official, Sarah read over the phone from a blue pamphlet handed out to parents when their child enrolled at the Hershey School: "Milton Hershey School provides medical, dental, psychological, behavioral and social work services for students while on campus." Why couldn't the Hershey School counsel her daughter instead of terminating her? The Hershey School staffer said that counseling wasn't an option for her daughter. Sarah suspected they wanted to expel Kayla so they wouldn't have pay her the $39,000 in Hershey School college aid she'd already earned.

Sarah eventually realized she couldn't convince the school to keep Kayla, and she scheduled a time to get her. The date was March 2, 2012, two weeks after the graffiti incident had occurred. "This was her future," Sarah said in an interview only a few weeks later, "down the toilet....We never thought in a million years this would happen." Because she was late arriving to pick up Kayla, the Hershey School threatened to report her daughter to county services as an abandoned child. Sarah retained a voicemail from a county official asking about Kayla.

There were other problems. Kayla had entered the Hershey School in 2009 on no medications. While there, school's medical staff prescribed her multiple medications for her moods and behavior (paid for by the School). When Sarah picked up Kayla, an employee at the Hershey School handed her a 30-day supply of the pills in a bag, one of which was Seroquel, an antipsychotic medication used to treat bipolar disorder and major depression. They told her she would have to get the refills. The Hershey School gave her no medical records.

With the 30-day clock ticking to refill Kayla's medications, Sarah scheduled an appointment with her Medicaid-covered family doctor. He evaluated Kayla and refilled the two most powerful medications because he "felt it was medically important not to drop them," Sarah said. Months later, Sarah still hadn't gotten an appointment with a Medicaid-covered psychiatrist, and she didn't get Kayla's medical records from the Hershey School until July—four months after the institution terminated the girl's enrollment.

Sarah said her experience with the Hershey School was a "huge disappointment. It wasn't at all what it was advertised." She thought that when Kayla got into Hershey, everything would be fine. The school had rigorously screened her daughter and only accepted her when everything checked out. "They should have the lowest kick-out rate ever. The kids are almost perfect," said Sarah. But over time, Kayla's mother became concerned about how the institution treated students. "They constantly have the kids on a teeter-totter as to whether they would be kicked out. It was like a joke in our family with Kayla—oh, don't get kicked out."

After the expulsion, Kayla lived with an aunt and uncle. She said in a phone interview that she was moving on with her life. She was getting A's in her new public school, and was singing with a church group. She was weaning off the prescription drugs. She had mentioned the sexual gossip at the dinner table in her student home, she said, "because it didn't sound like something that should be happening at a school."

The Hershey School didn't provide Sarah with a formal written explanation for why it terminated Kayla, though one of Kayla's medical documents provided a partial explanation. A Hershey School medical staffer wrote that Kayla made a "verbal allegation of inappropriate behavior by an MHS staff, which led her to be readmitted to the [Health Center] as a home-life admit. At this time, her enrollment was formally reviewed and her enrollment was terminated."

She was gossiping at the dinner table. For this, she lost $39,000 in college aid, had her life uprooted, and an expulsion letter made part of her academic record. She couldn't defend herself against the accusations of malicious gossiping by pointing to the fact that the gossip was related to the Silverbrook graffiti incident, because neither she nor her mother could participate in the expulsion process. And who were the people who expelled her for allegedly gossiping about a Hershey School staff member? Those also were Hershey School staff members.

Sarah wanted Kayla's college scholarship aid restored because she felt it was unfairly taken from her daughter. But "I would not send her back," she stated. "I don't trust them anymore because they are always trying to hide things. It's always a big run-around."

IN EARLY MARCH 2013, a Hershey School senior punched a boy in a deserted hallway between classes. A school surveillance camera captured the punch—there are over 600 cameras on campus, more than most towns. The boy who'd thrown the punch, a student from West Philadelphia, admitted that it "looked bad" on camera. He seemed to jump unprovoked and clock the boy. The West Philadelphia boy then ran after the other boy and swung again, but didn't connect.

The Philadelphia boy and another boy from a small Pennsylvania city had been friends on the basketball team but later fell out over a prank. Someone had flashed a girl, pulling up his shirt; the girl didn't know which one. No one was punished. Afterward, though, the teammate began calling the Philadelphia boy a snitch, saying he wouldn't take the blame if it came to that. They shoved each other at the high school. Administrators told them to cool it, warning them they'd call the police if anything more happened.

On the day of the incident, the two boys exchanged glances in the hallway and agreed to meet in the bathroom. The Philadelphia boy went to the bathroom; the other boy wasn't there. As he was returning to class, he encountered the other boy in the hallway.

Hershey School administrators called the Derry Township police, and a detective drove the Philadelphia boy to the station. When he returned to campus, he was immediately placed in the medical center with his enrollment under review.

The Philadelphia boy's mother, Sondra, thought punching the other boy was wrong. Her son shouldn't have hit him. But no one was seriously hurt, and the punch didn't seem like something he should be expelled for. They weren't getting along. She thought the school could have defused the situation. Her son had enrolled at the Hershey School in first grade, and now had only three months left before graduation. Four colleges had accepted him for the fall and he'd earned $76,000 in college aid through the scholarship program, thanks to good grades and a top-level, "Spartan" behavior record. Her son also apologized. But a week later, the school terminated him without a formal hearing; neither his mother nor the boy could explain the circumstances and the slights leading up to the incident.

Sondra told her son's story in the dining area of a Whole Foods Market in Philadelphia, where she met with me several days after the termination.

She was confused and upset. Sondra was nicely dressed in an outfit completed with a hat. Her son also was a very good-looking boy, dressed in a polo shirt—thin, athletic and courteous. He hadn't gotten into serious trouble before. The school had informed him it would call the police if he fought with the other boy. But he had not been told he would be expelled. He seemed embarrassed and remorseful, not arrogant and trash-talking.

Why hadn't the school called her earlier to tell her there was a problem with the two boys? "I asked why they didn't counsel him. Why didn't they call the boys' parents so we could talk with them? What are you not telling me?" The school sent her a form expulsion letter.

The termination dumped the West Philadelphia boy, after 12 years in the highly structured and rural Hershey School, into the violent and chaotic Philadelphia public schools. In addition, her son hadn't taken African-American history courses in Hershey. The Philadelphia district required African-American history to graduate. Sondra asked the Hershey School whether her son could obtain a diploma if he was home-schooled his final three months. The Hershey School said no.

Sondra explained to the Hershey School outplacement staffer that she was having trouble finding a new school for her son this late in the school year so that he could obtain a high school diploma and attend college that fall. The Hershey School staffer responded that the Philadelphia public schools simply had to accept her son. Then the staffer told Sondra of another option: the federally funded Job Corps for at-risk children and delinquents. Here was a multi-billion-dollar Trust funded by the nation's chocolate profits, which existed to educate and raise orphans and poor kids, booting out a student after 12 years in its institution, spending more than a million dollars on him, and then recommending that he finish his education in a federal program. "There is no way I am sending him to Job Corps," the mother concluded.

EACH OF THESE STUDENTS faced devastating consequences for their behavior. For Abbie Bartels, the consequences were fatal. Their alleged behaviors fell along a range of concern—from gossiping and hitting another boy, to signs of emotional difficulties. But clearly these behaviors could have been tolerated, understood as falling within the bounds of adolescent difficulties, or at least handled in a more forgiving way.

The Hershey School operates within a founding mandate to help poor children, and it is not surprising that their students would sometimes exhibit behaviors indicative of emotional difficulties. It falls to the School, with its massive financial resources, to have procedures and programs in place that will help its hardworking students make it to the finish line—high school graduation. Instead, these stories reveal how in its zeal to police behavior, the Trust has pursued policies that punish and cause harm to the very children it has committed to serve.

12

ZIMM'S PALACE

Greed and a Decade of Soaring
Trust Board Compensation

WHEN LEROY ZIMMERMAN joined the board of the Hershey Trust Company in 2002 as part of an Orphans' Court- and Attorney General-forced reorganization, he was a man who was used to wielding power. Coming from humble beginnings, he had learned lessons early on which he drew on as he rose from success to success, including serving two terms as Pennsylvania's Attorney General in the 1980s. A consummate power broker in state-level politics, he would end up using his position with the Trust as a congenial platform to wield his personal brand of influence, and would be compensated in total about two million dollars while doing it.

LeRoy Salvatore Zimmerman grew up on Harrisburg's ethnic south side in the 1930s and '40s. His dad walked out on his mother, the former Amelia Magaro, and she raised him as a single mother. Roy was a good boy who cut lawns, delivered groceries, sold gardenias to men in local bars, and dug graves for $1.10 an hour. Amelia worked as a clerk for the Dauphin County Recorder of Deeds by day, and at night answered the phones as a receptionist at the local YMCA. "There, at 10 o'clock each night [Roy] would meet her and they would walk home together to the apartment above the grocery store at Second and Chestnut," said a magazine profile on Zimmerman written at the height of his political career. Zimmerman attended Villanova as an undergraduate and went on to Dickinson Law. He got a job at the Dauphin County district attorney's office and in 1965, local judges appointed him to complete the unexpired term of District Attorney Martin Lock, who had died of cancer. Zimmerman won the next general election and kept on winning.

During the 1970s, the period of Zimmerman's rise to power, more than 300 Pennsylvania public officials were found guilty, admitted guilt or pleaded no contest to corruption charges, resulting in a drumbeat of sensational headlines for the state's newspapers. Lawmakers responded to the public outrage by enacting new ethics and wire-tap laws and campaign finance reform measures, creating investigating state grand juries, and establishing a crime commission. Voters approved a referendum amending the state constitution to create an elected attorney general who would be independent of the governors—up till then, they had been appointed by the governor.

In 1980, Zimmerman, then in his mid-forties, ran in the election to head the new Office of Attorney General, and won. He hired the staff and, generally, earned good marks in his first three years on a range of initiatives, including cracking down on deceptive marketing by Pocono resort operators, price-fixing at auto inspection garages, and reining in overzealous debt collectors. An Everyman's Attorney General, his anti-shoplifting campaign featured a gravel-voiced cartoon hound, Inspector McGruff, taking a bite out of crime. He also exercised broad oversight responsibility as *parens patriae*—the Commonwealth's protector of children and the disadvantaged—of the Trust and the state's other charities.

Harrisburg's entrenched corruption seemed to recede with Zimmerman as attorney general and former federal prosecutor Dick Thornburgh as governor. Zimmerman also investigated job-selling by officials in the auditor general's office, and helped prosecute lottery fixers.

As a Pittsburgh magazine put it: "Harrisburg is Roy Zimmerman's town: From St. Patrick's Cathedral, where he served as a page to Bishop George L. Leech and where, in the shadows of the massive floodlighted capitol, he played scrub football, to the YMCA, where the late congressman John C. Kunkel, a neighbor for whom he did chores, bought him a membership every year from early in grade school until late in college...from Bishop McDevitt High School to the Dauphin County Courthouse, where for 16 of the 18 years he worked there, he was district attorney."

On January 12, 1984, LeRoy Zimmerman announced his run for a second term as attorney general in the capitol rotunda accompanied by the "Kennedy Republican" William W. Scranton, whose fame still ran like an anthracite coal seam through Pennsylvania Republican politics. Scranton would chair Zimmerman's campaign and help him raise one million dollars—a huge endorsement from the GOP establishment.

Then came the CTA scandal.

It began as the campaign season was opening, in early 1984, when the head of Computer Technology Associates (CTA), John R. Torquato Jr., began a money-greased pursuit of a no-bid state contract. The contract was to carry out a project documenting overpayment of Social Security taxes to public school employees, and it was valued at $4.6 million. Though Torquato's business was based in California, he was the son of a local political boss, and knew how to feed at the Harrisburg trough. He enlisted Dauphin County Republican William Smith, who targeted state treasurer R. Budd Dwyer with "campaign funds." Smith told Dwyer in a March meeting of the quid pro quo: "Mr. Torquato has authorized me to tell you that if CTA gets the contract, they'll make a $300,000 contribution to [your] campaign." An uncomfortable moment passed between the two men. "Beads of sweat broke out on his forehead," Smith said of Dwyer. "He just didn't say anything....I was nervous, and he was nervous. We were both in a kind of distressed state there." Dwyer awarded the contract on May 10th. In late May or early June, Smith offered the Zimmerman campaign a contribution of $150,000 in exchange for a favorable letter on the CTA contract. Smith later called the offer "a gratuitous, off-the-cuff remark."

The FBI got wind of the contract and its basis in shady campaign donations before it could be executed. Dwyer voided the contract. He also publicly confirmed the existence of the federal investigation. On October 23rd, U.S. Attorney David D. Queen indicted Smith, Torquato and three others for "a large-scale organized effort to bribe state officials." Neither Dwyer nor Zimmerman was part of the indictment, though Queen disclosed that a top Zimmerman aide had been offered a campaign contribution in return for a supportive letter. Zimmerman told a hastily scheduled news conference that he hadn't accepted the campaign funds, nor did he write the letter. His spokesman later acknowledged that the Office of Attorney General didn't open an investigation into CTA until after Dwyer voided the state contract and disclosed the federal investigation—a very delayed response for the state's top law-enforcement official.

Thornburgh stuck by Zimmerman in his re-election campaign, and the incumbent attorney general squeaked out a second-term victory over Democrat Allen E. Ertel, beating him by only 40,000 votes out of nearly five million cast. But the CTA scandal was just beginning to play out in Harrisburg. Smith and Torquato cooperated with the prosecutors, who went on to charge Budd Dwyer and former state Republican Chairman Robert P. Asher. In late 1986, a federal jury in Williamsport convicted Dwyer and Asher on 11 bribe-related offenses. Each faced a maximum sentence of 55 years, and fines totaling $65,000. Despondent over the damage to his reputation and potential loss of his state pension, Budd Dwyer called for a press conference on January 22, 1987, the day before sentencing. He accused prosecutors of going after him while protecting Zimmerman. As the TV news cameras rolled, Dwyer pulled a .357 handgun out of a manila envelope and waved it around. He then placed the gun in his mouth and pulled the trigger.

Journalists William Keisling and Richard Kearns watched these events unfold. Keisling, though young, was already a seasoned journalist with experience at the muckraking weekly *Harrisburg Independent Press*. He had investigated the Three Mile Island nuclear accident, turning his work into a book. He'd moved on to an editing position at Rodale Press. Keisling knew there was a big story in the events leading up to Dwyer's death, and knew it offered a chance to expose government wrongdoing. He obtained a confidential transcript of an FBI recording with Harrisburg police chief Bruno Favasuli, in which the chief seemed to mention Zimmerman's having accepted money from gamblers. "I mean, Jesus Christ, they can get LeRoy Zimmerman, they can get any of them guys, if they want to," Favasuli told Norman Bonneville, who was wearing an FBI wire in December 1979. Zimmerman seemed to them to offer a wealth of material for a profile.

William Keisling and Richard Kearns traced LeRoy Zimmerman's family history through old Polk city directories, immigrant records, marriage certificates, court records and real estate records. His grandfather was "Georgie the Peanut Man," so beloved that one of the Harrisburg newspapers published his obituary on the front page. Johnny Magaro also fascinated Keisling and Kearns. Harrisburg cops arrested Magaro, Amelia's half-brother and Zimmerman's uncle, numerous times between 1931 and 1957. The last time, when he was proprietor of the Court Hotel across the street from the Dauphin County Courthouse, police charged him with pandering, corrupting the morals of a minor, prostitution, bookmaking, pool-selling and running a gaming house. A Harrisburg detective testified, "The reputation of the Court Hotel is one of allowing minors to hang out in the place; allowing people of ill-repute to hang out there; prostitution, girls taking fellows upstairs from the barroom. That about covers it." A judge sentenced the fast-talking Magaro to three to six years in Rockview. Court officials paroled him in March 1960. City directories listed him, Amelia and his nephew, Leroy Zimmerman, as living together.

Keisling and Kearns kept digging and learning more. "We were introduced from one cop to another," said Keisling of his research for the book. "I was like 27 or 28 years old and these cops were kind of amused by us." Five retired police officers told Keisling and Kearns that Johnny Magaro had run a numbers racket in Harrisburg—and recalled how his nephew, as Dauphin County District Attorney, seemed to turn a blind eye. On one occasion, they were told, Sergeant Sam Orlowsky screamed so loud at Zimmerman over his foot-dragging that Orlowsky burst a blood vessel in his eye. Orlowsky handed over to the authors a 1965 film that he claimed was evidence of a Magaro associate paying off the Steelton police chief.

At first, Keisling and Kearns attempted to publish the story as an investigative news piece—they approached *Philadelphia* magazine, the *Philadelphia Inquirer*, the *Daily News* and the Harrisburg *Patriot-News*, but with no success. Keisling decided to self-publish under his Yardbird imprint, named in homage to Charlie Parker. The book came out as *The Sins of Our Fathers: A Profile of Pennsylvania Attorney General LeRoy S. Zimmerman and a Historical Explanation of the Suicide of State Treasurer R. Budd Dwyer.* The first 250 books sold out. Keisling heard that state employees were making copies of *Sins of Our Fathers* on state copy machines to pass around. He asked his printer for second and third print runs. The 132-page *Sins of Our Fathers* has sold several thousand copies over the years.

Along with telling Zimmerman's story, the authors observed: "Politics in Pennsylvania had always been dirty, some say among the dirtiest in the nation. But when Dwyer blew out the lights in front TV cameras, politics here suddenly had sunk to new levels—not just ugly, not just dirty, but deadly. In the end, we find the events leading to Dwyer's death had their roots in a century of Harrisburg history. The signposts leading to his death had been in place for decades. We would discover a long tradition of Harrisburg politicians playing ball with one another."

FIFTEEN YEARS had passed since Budd Dwyer "blew out the lights."

Joe Berning, one of the most dedicated members of the Hershey alumni's "Orphan Army," was driving back to Hershey in the midst of the furor over the direction of the School and the chocolate company sale during the summer of 2002. On his way to the Homestead, he cut through a neighborhood of Trust-owned executive mansions on Para Avenue. At the rounded-off corner of Para and East Granada Avenues, Berning saw cars lined in a semicircle. Berning drove past. He drove past again. "I was coming around there and I ran into this big line of cars," he recalled, "and the first thing I said was, 'What the fuck is going on?'" It had to be something to do with the Trust, he thought. Why didn't alumni leaders know about it?

Berning scribbled down the license plates. He learned the next day that all the owners of those vehicles were retired Trust board members or retired Hershey business executives. Could this be a secret meeting? But the owner of one vehicle with the vanity plate OAG-1 was someone else—not a retired Trust board member, or a business executive in one of the Trust-owned entities. Berning figured it out: OAG stood for Office of Attorney General. The "1" stood for first. The owner was LeRoy Zimmerman, Pennsylvania's first elected attorney general, hence the vanity plate, and "the most experienced player in the Harrisburg game."

The puzzle pieces fell into place several months later. When the proposed sale of the chocolate company fell apart and Judge Warren Morgan and Attorney General Mike Fisher forced William Lepley's ouster, Zimmerman was elected to the Trust board with other Hershey civic boosters—among them, chocolate company CEO Richard Lenny and former *Patriot-News* publisher Raymond Gover. They began the process of stabilizing the organization, calming the alumni and looking inward to develop the Hershey School with hundreds of millions of dollars in construction contracts. Nothing would soothe Hershey like economic development, and nothing would please the alumni like making room for more students. On March 3, 2004, the *Hummelstown Sun* published an article quoting Hershey School officials as saying the institution would add 500 students and would finally break through the Trust-imposed ceiling of 1,500 to 1,600 students. "As we go from 1,300 students to 1,800 students, there's going to be additional housing needs, transportation needs," the school's spokesman, Michael Kinney, told the *Sun*, "and this includes building new houses." About 50 new homes would have to be built to accommodate the 1,800-student goal. The enrollment goal would later be revised upward to 2,000 students.

But somehow the historically land-rich Trust now found itself short of real estate for its ambitious plans for more students. The Trust had repurposed or sold huge chunks of Milton Hershey's 10,000 acres of farms for roads, the medical center complex, housing, a municipal building, and retail stores over the decades. The Trust-owned for-profit Hershey Entertainment seemed particularly land-greedy. To make possible its expansion plans, Hershey Entertainment had taken over properties including the Fairway farm, which became the Giant Center—a state-subsidized, 10,500-seat arena with 40 luxury boxes and 688 club seats that was constructed between 2000 and 2002 for $98 million. The school also lost the Longmead farm, to create overflow parking for the antique auto show; the Westmoor farm, for the 665-room Hershey Lodge; the Sunset and Maple Lawn farms, for the Hershey Country Club; Broad Acres, for Chocolate World parking; and Rolling Green for apartments.

Hershey Entertainment seized the orphans' rustic Camp Swattee on the Swatara Creek, too. In 1977, during a dispute over taxes with Derry Township, the Trust had maintained that the camp was intrinsic to the Hershey School's activities with the orphan boys. "Camp Swattee is a campground facility used almost every weekend by the School's students, who camp overnight in cabins, fish, hike, and take part in other camping activities as part of their education in natural sciences." The camp, the Trust told the court in the tax dispute, "is used almost exclusively by students."

But by 2003, the Trust had repurposed the property for Hershey Entertainment's "Sweet Lights" Christmas extravaganza, charging $20 a car for admission to the drive-through holiday experience. This transformation of a camp for students to the grounds for a holiday show would be part of the alumni association's lawsuit seeking to reinstitute Attorney General Fisher's cancelled reform package. "Among the last straws for us was Sweet Lights," said two-term alumni association president John Rice in 2003, in a statement announcing the suit filed in Dauphin County Orphans Court by the alumni association to appoint a guardian and trustee over the Trust. "The land that they're taking around Camp Swattee for this project has been central to [Milton Hershey School] students' lives for decades. Now they want to convert that to [Hershey Entertainment] use, too. Haven't they taken enough land already?"

Commonwealth Judge Dan Pellegrini decided in favor of the alumni, and in his January 2005 opinion he wrote, "Some of the land formerly designated for school use was closed, sold, or abandoned or transferred to [Hershey Entertainment], thereby reducing the amount of homes that could house roughly 310 orphans."

The for-profit Hershey Trust Company seemed very willing over the years to transfer property to the for-profit tourism company, in moves that returned little in dividends —in many years, none at all—to pay the Hershey School's bills for orphans and poor kids. Now the Trust looked to replenish its land holdings for future growth, using tens of millions of dollars in school funds.

And Trust officials spoke of the need for additional property, not to make room for student homes but also as a *buffer* for student safety—a cushion between the Hershey School's campus and residential homes and local businesses. One of these cushions was the Pumpkin World roadside stand off busy Route 39 north of Hershey, which sold country crafts and vegetables to tourists. A local developer was proposing a "Jungle Joey" water park with a 125-room hotel on the 27-acre site when the Trust swooped in and bought it in 2006 for a total of $8.6 million with school funds, a sum more than nine times greater than the property's fair-market value, for buffer land. Many viewed the Trust's Pumpkin World purchase as protecting HersheyPark from a possible new competitor, not benefiting impoverished students.

Almost 200 acres of additional buffer land came on the market in the form of a money-losing luxury golf course near Pumpkin World. Doctors, lawyers and business executives had invested in the venture that converted a farm into a luxurious private golf course. The investment group lured disenchanted golfers from the Blue Ridge Country Club in Harrisburg and the Hershey Country Club as members. They bought "equity"—part ownership in the venture—and golfed without the distractions of a public course. Original investors, one of whom was the chocolate company CEO Richard Lenny, loaned the project additional money to keep it afloat.

But Wren Dale had failed to attain the critical mass of membership necessary to maintain itself; over 16 months, the golf course had lost close to one million dollars while carrying almost eight million dollars in debt. Even so, the investor group filed with the Pennsylvania Department of State to convert the non-profit organization into a for-profit company, and opened negotiations to sell the Wren Dale course to the Trust. The two sides seemed far apart on the price. The Trust hired an independent appraiser who placed a $6.2 million value on the property if it were sold to a housing developer, and four million dollars if it were operated as a golf course. Yet, in 2005, the Trust agreed to pay a whopping $12 million for the property. The Hershey Trust Company issued a press release on October 21st:

Hershey, Pa., Oct. 21 /PRNewswire/—Hershey Trust Co. and the owners of the Wren Dale golf course today announced an arrangement that ensures the long-term future of the championship-caliber course and *provides an open buffer of green space* for the planned expansion of the Milton Hershey School campus.

Wren Dale is located in South Hanover Township. The 180-acre property is adjacent to the site of a proposed expansion of the Milton Hershey School.

The Trust and owners of Wren Dale have signed a lease agreement. In a separate agreement, the Trust has signed an option to buy Wren Dale. Financial terms were not disclosed.

"This opportunity was simply too good to pass up. As the School continues to expand and enroll more students, our top priority is to ensure that our students have the proper environment," said Robert Vowler, president of the Hershey Trust Co. "That is at the heart of the Deed of Trust, and we believe that preserving this open space is critically important as the School continues to grow."

Vowler added, "Wren Dale is right next to where Milton Hershey School will be housing many Middle Division kids and, obviously, open space like this will provide an *appropriate buffer* for our students."

The School's Centennial Strategic Plan calls for enrollment to increase to 2,000 students by no later than 2013. The School now serves approximately 1,300 students. The agreement, coupled with recently approved zoning changes on land Hershey Trust owns in South Hanover Township, will ensure more *open space and more green space in the community.*

"This relationship makes sense for the School and the Trust, and the community can rest assured that this property will remain *open space.* This will not become another housing development. We think everybody wins," Vowler added.

Wren Dale, which opened in 2000, has earned a tremendous reputation among golfers from all parts of the country as one of the most challenging and beautiful layouts in the Central Pennsylvania region.

The course was designed by the award-winning architectural firm of Hurdzan-Fry of Columbus, Ohio. The agreements allow the current day-to-day operations to continue under John Caporaletti's management firm Caporaletti Golf Management under a long-term contract.

Wren Dale will continue to be managed as a premier, semi-private, golf-only facility, with a membership program distinct and separate from the other area clubs.

"Our top priority was to make sure that this course would remain open and not bulldozed to make way for yet another housing development," said Barry Fell, president of Wren Dale [author's italics].

"We poured our hearts into building this course and we're thrilled that the Hershey Trust Company recognizes the value in this course and has entered into this relationship with us. We're confident that the Trust and Caporaletti's management will operate a world-class facility," Fell added.

THE GOLF COURSE DEAL closed in 2006, during LeRoy Zimmerman's first year as head of the Hershey Trust. Richard Lenny was chief executive of the chocolate company, a member of the Trust board and a part owner of Wren Dale. But his part-ownership of the golf course wasn't mentioned publicly.

Hershey School president John O'Brien wrote to Hershey Trust Company officials in September 2005 to applaud the decision to purchase the golf course for buffer land with school funds for impoverished kids. "I... formally request that you continue to purchase buffer lands around our School operations and homes when it is feasible to do so. With the recent zoning approval of our plan to put homes in South Hanover Township, we are especially concerned about the high-density residential and commercial development which is being considered for lands contiguous to our property. One only needs to look at the problems of the Rockledge Development... to appreciate the value of significant buffers."

O'Brien distanced himself from the letter in an interview with me. A Hershey Trust Company official had asked him to write this letter and he had agreed, he told me. Everyone in Hershey knew the golf course was losing money, and O'Brien had believed the Trust could purchase it at a distressed price, sub-divide the land for buffer and resell the remaining land to a developer. Others, though, saw the deal differently: as the Trust bailing out some very influential local investors in a friendly deal in which nobody lost face.

The Trust's next actions appeared to support the idea that it was interested in actually running a new high-end golf course. Following the sale, the Trust finished landscaping the course, and renamed it Hershey Links. The Trust also constructed a Scottish-themed clubhouse with a public restaurant and a sit-down bar on the golf course property; school funds paid for the five-million-dollar price tag. This brought the total cost to $17 million for a property originally appraised at four million dollars. Hershey Entertainment leased the golf course at below-market rates and marketed it as a tourist attraction. At the least, it looked like an unhealthy intermingling of for-profit business and charitable assets meant for orphans and poor kids.

Activist alumnus Ric Fouad complained bitterly about the golf course in letters to Attorney General Tom Corbett. Others asked why the Trust had opened the course to the public, if the intent was to protect students with "buffer" land. How could golfers winging balls next to student group homes and a public restaurant/bar be considered safety precautions? Did the Trust really need a fourth golf course? Why not plant trees on the unfinished golf course?

The school for impoverished kids from Philadelphia and rural Pennsylvania didn't have a golf team—but Leroy Zimmerman, the Chairman of the Hershey Trust, did like to golf. In addition, he and other Trust board members distributed free Hershey Links passes to friends and others—a little in-kind golf diplomacy on the school's dime.

AS HEAD of the multi-billion-dollar Trust with tentacles throughout the Harrisburg area, LeRoy Zimmerman quickly consolidated economic and political power, and a stream of directors' fees. He joined the board of Hershey Entertainment, which operated Hershey Links, the Hershey Country Club, HersheyPark, the Giant Center and other assets. He seemed particularly enthralled with the four-star Hotel Hershey: he championed a $70-million modernization and upgrade that added a spa, detached cottages, a new restaurant and an outdoor skating rink. After the expansion was done, someone hung a big banner printed with the words "Zimm's Palace" above the hotel's front doors. Smiling Trust board members posed for pictures with the palace's politically powerful namesake.

Zimmerman hosted a Republican fundraiser at Trust-owned High Point mansion, Milton and Kitty's former home. Bush political advisor Karl Rove came to the event. The gala was catered by Hershey Entertainment. Participants got to ride the HersheyPark amusement rides after the park closed

While the old Wren Dale golf course was having its makeover in 2007, Zimmerman helped lead a major reorganization of the chocolate company board. Replacing what had been an independent board were himself, former Pennsylvania governor Tom Ridge and Philadelphia-area investment manager James Nevels—all three prominent Republicans. As board members, they each earned about $200,000 a year in directors' fees. Nevels was later elevated to the position of chocolate company board chairman. Zimmerman framed the chocolate company board shake-up as the Trust acting in the best interests of poor kids and orphans, saying in a statement, "The Hershey Trust, which is obligated to manage its assets solely for the benefit of Milton Hershey School…has made it clear that it is not satisfied with the company's recent results." Harrisburg insiders viewed it as the GOP establishment tightening its grip on the super-rich charitable Trust and a Fortune 500 company.

Boosting profits at the chocolate company entailed closing the downtown Hershey plant and relocating production lines to a low-cost Mexican factory, slashing local factory jobs. Zimmerman planned to redevelop the vacant 2.2-million-square-foot Hershey factory into condos, retail stores, a hotel and a retirement community with up to $100 million in Hershey School funds, another big construction project and local economic boost. This would remove the last concrete local tie to Milton Hershey's original chocolate-manufacturing venture in downtown Hershey.

But the redevelopment project appeared rife with conflicts. Zimmerman sat on the chocolate company board, which was selling the factory site, and at the same time chaired the Hershey Trust Company board that would finance the project with surplus school funds. In addition, his son-in-law, Anthony Seitz, was a part owner in a government relations and lobbying firm that briefed Hershey organization officials on a downtown redevelopment plan at the Hershey Lodge in 2009. Companies controlled by the Trust paid Seitz's firm $290,000 in fees, according to a Trust tax filing with the Internal Revenue Service.

Zimmerman now received compensation through directors' fees at the Hershey Trust Company, the chocolate company and Hershey Entertainment, totaling about $500,000 a year. His aggregate Hershey-related compensation over his tenure was heading toward two million dollars. Hershey Trust Company spokeswoman Connie McNamara said Zimmerman was properly compensated because of his service on "three distinct boards with separate and distinct responsibilities." She continued, "It is absolutely false to portray his entire compensation as in the service of a charity."

THE HAPPY DAYS were winding down, though. Cracks in the national economy widened into a chasm on September 15, 2008, when the Lehman Brothers investment firm filed for bankruptcy protection. America's house-of-cards boom economy, built largely on subprime mortgage deals and other debt, began to topple. Credit tightened and consumer demand for cars, appliances and homes collapsed. Unemployment soared. The stock market tanked. Poverty spiked. The Great Recession was on.

In the Depression, Milton Hershey had responded to the hard economic times by buying and constructing new student homes and adding hundreds of orphan boys. The Zimmerman-led Trust finished construction of the five-million-dollar, Scottish-themed clubhouse on the just-bought luxury golf course. Then Hershey School president Anthony Colistra, formerly a board member and Trust head, disclosed that the institution was suspending its goal of enrolling 2,000 students by 2013 because of the national economy. In 2010, the *Philadelphia Inquirer* published stories under my bylines on Zimmerman's board compensation and the acquisition of the golf course at the inflated price. Attorney General Tom Corbett, Zimmerman's friend and political ally, launched an investigation. Many viewed it as political grandstanding and media spin. The white-haired AG was now running for governor—the general election was three months away. If he were investigating the Trust, Corbett wouldn't have to answer questions about the Wren Dale/Hershey Links golf course deal or his oversight of the multi-billion-dollar charity at gubernatorial campaign stops.

Tom Corbett won in November, beating Allegheny County chief executive Dan Onorato with 54.4 percent of the vote. Those who were skeptical of Corbett's Trust investigation into the golf course purchase before the election became even more skeptical after the election. On January 17, 2011, Governor-elect Corbett held his "Benefactors Dinner" to thank those who contributed funds to his inaugural festivities at "Zimm's Palace," the renovated, Trust-owned and Trust-modernized Hotel Hershey.

A website explained the donation levels that would pay for Corbett's inaugural festivities: $5,000 for the bronze level, $10,000 silver, $15,000 gold, and $25,000 platinum. The highest rank was $50,000—the diamond level. A diamond contributor got four tickets to the Benefactors Dinner. Corbett, whose campaign was partly financed by gas companies involved in lucrative fracking projects around the state, would be there with his wife Susan, shaking hands with attendees in the Hotel Hershey's Foundation Room. Among those pledging at the diamond level were Corbett's core backers: Talisman Energy of Alberta, Cabot Oil & Gas of Houston, NiSource Gas and Storage, PPL, Duquesne Light, PECO, Exelon and Alpha Natural Resources.

Corbett spokesman Kevin Harley said after the event that there was no discount or special treatment accorded to Corbett's team for holding the Benefactors Dinner at the Hotel Hershey. The "inaugural committee paid whatever the sticker price was at the hotel, and nothing comped....I'm sure it was a nice dinner. They were treated like any other party that would make use of the facility."

FOR DECADES, the self-perpetuating Trust boards had operated mostly secretly, and largely accountable only to the complacent Office of Attorney General and a napping Orphans' Court. Now one of those Trust board members stepped forward to expose the Trust's activities. This board member had inside information and a name everyone would recognize: Reese.

Bob Reese's grandfather, H.B. Reese, relocated from the York area as a paid farmer for Milton Hershey and then started his own candy company in 1919 in his home on West Caracas Avenue. H.B. Reese thought that if Milton Hershey could make all that money with chocolate, he could at least support his family with a small candy business. He sold boxed chocolates door to door. H.B.'s wife Blanche had had the idea for the peanut butter cup. She thought it would be a healthy treat for kids. H.B. got along with Milton—they were both guys with elementary-school educations who risked it all as entrepreneurs. Milton didn't view H.B. as a threat, and supplied him with chocolate coatings. H.B. bought the house next to his original house on West Caracas Avenue to expand production, a seeming violation of Hershey's no-factory zoning decree for his model town. "Mr. Hershey could have shut him down any day of the week, but he didn't do it," Bob Reese recalled.

During the World War II sugar shortage, Reese eliminated all the specially filled chocolates from his product line, except for peanut butter cups. The company sold the "penny cup" and the "nickel cup." Sales really took off. H.B. Reese passed the company down to his sons, one of whom was H.B. Reese Jr., Bob's father. The sons negotiated the sale of the peanut butter cup company to Hershey Chocolate in 1963.

Bob had been born in 1950 in the old Hershey Hospital on Route 322. He grew up on the well-to-do east side of Hershey on Para Avenue, and his family may have been the only one in the neighborhood not directly employed by Trust interests. Hershey President Sam Hinkle and his family lived several houses away. Bob fished in Spring Creek and hung out in the Trust-owned Community Building with its beautiful indoor swimming pool. He toured the chocolate factory with friends: "All the ladies knew us." He wandered through HersheyPark. It was an idyllic childhood, Bob says. He attended Hershey public schools, and of the approximately 250 kids in his public elementary school, all but a small number graduated with him from Hershey High in 1968. The town had everything, even a Trust-owned department store that perhaps didn't have the fashionable selection of John Wanamaker's in Philadelphia, but had all the clothes you would need in central Pennsylvania. His dad loved hockey and during the winter months, Bob would be a "rink rat." One day a kid accidentally slashed Bob in the right eye with his stick during a game, detaching Bob's retina. He gradually lost his eyesight in that eye.

Bob Reese attended Harvard College and read history at Cambridge. He got his law degree at Georgetown. He specialized in federal taxes and served as assistant counsel on the House of Representatives' powerful Ways and Means Committee. Hershey Foods chief executive William Dearden asked Reese, whose family still owned substantial stock in the chocolate company, to join the company as one of its first in-house attorneys in 1977.

Dearden was transforming Hershey Foods after years of strategic drift that sapped the company's market power. The chocolate company hadn't expanded internationally after World War II as Coca-Cola did, and it hadn't introduced new chocolate bars as Mars had. The solution was to buy brands. Bob Reese negotiated candy deals that brought Kit Kat and other high-recognition brands into the Hershey portfolio. The company promoted him to general counsel and senior vice president. When Trust head William Lepley considered selling Hershey Foods in late 2001, Reese realized he would be part of the team asked to negotiate the sale. He couldn't do it. The company was the heart of the town; many people he knew could lose their jobs. He'd be selling his namesake—Reese's peanut butter cups. He retired and relocated to Colorado to do legal work for Peter Coors, whose family trust owned the brewing company.

But the pull of the candy company was still strong. The Trust asked Reese to join the board when it revived merger talks with British candy company Cadbury in 2007. Reese knew Cadbury chief executive H. Todd Stitzer from the late 1980s when Hershey Foods had bought rights to Cadbury's U.S. brands. Now they were talking about a global merger, and a Hershey/Cadbury combination seemed ideal. There would be minimal employee cutbacks globally. The Hershey Company already manufactured the Cadbury products in the United States because of a prior licensing deal. Hershey Chocolate had no European plants. Hershey could access Cadbury's overseas candy-distribution channels to introduce Reese's peanut butter cups to a global market. The combined company could jointly market Good & Plenty, Jolly Rancher and other Hershey sugar candies in places such as India and South America, where chocolate tended to melt on store shelves. Cadbury proposed that the Trust retain control of the merged entity in a stock-and-cash transaction and that the merged corporate headquarters would remain in Hershey. "When you did the numbers back then, it looked pretty good," Bob Reese recalled. But the deal fell apart over issues of who would run the combined company—the Hershey top executives or the Cadbury top executives.

A skilled executive and lawyer, Bob Reese joined the Board of Managers that administered the Hershey School, and he ran banking operations for the Hershey Trust Company. As with the other Trust board members, Reese wasn't an expert in child care. But as he listened to the presentations by Hershey School officials, he became concerned. The school had expelled a 14-year-old girl who had suicidal thoughts in 2010, several years before Abbie Bartels had taken her life. He didn't think expelling a girl for suicidal thoughts sounded right. The Hershey School was one of the richest child-care charities in the world. Why couldn't it treat her? Reese also wanted the school to thoroughly investigate the Charles Koons sexual abuse case.

The Trust's management of the school's financial assets particularly irked him, and he voiced strong opinions in the board meetings. Reese also spoke with the Office of Attorney General over a period of about two years. His conversations leaked back to other Trust board members—Zimmerman still had contacts among top officials at the OAG. In late 2010, Trust board members spoke with Reese about him stepping down from the Hershey Trust Company board, and thus also the Board of Managers for the Hershey School, but remaining on the boards of Hershey Entertainment and the M.S. Hershey Foundation. Because of his conversations with the Office of Attorney General, they asked him to sign a non-disclosure agreement. Reese refused. He realized he might be ousted.

In early February 2011, Reese filed a formal petition with the Dauphin County Orphans' Court, dropping the document off with OAG officials. Because he was still on the Trust board, Reese had legal standing to sue the charity under state law. The petition claimed broad fiduciary failures at the Trust, noting that board members passed out free passes to the Hershey Links golf course, lodged extra nights at the expensive and refurbished Hotel Hershey, and treated themselves to spa treatments and limo rides.

The Trust also didn't seem to be managing Hershey Entertainment for the benefit of poor children, Reese claimed. The $70-million Hotel Hershey modernization was "opposed by financial management of the 100-percent owned subsidiary because the investment would never have a payback to justify it. Even with the huge investment, Hotel Hershey loses money," Reese noted in the petition. Hershey Entertainment should be paying dividends to support the Hershey School. But Reese claimed that Hershey Entertainment "as a whole has a net loss, did not pay any dividends to the Charity, its sole shareholder, for several years and even when it did pay a 'token' two-million-dollar dividend to the Charity in 2010, it had to borrow the money to pay the dividend." Reese also described the $17 million golf course transaction and the flawed, $36 million Springboard Academy, which had opened in 2007 and closed soon after. The experimental facility had been meant to boost retention, but had showed little in positive results.

Compensation for directors of the Hershey Trust Company had soared to more than $100,000 a year from $35,000 a year over the past decade. Reese asked whether this was reasonable compensation, based on the fact that Trust board members worked an average of five hours a week and, technically, ran a charity and a small for-profit bank that managed charitable assets. The Trust board didn't even make investment decisions for its portfolio. It paid an outside firm millions of dollars to manage the funds.

The day after Bob Reese filed his petition, the Trust board voted to oust him. The Trust board members retained 16 lawyers at firms in Philadelphia and New York to defend themselves. The attorneys' first response was to attack Bob Reese. "Reese's petition," said one legal response, "is a vindictive abuse of process. Indeed, though Reese portrays himself as a white knight... his true motive is apparent: a vendetta against his former colleagues for not re-electing him to his positions on the board."

Before filing the petition, Reese couldn't seem to get the attention of the Office of Attorney General, no matter what he did. After he filed the petition, the staff at the Office of Attorney General called regularly, seemingly weekly, promising to look into each of his claims. They assured him they would get to the bottom of it. Meanwhile, though, he came to believe the Trust's high-paid lawyers could keep his case and concerns bottled up in Orphans' Court for years with technical objections and without dealing with the substance of his claims, draining hundreds of thousands of dollars, perhaps millions, in legal fees out of the school's assets. Reese withdrew the petition. "It is not in the best interests of the School and its mission to have funds diverted to court litigation," he said in a statement, "when the Attorney General's Office is now actively reviewing the matters."

13

REFORM SLIPS AWAY AGAIN

Attorney General Kane Quickly Closes the Investigation

"You want somebody tough enough to tell the Harrisburg boys 'enough is enough'; you need someone to send them a prosecutor, not a politician."

—Kathleen Kane, candidate for
Pennsylvania Attorney General

OVER EIGHT ELECTION CYCLES from 1980 through 2008, Pennsylvania voters elected white Republican men—Roy Zimmerman, Ernie Preate, Mike Fisher and Tom Corbett—to head the Office of Attorney General as the state's top law enforcement official and exercise *parens patriae* power over the multi-billion-dollar child-care Hershey Trust.

The winds of change began to blow in 2011 and 2012 with Democrat Kathleen Kane, a prosecutor in Lackawanna County. Brunette and telegenic, Kane gained credibility speaking on Chris Matthews' cable talk show *Hardball*. She positioned herself as a Harrisburg outsider and tough prosecutor who would get to the bottom of the sensational Jerry Sandusky case at Pennsylvania State University. This major child sex abuse case had finally come to the Office of Attorney General, years after an assistant Penn State football coach wandered into the athletic showers in 2002 and claimed to see Sandusky having sex with what looked like a 10-year-old boy. The assistant coach reported the incident to legendary football coach Joe Paterno, who reported it to Penn State administrators. Little was done. When complaints about Sandusky reached then-Attorney General Tom Corbett, he began a methodical investigation, but no charges had been brought by the time Corbett was elected governor in 2010. Conspiracy theories abounded as to why Sandusky was not prosecuted more quickly. Some believed that Corbett feared alienating potential campaign donors, or upsetting the potent Penn State alumni voting bloc come November. Corbett said the investigation couldn't be rushed. Candidate Kathleen Kane accused Corbett of letting a pedophile wander freely in central Pennsylvania. "You don't put a case like that before a grand jury," she told the *Times-Tribune* in Scranton. "That was leadership. Somebody made that decision that they're going to drag that out. Somebody made that decision that they're going to cloak it in secrecy. And I never would have done that. It has never taken me three years to take a pedophile off the streets."

Kathleen Kane had prosecuted child-abuse cases in the Lackawanna County district attorney's office until the siren call of politics pulled her away. Kane campaigned in Pennsylvania for Hillary Clinton in her first run for president. In the 2012 election cycle, Kane believed the Republicans were vulnerable at the Office of Attorney General, even though they'd won each time since LeRoy Zimmerman's victory in 1980—the year the position was established. She got a big boost from her husband, the trucking company executive Christopher Kane, who contributed about two million dollars to the campaign. "I have been on the frontline of crime for over 20 years," Kane, 45, said in a video as she gained political momentum. "I have experience from child abuse to elder abuse, robbery, violent crime, rape and murder. Right from the crime scene, through the investigation, right to the very end, when they are being taken out of this courtroom in shackles."

Patrick Murphy, 38, challenged Kane in the Democratic primary. He was a former two-term congressman from the Philadelphia suburbs and an attorney in the Army's Judge Advocate General Corps. An Iraq war veteran, Murphy had sponsored legislation repealing the "don't ask, don't tell" policy that barred gays from serving openly in the military, and he had broad support among Pennsylvania's Democratic Old Guard—organized labor, former governor Ed Rendell, the Democratic congressional delegation and the *Pittsburgh Post-Gazette*. Kane secured the endorsements of the *Daily News* and the *Inquirer* in Philadelphia, as well as former President Bill Clinton, who recorded robo-calls for her.

Kathleen Kane stunned the Democratic state machine. She won the primary without the Philadelphia Democrats. She now faced Republican David Freed, the Cumberland County district attorney who had been endorsed early in the primary season by the unpopular Tom Corbett. Freed also was married to LeRoy Zimmerman's daughter, making the powerful Republican his father-in-law. The Office of Attorney General hadn't concluded its investigation into the Hershey Trust's purchase of the Wren Dale golf course and the claims of misconduct in Bob Reese's petition. Because Zimmerman headed the Trust, David Freed would in effect be investigating his father-in-law if he won the election. Freed responded to the possible conflict-of-interest issue by saying that he would appoint an independent special prosecutor to finish the task if he was elected. Kane told voters she didn't have a conflict.

Everything seemed to go right for Kane. Corbett's popularity sank with the Sandusky revelations. Harrisburg's politics stunk like an open sewer: the city council filed for municipal bankruptcy in late 2011 because of a trash incinerator that spewed millions of dollars in fees for politically connected law and financial firms while saddling with city with $310 million in debt, "more than quadruple its annual budget," the *New York Times* reported.

Corbett appointed attorney David Unkovic to restructure the city's debt, but Unkovic resigned and called for a fraud investigation. "I believe the disdain for the law is so embedded in Harrisburg's political culture," he wrote in a letter, "that it constitutes a very insidious form of corruption."

Kathleen Kane titled her 30-second fall TV ad, "Cleaning Up Harrisburg," and told voters, "You want somebody tough enough to tell the Harrisburg boys 'enough is enough,' you need someone to send them a prosecutor, not a politician." Bob Reese contributed $100,000 to her campaign. More than three million Pennsylvania voters voted for Kane in November. Her Republican opponent, David Freed, pulled 2.1 million votes. A color-coded map published by Kane's hometown Scranton newspaper showed how Kane captured the state's metro areas: Scranton, Wilkes-Barre, Philadelphia, Allentown, Pittsburgh and Erie. But she also captured Harrisburg and Hershey, and Republican areas around Penn State. Freed won the staunch Republican-stronghold rural districts. Democratic leaders called Kane the future of the state party.

THOSE WHO WANTED to reform the Hershey Trust rejoiced, believing that Kathleen Kane, who campaigned as a child advocate, could bring fundamental change to the multi-billion-dollar, underachieving charity. And Kane didn't have to wait to take actions to reform the organization. She had an immediate vehicle: the ongoing Office of Attorney General investigation into the purchase of the luxury golf course and business practices launched under AG Tom Corbett. But the would-be Trust reformers grew concerned when Kane didn't publicly state her intentions for the Trust investigation during the final months of her campaign, though she seemed to use the

Trust for political advantage over David Freed because of his relationship to Leroy Zimmerman.

Concerns deepened to anxiety after her victory, when Kane hired Democratic insider Adrian R. King Jr. of the Ballard Spahr law firm in Philadelphia as her top aide. King had been deputy chief of staff to former governor Ed Rendell and, more importantly perhaps, he was the brother-in-law of John Estey. Estey had been former governor Rendell's chief of staff, and he had chaired the patronage-rich Delaware River Port Authority that collected hundreds of millions a year in tolls on the bridges between Philadelphia and South Jersey. After leaving Rendell's administration, Estey launched a new legal-services department at Ballard Spahr. Supreme Court Justice Ronald D. Castille soon hired him to help persuade Rendell to release $200 million in state funds for a new Family Court building to be constructed in Philadelphia.

In 2011, the Hershey Trust Company hired Estey as its acting general counsel. The organization faced tough negotiations with the Office of Attorney General on a range of issues as part of the investigation—the acquisition of the golf course, its business practices and board compensation. The Trust also would have to deal with the Justice Department's discrimination investigation over its rejection of the boy with HIV. Hershey Trust Company spokeswoman Connie McNamara said that Estey held the positions of acting corporate secretary and acting chief compliance officer, in addition to acting general counsel. By early 2013, Estey had resigned his position at Ballard Spahr and was one of the top full-time executives at the Hershey Trust Company, the state-chartered bank that controlled Milton Hershey's financial estate and charitable legacy. The relationship between Adrian King, the top aide in a state agency investigating the Trust, and one of the organization's top executives, John Estey, seemed too cozy for some observers. An OAG spokeswoman, Carolyn E. Myers, said later that King was recused from any dealings with the Trust and the school to avoid a conflict of interest. "[King] had no participation in this matter whatsoever," she added.

Kathleen Kane also retained Mark Pacella as head of the charities and non-profits section at the Office of Attorney General. Trust reformers viewed him as well-meaning but ineffectual. He answered phone calls and seemed genuinely concerned about child welfare. But he couldn't seem to make any meaningful steps toward reforming the multi-billion-dollar organization. Pacella had now served under Republican Attorneys General Mike Fisher and Tom Corbett. During Pacella's tenure, the Trust hired two Hershey School alumni with no professional experience in residential education as school presidents. Student expulsions had soared. The Chapin Hall research project had gone nowhere after the Trust spent about two million dollars on it. Hundreds of millions of dollars had been spent on construction in Hershey. By late 2012, Pacella had been investigating the Wren Dale/Hershey Links golf course deal and the other claims in Bob Reese's petition for two years. How long did such an investigation need to be? The Office of Attorney General had issued no subpoenas and had taken no formal depositions.

The investigation—some called it a civil review—came down to a judgment call:

- Should the Trust have paid $12 million for a golf course and subsequently spent five million dollars to construct a restaurant/bar on the property?
- Did the Trust, with 10,000 acres and several other golf courses, need a new golf course?
- Did an insider improperly benefit?
- Did the Trust need the Pumpkin World property, which cost about $10 million?
- Should the Trust have modernized the Hershey Hotel?
- Why weren't there any child-care experts on its board?
- Should Trust board members be so highly compensated?
- Was the Trust making decisions prudently and for the welfare of poor children and orphans?
- Was the for-profit Hershey Entertainment supporting the charity's mission?

The truth always comes out," Kane had told the Scranton newspaper when she discussed how she would investigate Corbett's handling of the Sandusky investigation at Penn State as attorney general. "It just takes that person willing to dig deep and to find the truth and to just keep chasing the facts."

She would not be willing to keep chasing the facts in Hershey.

A MONTH INTO Kathleen Kane's term, the Hershey School announced that it would close the hugely expensive Hershey Links golf course and build new student homes on the property it had purchased just a few years before.

According to the press release reprinted here in full:

Hershey, PA—The Milton Hershey School announced today that it will seek township approval to build additional student homes as part of its long-planned North Campus expansion on the site of the Hershey Links Golf Course and Pumpkin World properties.

This is the next step in the School's efforts to increase the number of students it serves now and in perpetuity. The property was purchased in 2006 with the goal of building additional student homes for middle school students.

"This is an exciting time for the Milton Hershey School as we continue our efforts to serve more children consistent with our Deed of Trust," said MHS President Dr. Anthony Colistra '59. "For nearly a decade, we have been focused on expanding our campus for that purpose."

"We purchased this property as part of our plan to one day build additional student housing on it," he said. "It is located immediately adjacent to our existing campus, and as we have said from the start, it provides an ideal opportunity to expand the campus so that we can serve more students."

With the Milton Hershey School now ready to move forward with its plans to construct new student housing, Hershey Links will close at the end of the 2013 season. A Master plan for the site, first developed nearly a decade ago by the Washington, DC-based architectural firm of Bowie Gridley, has long envisioned the development of new homes for the School's middle school students on the Venice tract located along Route 39 in South Hanover Township. Thirty-two student homes have been added to the North Campus, and with today's announcement, the School will seek approval to build additional homes.

Milton Hershey School, founded in 1909 by chocolate magnate Milton Hershey and his wife Catherine, provides a home and education to more than 1,800 children from pre-kindergarten to 12th grade who come from families of poverty.

WHAT HAPPENED to the buffer land? What happened to the details in the October 2005 Trust press release on the plan to run a championship-caliber golf course? Why would the Trust construct new homes on this high-cost acreage? A master plan drafted by the Bowie Gridley Architects and published in July 2006 described the Hershey Links golf course as buffer from housing developments, because the next cluster of new student homes could be built on the Trust-owned Manada farm down the road. There were two additional Trust-owned farms in the vicinity: Green Hill and Swatara. Insiders speculated that the Trust was closing the Hershey Links golf course so it could now tell the Office of Attorney General that the school funds expended on it would, in fact, be directly applied to helping poor children.

Milton and Kitty's 1909 Deed said the orphans' fund was to be *exclusively devoted* to the Hershey School. Golf course land—albeit very expensive land—could be used for student homes. But how could the Trust justify the expenditure of five million dollars in school funds on the beer- and food-serving restaurant on the golf course? One solution might be for Hershey Entertainment to purchase the restaurant/bar for five million dollars, replenishing what the school paid to construct it. But that would be a very expensive restaurant/bar for Hershey, and Hershey Entertainment apparently did not make the offer. Now, Lisa Sculling, a Trust spokeswoman and a former TV news reporter, said the restaurant/bar would be repurposed for poor students. Sculling didn't exactly say how in an email to me:

> The club house [Highlands] was built to be a multipurpose structure in anticipation of transition to School use. Even its location was selected with future school use in mind. When originally planned, the club house was to have been located along Route 39, a preferred site for golf and business purposes. But the club house eventually was built in a different location, further from Route 39 because that site was deemed a better fit for eventual conversion to school use. School needs were taken into consideration when developing utility lines.
>
> The building presents a number of viable and useful options when it comes to future use. We are confident that we can utilize that structure in a way that benefits our students. Indeed, the club house was original designed with this option in mind.

Homeowners near the Hershey Links property organized themselves as the Concerned Citizens of South Hanover Township. They complained that the Trust seemed to have misled them about their development plans in 2005.

ON MAY 8, 2013, the Office of Attorney General and the Trust emailed separate press statements announcing that they'd settled the investigation. Kathleen Kane found no breach of fiduciary duty, and no Trust board members would lose their well-paid positions. Trust board members wouldn't be personally surcharged millions of dollars to recoup money for wasteful spending of charitable funds for poor kids. But the Trust agreed to a relatively modest slate of reforms, for the third time in 19 years.

Kane didn't hold a press conference to answer questions. Instead the Office of Attorney General filed a document with the Dauphin County Orphans' Court titled "No Objection to Confirmation of Accounts" that explained its decisions and formally justified the Trust's expenditures. According to it, the Wren Dale/Hershey Links golf course was a prudent purchase because "notwithstanding the property's previously appraised value, the $12 million purchase price was consistent with the property's fair market value as compared against *at least one comparable property* and in light of the School's intended long-term use of the property." [Italics added.] The OAG did not give the location of that "one comparable property" and it didn't say how government lawyers, untrained as economists or property specialists, overrode a professionally prepared appraisal. The Office of Attorney General didn't mention the $5 million expended for the construction of the Highlands bar/restaurant and club house that opened in 2009, and was now scheduled to close in 2013.

Richard Lenny, the chocolate company's chief executive, owned a small equity stake in Wren Dale and so had benefited from the Trust's purchase of the golf course. The Office of Attorney General explained: "Although no disclosure of the former Manager/Director's interest in the golf course was documented in board minutes, his interest was already known within the School and Trust Company. Moreover, the evidence was insufficient to conclude that the interested Manager/Director had participated in the vote to purchase the Wren Dale property or otherwise influenced the transaction, which was pursued to further the North Campus Expansion Project of the School." The reasoning here echoed Fred Speaker's report from 1994 as it related to Trust board member William Alexander, whose construction firm won the huge contract to centralize the Hershey School's campus. Then, the Trust had argued that Alexander had not participated in the board discussions on the contract. According to Kane's agreement, the Trust would now inform the Office of Attorney General thirty days prior to any real estate transaction of more than $250,000.

The Trust also agreed to implement yet another conflicts-of-interest policy, explicitly mandating that Trust board members could not profit from private information about any Hershey entities: the chocolate company, Hershey Entertainment or the Hershey Trust Company. They could not accept personal favors or services from suppliers to the Trust-related businesses. They couldn't do business with the suppliers to those businesses. And Trust board members or family members could not make political contributions to the Pennsylvania attorney general candidates, or those seeking to be a Dauphin County Orphans' Court judge.

Soaring compensation for Hershey Trust Company board members seemed obscene for service on a charitable board, where the norm is voluntary service, and in many cases involves a financial commitment from board members. The Trust argued that its board members should be compensated because, based on the 1909 Deed and other incorporation documents, the Hershey Trust Company was a for-profit bank designated to manage Milton Hershey's estate and not a classic non-profit organization managing an endowment. The old conundrum, with its roots in Milton Hershey's unusual symbiosis of his profitable and charitable ventures, would not go away.

The Office of Attorney General stated in the court filing, "The Trust Company has consistently hired independent consultants to conduct salary surveys based upon comparable responsibilities and workload and to provide recommendations regarding the appropriate compensation for both its board members and executive staff; while their compensation has increased considerably over the past decade (including the additional perquisites alleged), it has generally amounted to less than the 75th percentile of the relevant peer groups." But those relevant peer groups were for-profit corporate boards in the finance industry (such as regional banks), not non-profit boards. And it even seemed questionable that these were comparable peer financial institutions. Basically all of the Hershey Trust Company's assets— the billions of dollars that made it look like a substantial bank—were charitable assets earmarked for poor kids.

Nonetheless, the Trust told the Office of Attorney General it would curb its appetite for higher directors' fees. Hershey Trust Company board members would earn $30,000 a year as base compensation—a seemingly reasonable amount. In addition, these board members would be paid $4,500 a day for meetings over four hours. The Trust board chairman would be paid a $10,000 retainer. Trust committee chairs would be compensated an additional $5,000. Because compensation would be a package made up of the base pay and stacked add-ons, total compensation would be significantly higher than the $30,000 a year. If, for instance, the Trust board met for ten days a year, Trust board members would be paid an additional $45,000, bringing compensation to $75,000. Add a committee chair, and the amount would reach $80,000.

Kathleen Kane's agreement forbade a Trust board member from holding three Hershey-related fee-paying board seats at one time, so-called triple-dipping. LeRoy Zimmerman earned $500,000 a year in directors' fees this way. But Kane's agreement allowed Trust board members to double-dip: one Trust member could simultaneously hold seats with the Hershey Trust Company and Hershey Entertainment. Three Trust board members could simultaneously hold board positions with the Hershey Trust Company and the chocolate company. The chocolate company board seats still paid at least $200,000 a year. Those three Trust board members at the time of the agreement were James Nevels, the chocolate company's chairman; Robert Cavanaugh, the Trust head; and James Mead.

Trust board members who held board posts in Hershey Entertainment or the chocolate company wouldn't receive the $30,000 base compensation that went with a board seat with the Hershey Trust Company. But they could be paid the $4,500-a-day fee for attending meetings. The restriction—withholding the $30,000 Hershey Trust Company board compensation—wouldn't take effect until 2015.

The Office of Attorney General had to be consulted on future compensation changes. If it was seeking to hike board pay, the Trust had to submit the names of five consultants who would offer formal recommendations. The Office of Attorney General would specify three acceptable ones. While all this might make some difference, when one did the compensation math and looked at the loopholes, Kane's 2013 agreement did not seem like a major reform.

The petition submitted by Bob Reese in 2011 exposed lush travel and hospitality perks. The Trust agreed to a travel-reimbursement policy that banned members from flying first class and charging personal items to the charity. "Gift shop purchases, in-room videos, personal phone usage, spa services, local sightseeing, entertainment or recreational activities such as golf that are unrelated to the business purpose of the trip, and other incidental expenses will not be reimbursed, but must be charged to a Manager/Director's personal credit card. In the event that any such charges are billed to a hotel room, the Manager/Director must reimburse the Trust Company for the charges" within sixty days, according to the new policy submitted to the court.

The Trust also wouldn't cover extra meals for board members. The Trust could pay for spouses and children to attend the Milton Hershey School graduation in June, but spa treatments at the Hotel Hershey had to be reported as taxable income.

As it regarded child care, the Trust had constructed the Springboard Academy to boost student retention among middle school students at a cost of $36 million and then closed it several years later—seemingly a huge waste of money. The Office of Attorney General noted that "Springboard Academy was a project intended to improve the School's retention rate of new students and consisted of two newly constructed 'off campus' buildings with dedicated staff members. The program opened in the fall of 2007 and was ended in the spring of 2010 because the School's administration concluded that its costs were exceeding the costs of the School's traditional program without achieving commensurate improvements in new student performance and retention. The Commonwealth concluded that the *Springboard program had not been well-conceived initially* and that the School's administration should have provided more detail and analysis to the board on both the concept and the implementation of the Springboard program" [italics added].

It was $36 million down the toilet. But who cared? They made a mistake. Those two projects—Wren Dale/Hershey Links and Springboard—cost an estimated about $55 million to $60 million over about five years when one considers the operating losses at the golf course.

At this point, one of the nation's wealthiest child-care charities had no national experts on at-risk children, residential education, childhood education, child psychology or poverty on its board, even though William Lepley had said in 1994 that the Trust would appoint board members who would advance the charity's mission, His promise that board members would be limited to ten-year terms had also not materialized.

Kathleen Kane now said that the Trust had to use its "best efforts" to correct the deficiency: "As the Boards reach their authorized size, they shall follow best governance practices in allocating responsibility among Manager/Directors for leadership positions, Committee assignments and appointments to the Boards of related entities."

The Trust's glowing press release on May 8, 2013 pledged a renewed commitment to poor and needy children with its billions of dollars in charitable assets. "There was no wrongdoing on the part of the Board," crowed

Trust chairman Robert Cavanaugh. "We believe that the decision to purchase this property [Hershey Links/Wren Dale] was the right decision for the long-term future of the school. The Board has always sought to meet the best interests of the School and the Trust. Thanks to the leadership of the Attorney General, we believe we are setting a course that enhances our ability to service children in need in perpetuity."

Activist alumnus Joseph Berning downloaded the Office of Attorney General and court documents on May 8th. The next day, he emailed reformers, alumni friends, media and others his analysis:

> Clearly, this press release is the by-product of TWO YEARS of heavy duty 'negotiations' between the Trust's high-priced Philadelphia lawyers and completely impotent and under-funded Attorney General's office.
>
> In essence, same shit—different decade!
>
> This press release was particularly helpful since all of the documents are attached for download. The most complete and helpful is the first one—the [Orphans' Court] Filing. Please download it and read it very carefully.
>
> I find it shocking (and troubling) that while the OAG says the Managers didn't break the law, they somehow felt the need to enter into a settlement 'agreement' that includes no less than 16 areas of concern, including governance reform, conflicts of interest, excessive compensation, limiting real estate deals, serving the right children, and a systematic monitoring of their actions—not to mention the self-correcting they have already recently done, like firing more than a half-dozen employees who violated these provisions, and getting rid of the conflicting wealth management division of the Hershey Trust. But then again, they didn't do anything wrong—did they?

Kathleen Kane told reporters at a press forum in Harrisburg a week later that the Trust's business decisions were "not criminal conduct, and for a variety of reasons, it was non-prosecutorial." But the Office of Attorney General had not been investigating possible criminal conduct, such as Jerry Sandusky's sexual abuse of young boys or politicians taking bribes. Kane had been investigating violations of trust law or civil violations—what came down to judgment decisions. Were beneficiaries of Milton and Kitty's philanthropy being properly served by the Trust?

After deciding that the Trust board members hadn't spent recklessly or improperly from Milton and Kitty's orphans' fund, Kane noted, "We then had to decide what is going to make this $10 billion children's charity work better for those kids." She said there were "some sticking points, but I believe we stuck to our guns and that the reforms they agreed to—I think— are setting a new standard for charitable organizations. Because they are tough. They changed the composition of the board so that we are dealing with the actual mission of the charity—at-risk residential children."

The Office of Attorney General/Trust agreement, as a matter of fact, did not change the composition of the Trust board. OAG spokeswoman Caro- lyn Myers later clarified Kane's statement regarding the board composition, saying, "The Office of Attorney General did not find a breach of fiduciary duty following the investigation but did find some questionable decisions were made. An agreement was reached for standards of conduct moving forward to put the focus of the Trust and School on the children that if broken, could result in a board member's ouster."

Having closed the books on the investigation, Kathleen Kane visited the Hershey School in June 2013 for a photo op. The Office of Attorney General posted a photo on its web site of Kane with eight smiling young children and two houseparents.

Later that same month, Hershey School officials told Julie Bartels that her depressed and possibly suicidal daughter Abbie couldn't participate in her Hershey School eighth-grade graduation and student home barbecue. Abbie told her mother it was okay, though she had written colorful and sentimental goodbye notes to her friends. Days after the graduation and barbecue, the distraught 13-year-old girl who enrolled in the Hershey School as a kinder- gartner hanged herself in the closet of her second-floor bedroom in her home in Newport, Pennsylvania, just across the street from a dollar store.

Anthony Colistra retired as president of the Hershey School in July, shortly after Abbie's death. The Trust said the resignation was unrelated to the suicide. Meanwhile the Trust appointed John Estey—the former chief of staff to governor Ed Rendell and chairman of the patronage-ridden Del- aware River Port Authority—as the interim president of one of the nation's richest child-care charities and the nation's largest boarding school.

Joe Peters, the spokesman for the Office of Attorney General, said in the fall of 2013 that the agency was "saddened to learn of the death of Abbie Bartels. The goal of Milton and Catherine Hershey in creating the Milton Hershey Trust was to ensure that the children would go to the Milton Her- shey School to emerge better and stronger than when they entered."

14

SLAVE LABOR IN THE COCOA LANDS

Hershey Profiting Off the Toils
of Children in West Africa

CHILD SLAVE LABOR in the cocoa lands has been a concern for years among global activists concerned with fair trade and Third World child exploitation. Reports of child slave labor in the cocoa farms of West Africa first surfaced in 1998 in an Ivory Coast newspaper. A British documentary in 2000 claimed that hundreds of children in Burkina Faso, Mali and Togo were purchased from their parents and sold as slaves to Ivory Coast cocoa farmers. In 2001, Sudarsan Raghavan and Sumana Chatterjee of the Knight-Ridder newspapers published a multi-part, exhaustive investigation on child labor in the cocoa lands. Their first piece, datelined from Daloa, Ivory Coast, began:

> There may be a hidden ingredient in the chocolate cake you baked, the candy bars your children sold for their school fundraiser, or that fudge-ripple ice cream cone you enjoyed on Saturday afternoon. Slave labor.... Forty-three percent of the world's cocoa beans, the raw material of chocolate, comes from small scattered farms in this poor West African country. And on some farms, the hot, hard work of harvesting the fruit is done by boys who were sold or tricked into slavery. Most are between 12 and 16; some are as young as nine. Many are lured from their hometowns with the promise of good-paying jobs and taken to Ivory Coast and sold by traffickers to farmers for less than $50.

The number of child slaves was unknown, but the stories noted that between January and May 2001, 324 enslaved minors were repatriated to Mali from Ivory Coast.

Seventy percent of the world's cocoa is grown and harvested in West Africa. The use of forced child labor had been acknowledged by governments, NGOs, industry, and labor officials since the late 1990s, and has been called among the "worst forms of child labor." Traders trafficked boys into the cocoa lands of Ivory Coast, Mali, Benin, Burkina Faso and Nigeria. Boys who were trafficked work alongside others who chose this arduous work, handling machetes and hauling heavy bags of harvested cocoa. They received no schooling, and many believe they were doomed to work in cocoa harvesting for the rest of their lives.

The emergence of stories like this posed an ethical and public relations dilemma to the worldwide chocolate industry—one that should have been particularly acute for Hershey Chocolate, with its longstanding fiduciary mission to serve the needs of poor, disadvantaged children. In fact, it took years of political, media and legal pressure coming from outside the corporation to force Hershey to grapple with this unacknowledged tragedy in the chocolate manufacturing chain.

ALY DIABATE, 11, had been enticed to work on one Ivory Coast farm with the promise of earning money for a bicycle. But he found himself among other boys forced to work by Le Gros, or the Big Man. He was never paid for his work, and later learned he had been bought for $35. The boys worked 12-hour days and slept on wooden planks in a locked room. They had to pee in a can. Managers beat them with bicycle chains.

To harvest the 400 beans to make a pound of chocolate, boys cut pods from cacao trees, sliced them open and scooped out the insides. They spread the beans in baskets or mats for fermenting. After this, they dried the beans in the sun, bagged them and loaded them onto trucks for shipment to global markets.

Hershey Chocolate and chocolate industry officials at first denied the existence of forced child labor in West Africa. But Ivorian officials confirmed media reports in early 2001 when they disrupted a slave-labor smuggling ring in Bouake. In mid-2001, as the Knight-Ridder series was being edited for publication, Hershey Chocolate general counsel and senior vice president Bob Reese said for publication: "We're not going to sit here and say it's not happening if the Ivorian government says that it is happening."

Reese added, "No one, repeat, no one, ever heard of this. Your instinct is that Hershey should have known. But the fact is we didn't know."

Reese had responsibility for public affairs and public relations in addition to legal affairs. He realized slave child labor could tarnish the feel-good Hershey brand and questioned officials in the company's commodity-buying group after publication of the newspaper articles. Those officials acknowledged the existence of child labor in the cocoa fields. But there were concerns that doing something about the child labor issue could boost cocoa prices. Reese told the company's chief executive, Richard Lenny, that the company had to address it.

The U.S. House of Representatives responded swiftly to news of forced child labor in the West African cocoa lands, voting by a margin of 291 to 115 to attach a rider to a farm bill setting aside $250,000 for the Food and Drug Administration to develop "slave-free" labeling for chocolate products. But the Senate opposed it. Seeking to head off the new regulations, the chocolate industry hired former senators Bob Dole and George Mitchell to negotiate a solution. Reese regularly traveled to Washington to meet with Mitchell at his Washington, D.C., law offices as part of negotiations in August and September 2001. Hershey Chocolate and other industry leaders came together to voluntarily police child labor on cocoa farms and, on September 19, 2001, formally signed an agreement with the intent of eradicating the worst forms of child labor by certifying cocoa.

Democratic Senator Tom Harkin of Iowa and Congressman Eliot Engel of New York sponsored the agreement, which carried the lengthy name, "Protocol for the Growing and Processing of Cocoa Beans and their Derivative Products in a Manner that Complies with ILO Convention Concerning the Prohibition and Immediate Action for the Elimination of the Worst Forms of Child Labor." Known as the Harkin-Engel Protocol, it set dates for accomplishing the mission to certify cocoa as cleansed of forced child labor. There were to be "credible, mutually acceptable, voluntary, industry-wide standards for public certification...that cocoa beans and their derivative products have been grown and/or processed without any of the worst forms of child labor" by July 1, 2005.

Richard Lenny, Hershey Chocolate's top executive, signed the protocol. Lenny would later be a part owner of the money-losing Wren Dale golf course that the Trust bought at an inflated price with school funds. Others from the industry joined with Hershey on the protocol: Guittard Chocolate Company, M&M/Mars Inc., World's Finest Chocolate Inc., Nestlé Chocolate & Confections USA, Archer Daniels Midland Company, Blommer Chocolate Company and Barry Callebaut. Other industry groups or officials also participated: the president of the Chocolate Manufacturers Association, the president of the World Cocoa Foundation, the national coordinator for the Child Labor Coalition, the president of the National Consumer League, the executive director of Free the Slaves, a director of the International Labor Organization, the general secretary of the International Union of Food, Agricultural, Hotel, Restaurant, Catering, Tobacco and Allied Workers Association, and the ambassador from Ivory Coast.

The International Cocoa Initiative was organized in 2002 as a partnership of charities, NGOs, trade unions, cocoa processors and chocolate brands. Meetings and discussions were held. But without headlines and a U.S. threat of government labeling, industry urgency faded. Reese advocated for the protocol at the top executive levels of Hershey Chocolate. But he retired in late 2001, after Trust head William Lepley said he would sell the chocolate company to diversify the charity's assets. Responsibility fell mostly to the media relations department.

By 2005, three years after the Harkin-Engel Protocol was agreed to, the senators who sponsored it were dismayed. "The Harkin-Engel Protocol established a framework to improve the living and working conditions for families and children who are growing, harvesting and exporting the cocoa we enjoy here in America," Harkin said. "I am disappointed that the July 1st deadline established in the protocol was not fully met."

Two industry leaders issued a statement. Lynn Bragg, the head of the Chocolate Manufacturers Association, and David Zimmer, secretary general of the Association of Chocolate, Biscuit & Confectionary Industries of the European Union, noted: "While we would like to be further along than we are in this effort, the building blocks are in place today for the development of a certification system which can be expanded across the cocoa-growing areas of West Africa, and for programs to improve the well-being of farm families. The Harkin-Engel Protocol will continue as the framework for these efforts to get the job done."

The chocolate industry pledged to achieve a certification system covering over 50 percent of the cocoa regions in Ghana and the Ivory Coast within three years. But the U.S. Department Labor seemed impatient and concerned with the progress on the protocol. The agency granted $4.3 million to Tulane University's Payson Center for International Development and Technology Transfer to monitor the implementation of Harkin-Engel in 2006. Three years later, the federal agency added $1.2 million.

Harkin and Engel released positive statements about the chocolate industry's implementation in 2008, noting that the industry had invested $10 million into the project over the previous seven years, or about $1.5 million year. But it was apparent that the industry was far from having a credible certification system that enabled U.S. consumers to purchase chocolate certified as untainted by forced child labor. Chocolate industry officials announced a new timetable for certifying chocolate as free of the worst forms of child labor: By 2020, 70 percent of the Ivory Coast and Ghana cocoa would be covered—that would be years after the original goal. The new goal was backed by 10 million dollars in U.S. government funding and seven million in additional industry funding. The chocolate industry could add three million dollars later.

But time seemed to be running out on the chocolate industry. European documentary filmmakers Miki Mistrati and U. Roberto Romano released the documentary film *The Dark Side of Chocolate* in 2010. The film opens with the narrator observing, "While First World kids are enjoying the sweet taste, [the] reality is rather different for Africa's children." It goes on to ask, "Is it true that young children work as slaves in the chocolate industry?" Mistrati traveled to a border crossing between Mali and Ivory Coast to find boys and girls being smuggled into the cocoa lands on motorcycles. One young boy who couldn't find his contact for his final leg of the journey to the cocoa lands sat sobbing on a bench. Interpol had busted a smuggling ring months earlier. With a hidden camera, the filmmakers captured young boys—perhaps 10 years old—harvesting cocoa with machetes. "The use of child labor in the cocoa industry is prevalent, this in spite of the international chocolate manufacturers signing a protocol in 2001 to the contrary," the film says. "There is no doubt of the extent of the problem. The chocolate manufacturers should know the facts."

The film quoted a top United Nations official saying there had been "some progress" from Harkin-Engel, but "in terms of real change, we see very little." The documentary was distributed free on the Internet and showed in colleges.

Tulane released its final report on the progress of the Harkin-Engel Protocol in March 2011, acknowledging unstable politics in the region and other obstacles. Still, researchers didn't believe the oft-delayed deadline for certifying cocoa, now set for 2020, could be met. Tulane had conducted a survey of households in Ivory Coast and Ghana in 2008 and 2009. Their results supported estimates that 819,921 children in the Ivory Coast and 997,357 children in Ghana worked in cocoa-related areas. The researchers also estimated that 32,514 children in the Ivory Coast and 6,243 children in Ghana had been helped by the protocol up to that point—a small fraction of the total number of children involved. The report concluded that the realities of a competitive marketplace could make it impossible for the chocolate industry to self-regulate child labor.

One option could be a U.S. law mandating that chocolate companies disclose cocoa sourced in West Africa to inform consumers, researchers said. A similar requirement was part of the Dodd-Frank Wall Street Reform and Consumer Protection Act: a provision in the law required companies to disclose minerals sourced from the war-torn Democratic Republic of Congo.

Industry officials trashed the Tulane report as harsh and lacking perspective. "[W]e reject the gratuitous criticisms of industry's commitment and approach to combating the worst forms of child labor in cocoa production in the Ivory Coast and Ghana," Ronald Graf, chair of the industry's Global Issues Group, wrote to the Tulane report author, Bill Bertrand. The Global Issues Group was an ad hoc industry organization, in which Hershey Chocolate participated. "There is scant new data from which to draw conclusions, yet the draft contains numerous subjective and editorial observations that are unsupported by fact and beyond the scope of Tulane's mandate."

Graf listed the chocolate industry's successes over the last decade: committing financial resources to Harkin-Engel, forming an advisory group, issuing a joint statement on the need to end forced child labor, signing a binding memorandum of cooperation, establishing the International Cocoa Initiative, and developing a credible public certification system. This, Graf wrote Bertrand, illustrated the industry's concern over the slave and forced child labor in the cocoa lands.

No other industry had attempted a similar voluntary certification initiative involving an agricultural sector as diffuse as Ivory Coast and Ghana cocoa farms, Graf wrote. In view of this, patience would be necessary. "There are no walls, auditors, guards or monitors that can track social conditions on each and every farm." He rejected the suggestion that individual companies, such as Hershey Chocolate, could organize separate certification systems. The ultimate goal was to certify cocoa from "bean to bar."

IN THE 11 YEARS after Sudarsan Raghavan and Sumana Chatterjee of the Knight Ridder newspapers published their stories, profits more than tripled at Hershey Chocolate. The nation's largest chocolate company reported profits of $207.2 million on sales of $4.6 billion in 2001, and profits of

$660.9 million on sales of $6.6 billion in 2012. Tens of millions of dollars of Hershey Chocolate profits now flowed each year to Milton and Kitty's trust fund to finance the Hershey School for impoverished American kids. Trust board members also were personally benefiting—growing rich over time, in fact—from Hershey Chocolate's part-time directors' compensation, made up of both fees and shares in the company.

Hershey School alumnus Robert Cavanaugh, who now headed the Trust board, had sat on the chocolate company's board since 2003, through the entire time that Hershey missed a number of deadlines to certify West Africa cocoa. Cavanaugh, a 1977 graduate of the Hershey School who lives in the Los Angeles area, chaired the chocolate company's compensation and executive organization committee and belonged to the governance committee, both platforms from which he could have voiced his opinion on Harkin-Engel. Corporate documents show that over Cavanaugh's board tenure through April 2014, he accumulated almost 40,000 Hershey Chocolate shares, valued at four million dollars.

Other well-connected board members also received generous levels of compensation during this period of failed oversight of an acknowledged human-rights issue. James Nevels, an African-American investment advisor with many government contacts from the Philadelphia area, joined the Hershey Chocolate board when the Trust seized control of it in 2007. Like other members of the Trust board, he was compensated handsomely for his role, receiving $1,800,799 in part-time directors' fees between 2008 and 2013. Nevels served as Hershey Chocolate's non-executive chairman. Former Republican governor Tom Ridge also joined the Hershey Chocolate board in 2007. Ridge had friends in the highest reaches of Pennsylvania government: he had given current governor Tom Corbett his big political break by appointing him to Ernie Preate's unexpired term as attorney general in the mid-1990s. Ridge also owned a block of company shares worth about $2.7 million.

At the same time, Hershey Chocolate continued to boast to investors and the public of its philanthropic legacy. The company wrote annually in its 10-K regulatory filing with the Securities and Exchange Commission:

> Our founder, Milton S. Hershey, established an enduring model of responsible citizenship while conducting a successful business. Making a difference in our communities, driving sustainable business practices, and operating with the highest integrity are vital parts of our heritage and shapes our future. The Milton Hershey School,

established by Milton and Catherine Hershey, lies at the center of our unique heritage. Mr. Hershey donated and bequeathed almost his entire fortune to the Milton Hershey School, which remains our primary beneficiary and provides a world-class education and nurturing home to nearly 2,000 children in need annually. We continue Milton Hershey's legacy of commitment to consumers, community and children by providing high-quality products while conducting our business in a socially responsible and environmentally sustainable manner.

Hershey Chocolate had now been riding its "philanthropic legacy" for decades, dating back to the 1930s when P.A. Staples testified in Washington that the company should be given special consideration because of its financing of the Hershey Industrial School.

Pennsylvania lawmakers had even granted special takeover protections for Hershey Chocolate in 2002, considering it a cherished state asset. This came after William Lepley's threat to auction Hershey Chocolate to the highest bidder to diversify the orphanage's assets. Based on the 2002 law, the attorney general had to be informed of a potential sale of the company to give him or her time to block a sale to protect local jobs and the community's interest. The unusual law seemed only to apply to Hershey Chocolate, and protected the company and its executives from a corporate raider or acquisitive rival. This special, state-granted protection in effect gave Hershey Chocolate greater corporate autonomy than other chocolate companies, and greater maneuvering room to take strong action to end its complicity with forced and slave child labor in its manufacturing chain.

Still, even with its special state-granted protections, Hershey Chocolate did not act as if it were morally obligated to take a leadership role in the industry on this issue. Hershey could have used its charitable legacy as an inspiration to take action, becoming a leader in efforts to deal with the horrors of forced child labor in the chocolate industry. Instead, its response during this period consisted of protesting its ignorance and participating as just one company among many in an industry task force.

IN JANUARY 2012, CNN broadcast *Chocolate's Child Slaves,* bringing another wave of publicity and national outrage. Later in the year, a Louisiana municipal pension fund acted to test the business ethics of one of its holdings: Hershey Chocolate. On October 4, 2012, the pension fund, LAMPERS, sent

Hershey Chocolate a letter asking for information on its cocoa sourcing. A LAMPERS lawsuit filed in the Delaware Court of Chancery the next month claimed that "by producing chocolate at its Pennsylvania factory that is the product of child and forced labor in West Africa, Hershey has flouted domestic and foreign law and placed at risk its century-old brand and reputation... There are substantial grounds to believe...that Hershey's chocolate empire is built on a foundation of a West African child labor force."

With the media, the courts and the government taking a closer look at child labor in West Africa, Hershey Chocolate announced a "watershed moment in our industry" on March 21, 2013. At least 10 percent of cocoa in Hershey's products would be certified by the end of 2013, 40 to 50 percent by the end of 2016, and 100 percent by 2020.

"Cocoa is the heart of our business and we care deeply that this key ingredient is grown in a safe, healthy and sustainable manner," said Hershey Chocolate chief executive John P. Bilbrey. "Through our Hershey 21st Century Cocoa Plan, we are taking meaningful and measurable steps and making a positive difference in the health and well-being of cocoa communities." One project was the "CocoaLink" mobile phone-messaging service to connect farmers with information on safety, child labor, crop-disease prevention and sustainable farming.

On the morning of May 21, 2013, five attorneys and a half dozen others convened on the top floor of the New Castle County Courthouse in Wilmington, Delaware, to argue the Louisiana pension fund case: Did Hershey Chocolate, the nation's largest chocolate manufacturer, controlled by a multi-billion-dollar child-care charity for poor kids, source its cocoa from West African cocoa farms that utilized forced child labor or child slaves?

Wilmington attorney Srinivas M. Raju of the Richards, Layton & Finger firm, representing Hershey Chocolate, told special master Abigail LeGrow of Delaware's Court of Chancery that the legal complaint filed by the pension fund was a "fishing expedition."

Yes, Hershey Chocolate was one of the largest cocoa purchasers in the world. But it didn't directly purchase cocoa from West African farmers, Raju told her. "Hershey purchases cocoa. From whom? From where? Who knows?" he asked. "All they are saying is that Hershey is a participant in the cocoa industry and they are not using 100 percent certified cocoa."

Hershey's third-party suppliers had agreed to a "supplier code of conduct" for ethical conduct, and the company participated in a government-approved industry group overseeing a cocoa-certification program to cleanse cocoa of forced child labor, Raju said in court. The group had failed to meet its goal of having the certification program running by 2005. Because the chocolate industry couldn't "collectively meet the goal does not mean mismanagement," Hershey's attorney told the special master. Missing a deadline isn't illegal. Anyway, the group's mandate for certifying cocoa was "a non-binding agreement." Child labor has been "a challenge for the international community for a long time."

Attorney Michael Barry of the Grant & Eisenhofer law firm represented the Louisiana pension system. If the company's corporate directors had knowingly sourced slave-produced cocoa, the firm could file a lawsuit over mismanagement. He spoke with emotion, arguing that Hershey couldn't use the "ostrich defense." Available industry information pointed to a pattern of cocoa from this region leeching into Hershey Chocolate's supply chain and into the mouths of American consumers—the attorneys would connect the dots later, he promised. Barry said there seemed to be a direct correlation between Hershey and "the site of the wrongdoing."

"The elephant in the room," said Barry, "is that everyone knows that child slaves are being used." Hershey's response was that "you can't sue us because everybody's doing it."

ON NOVEMBER 18, 2013, special master Abigail LeGrow dealt a setback to the Louisiana pension fund. Its attorneys had not "not alleged a credible basis from which I can infer wrongdoing" so that the legal complaint could advance in the Delaware court, she wrote. LeGrow denied the pension fund's request for information including Hershey Chocolate's board minutes. LeGrow noted Hershey Chocolate's avowal that it did not directly purchase cocoa from West African farmers, "because most of Hershey's products are processed from cocoa-derived products purchased by Hershey from large, multi-national corporations."

LAMPERS appealed the ruling. The following March, the Delaware Court's vice chancellor, Travis Laster, reversed LeGrow's decision, referring to the "horrific reality, which is undisputed for the purposes of today, of the use of child labor and effectively child slave labor in the cocoa trade."

Laster noted an indication "that one supplier, Cadbury's, has done some form of certification. Hershey's has not." At this early stage of the court process, he said, "Hershey's has to acknowledge that some of its cocoa is produced through child labor and as a result of individuals who were victims of human trafficking."

The Louisiana pension fund didn't need to produce evidence or specific facts of illegal activity but only to show that "there is possible wrongdoing." Laster said in court, "There's also a reasonable inference, one possible inference, that the [Hershey Chocolate] board knows some of its cocoa and cocoa-derived ingredients are sourced from farms that exploit child labor and use trafficked persons. The laws of Ghana prohibit exploitive child labor and human trafficking. The Children's Act prohibits the use of exploitive child labor," defining children as persons below the age of 18. "The Human Trafficking Act prohibits the use of a trafficked person and also includes a duty to inform."

Courts in the United States, Laster continued, "most notably in the recent *Doe v. Nestlé* decision recognized that it is possible for a U.S. corporation to be held liable for aiding and abetting violations of international law, such as the principle, hopefully universally acknowledged, against the use of child labor and human trafficking."

Judge Laster seemed unwilling to accept at face value that Hershey Chocolate knew nothing about the child-labor conditions in an area that supplied 70 percent of the world's raw cocoa. "Now, as I've already said, Hershey's response has been to argue that plaintiff hasn't proved wrongdoing. That's not the test. Hershey's also has said that there's no evidence related to it, i.e., directly to Hershey's involvement. I think you can draw the inference from Hershey's inability to represent that it currently uses only certified cocoa and it's undertaking to do so by 2020....I think you can draw the inference of knowledge from Hershey's cocoa sustainability efforts, which includes its eight 'on-the-ground programs' through which Hershey has contact with farmers in West Africa and high-level visits, such as visits by Hershey's chairman....You can draw the inference from a decision referenced in the complaint by Whole Foods to stop carrying Hershey's Scharffen Berger brand because of Hershey's inability to certify."

Laster was telling Hershey Chocolate—the nation's largest chocolate manufacturer, which is controlled by one of the wealthiest child-care charities in the world—that it couldn't bury its head in the sand with an ostrich defense on forced child labor and slave child labor in West Africa. Would the company take his decision to heart, and use it as a springboard to act in the spirit of Milton Hershey's desire to help poor, disadvantaged children? One can hope that its future behavior is not to be predicted from its past missteps.

Epilogue—HERSHEY'S SHAME

What to Do Now?

> *"I have never seen a place with so many resources in my life with such a great need where there has been such a great underachievement."*
>
> —FORMER MANHATTANVILLE COLLEGE PRESIDENT
> RICHARD BERMAN

FORMER ATTORNEY GENERAL Fred Speaker spoke of the role of the state's top law-enforcement official in his *pro bono* report absolving the Trust of wrongdoing in 1994. "Under Pennsylvania law," he wrote, "the Commonwealth and its Attorney General have the duty, as *parens patriae*, to oversee the operation of charitable trusts. It is a duty deriving from the nature of charitable trusts, which may lack beneficiaries with interests definite enough to sue for themselves. This representation serves a void-filling function…and the Attorney General is an indispensible party." Poor kids or their parents can't sue a multi-billion-dollar Trust to force it to deliver the charitable services. They don't have the financial resources of the Trust, resources that overwhelmed even Bob Reese, scion of the H.B. Reese Candy Company family. Poor families also lack the legal right, the so-called standing, to sue what amounts to one of the nation's richest, perhaps the richest, child-care charity. How can this be? The oversight duty falls to the Pennsylvania Office of Attorney General with a taxpayer-funded budget and legal responsibility under Common Law and legal precedent. But the state's top law-enforcement official has acted as anything but a protector of orphans and poor children. As attorney general between 1963 and 1966, Walter Alessandroni participated in the conspiracy to divert $50 million into the Hershey medical center and away from orphans and poor children—the first and perhaps biggest looting of the Trust, and also one that set precedent. Nine governor-appointed attorneys general followed Alessandroni:

H. Edward Friedman, 1966 to 1967; William C. Sennett, 1967 to 1970; Fred Speaker, 1970 to 1971; J. Shane Creamer, 1971 to 1972; Israel Packel, 1973 to 1974; Robert P Kane, 1975 to 1978; J. Justin Blewitt Jr., 1979; Edward G. Biester, 1979 to 1980, and, finally, Harvey Bartle 3rd, 1980 to 1981. Zimmerman was the first elected attorney general, followed by Ernie Preate, Mike Fisher, Tom Corbett and, finally, Kathleen Kane.

Over the period that these appointed and elected attorney generals held office, the town of Hershey boomed with the assistance of assets from the orphans' fund; real estate prices soared; the medical center hired thousands of employees; municipal tax revenues swelled, and an orphan-subsidized regional tourism company rose in assets and influence. But the sad Hershey School orphanage, the charity that effectively owns the town of Hershey along with Hershey Entertainment and controls Hershey Chocolate, couldn't fulfill a pledge to enroll 1,600 students a year and, moreover, enrolled closer to 1,000 kids many years.

Three of the most recent state attorneys general—Mike Fisher, now a federal appeals court judge in Philadelphia; Tom Corbett, who went on to become Pennsylvania's governor, and Kathleen Kane, who has expressed interest in a Pennsylvania Senate seat—have punted on the Trust. Fisher, at first seemingly a hero with his reform package of 2002, cancelled those reforms and agreed to the appointment of a new Trust board headlined by former attorney general LeRoy Zimmerman in what amounted to a backroom political deal. Corbett had failed to regulate this new Trust board through his first term and part of his second, as the Zimmerman-led charity spent hundreds of millions of dollars on construction, real estate and a golf course. Board compensation soared over the same period, as did student expulsions. In the waning days of his leadership at the Office of Attorney General, Corbett launched an investigation. Years later, Kane—the state's first Democrat to be elected attorney general—whitewashed the Trust's actions but negotiated reforms that did not structurally change the organization, although they garnered good headlines for her as a politician. Her reforms were in fact similar to reforms announced almost 20 years earlier.

After looking at the evidence, it's hard for me not to view the management of Milton and Kitty Hershey's trust fund over the last 50 years as a massive taking, or redirecting, of funds for orphans and poor children by the state's political establishment and Trust leaders to benefit local economic development and themselves. The examples: the Hershey medical center, repeated school construction projects, multiple golf courses, soaring board

compensation, the repurposing of farm properties, and Hershey Entertainment's failure to pay dividends to meaningfully help pay for charitable
services for poor kids. William Lepley, once head of the Hershey School,
told me in a 2012 phone interview: "Right now, everybody thinks they are
entitled to that money even though it's clear that it's for the kids. The way
for that school to be successful is that there has to be more independence
by the board that serves the school and its trust, and it has to serve children
beyond the borders of Hershey."

Lepley continued, "It's hard to get them to change because there is no
external pressure."

What he meant was that on public school boards, board members are
voted off if they don't respond to the needs of parents and students. The
Trust, however, is a self-appointing and self-perpetuating board, now made
up of politically connected individuals, lawyers, alumni and business people.

At this point it seems reckless—even dangerous—for the insular Hershey School to expand its enrollment in Hershey. The death of Abbie Bartels, the rejection of the 13-year-old, HIV-positive boy, persistent sexual
incidents, clear attrition, and what seems to be a deeply flawed educational
model based on boarding schools for rich kids, all point to systemic problems at an institution that operates under the legal protection of a weak
Office of Attorney General, a complacent Dauphin County Orphans' Court,
a derelict Internal Revenue Service, and the halo of the Hershey brand name.

PENNSYLVANIA HAS ALREADY squandered one of America's giant fortunes set
aside for orphans: Stephen Girard's. In the spring of 2013, Girard College
disclosed that bad investments and high costs were leading to insolvency,
and that the school would have to cut staff and students to remain viable
as a going concern. As recently as World War II, Girard College enrolled
more students than Hershey. "What happened to all that money Girard
had?" asked one Hershey School staffer. "The politicians and lawyers got
involved." A full accounting of what went wrong at Girard has yet to be
done, if it ever will be. Similar to the Hershey Trust, it has been administered by the local Orphans' Court. Milton and Kitty Hershey modeled their
charity after Girard College.

*One has to ask: Why does Pennsylvania have county-level Orphans'
Courts if those courts can't seem to protect assets bequeathed to
orphans?*

Richard Berman, a former president of Manhattanville College, was interviewed for the Hershey School president's post in 2002 and 2008. Both times the Trust had hired a search firm to find a qualified candidate. Both times the Trust ended up hiring alumni: corporate consultant John O'Brien and retired public school superintendent Anthony Colistra. In 2014, the Trust hired the third alumnus as president of the Hershey School, Peter Gurt. He was the admissions head at the Hershey School who testified in 1999 in Judge Morgan's court in support of diverting trust fund assets into the proposed research institute. Gurt also served as a high-ranking administrator at the school under O'Brien and Colistra over the last decade—the period of buffer land acquisition, the short-lived Springboard Academy and a harsh expulsion policy. The president's post at the Hershey School pays about $500,000 a year. "I have never seen a place with so many resources in my life with such a great need where there has been such a great under-achievement," Berman said in an interview. "It has been an underachievement in the number of kids helped and under-achievement in the success of those kids....Think about the number of kids whom they could have changed their lives, dramatically changed their lives. That's the real crime."

AFTER FOUR YEARS of reportage and writing, I believe that this institution, the Trust, urgently needs to be more transparent, more compassionate, more focused on poor children, and more accountable for its use of chocolate profits and its other financial resources. Here's how to reform this national treasure for millions of poor kids:

- Dissolve the Hershey Trust Company and fold its financial-management functions into the Hershey School so that the organization is structured like a typical private college instead of the complex organization created by Milton Hershey in 1909.
- Appoint independent experts in residential education, at-risk children, child psychology, educating poor children, staff development and institutional management to the new Hershey School board.
- Slash directors' fees at the Hershey School to $10,000, or zero as it is on most other charitable boards.
- Ban multiple board seats within the Hershey organization so that Hershey School directors focus on educating poor children and orphans.

- Immediately halt any Hershey School expansion in Hershey and re-evaluate the institution's child-care mission.
- Finish the multi-million-dollar independent Chapin Hall study to evaluate the benefits of the Hershey School.
- Disclose all financial settlements, without names but with narratives, of student-on-student and adult-on-student sexual abuse over the last 20 years.
- Investigate each drop-out or expulsion over the last decade. Publish a report that explains the reasons for the turnover. Post the report on the Hershey School's website so parents who are considering sending their children there can read it for themselves. Compensate students wrongly expelled or forced out.
- Spin Hershey Entertainment and Resort Company out of the current organization as the core asset of a new child-centered charity, forcing it to pay dividends to support the new charity's mission.
- Strip the Office of Attorney General and the Dauphin County Orphan's Court of oversight responsibility for the Hershey charity. Oversight could switch to the Department of Education, the Department of Public Welfare, or a new independent agency.
- Invest Hershey School assets, with the exception of Hershey Chocolate, in index funds to eliminate financial advisory fees and politically driven investment decisions.
- Insist that Hershey Chocolate independently develop and institute a certification program to eliminate the worst forms of child labor from its supply chain and products.

Over a century ago, Milton Hershey founded a school meant to benefit poor children, lifting them from the hard life he himself had known. He went on to set up an unprecedented arrangement that would pour the vast profits from his business ventures into this charitable venture, in perpetuity. After all this time, and so many gratuitous examples of misuse of the power and funds flowing from this legacy, it is time to make the changes necessary to allow Hershey's dream to continue into the future, helping the most possible children in the best possible way.

CAST OF CHARACTERS

Walter Alessandroni, Pennsylvania attorney general, agreed to the diversion of Hershey Trust assets into the Hershey medical school and hospital.

Abbie Bartels, a 13-year-old Hershey School student, hanged herself in her bedroom closet in June 2013 after the school refused to allow her to attend her eighth-grade graduation because of depression and reported suicidal thoughts.

Joseph Berning, class of 1973, an alumni activist and auto mechanic and an unofficial Hershey Trust historian.

Robert Cavanaugh, class of 1977, a California-based real estate investor and Hershey Trust chairman.

Anthony Colistra, class of 1959, Hershey Trust board chairman. He agreed to the purchase of the Wren Dale golf course and the Pumpkin World market with Trust assets. Colistra was later appointed Hershey School president.

George and Prudence Copenhaver, the first Hershey School administrator and the first Hershey housemother, were hired in October 1909.

Tom Corbett, Pennsylvania attorney general (2005 to 2011) and governor (2011 to 2015).

William E. Dearden, class of 1940, modernized the chocolate company's sales and marketing after rising to the top executive post. Under Dearden, Hershey developed new chocolate products and acquired several brands.

Cesar Escudero-Aviles, a Reading boy, sued in federal court in Harrisburg over his expulsion from the Hershey School.

John Estey, the chief of staff to former Pennsylvania governor Ed Rendell and the former chairman of the Delaware River Port Authority, is one of the top executives at the

Hershey Trust Company. Estey served as the interim school president for the 2013-14 academic year.

Mike Fisher, Pennsylvania's attorney general from 1997 to 2003, announced structural reforms to the Hershey Trust as he ran for governor in 2002, but then cancelled those reforms before they could be enacted in 2003. Fisher is now a federal appeals court judge in Philadelphia.

F. Frederic "Ric" Fouad, class of 1980, a New York lawyer and former president of the Milton Hershey School Alumni Association.

Ronda Goldfein, Philadelphia lawyer and AIDS activist.

Raymond Gover, former publisher of the Harrisburg *Patriot-News*. He was named to the Hershey Trust board in late 2002.

Peter Gurt, class of 1985, was appointed president of the Hershey School in June 2014. He is the third consecutive alumnus to head one of the nation's richest educational institutions. Gurt served as the Hershey School's second-ranking administrator during a time when expulsions rose substantially and the institution built the now-failed Springboard Academy at a cost of tens of millions of dollars.

John Halbleib, class of 1971, a Chicago attorney and former president of the Milton Hershey School Alumni Association

Catherine Hershey, born Catherine "Kitty" Sweeney, married Milton Hershey on May 25, 1898. She died in 1915.

John "J.O." Hershey, a former houseparent and no relation to Catherine and Milton. He rose to the top levels of the Hershey Trust organization.

Milton Hershey, founder of the Lancaster Caramel Company in 1887, and a pioneer in the development of mass-produced milk chocolate. Before his death in 1945, he bequeathed his fortune to the Hershey orphanage and school.

Sam Hinkle, former Hershey Chocolate executive and Hershey Trust board member. He advocated diverting Hershey Trust assets to the medical school.

Kathleen Kane, Pennsylvania's first woman Democrat to be elected attorney general. She campaigned saying that she wouldn't be one of the "Harrisburg boys."

Charles Koons 2d, a serial pedophile, regularly visited the Hershey School campus with his mother, a substitute houseparent. The Trust paid a settlement of three million dollars to five boys who claimed that Koons molested them on campus.

William Lepley, an Iowa educator hired to head the Hershey School in the early 1990s. He led the orphanage's transformation into a boarding institution that prepared students from deprived backgrounds for college.

Warren Morgan, a Dauphin County Orphans' Court judge, refused to allow the diversion of Hershey Trust assets into a research institute in 1999. He insisted that the school boost enrollment, and was instrumental in naming LeRoy Zimmerman and Raymond Gover to the Hershey Trust board in 2002.

James Nevels, a politically connected investment advisor and former head of the Philadelphia public schools' oversight board, serves on the board of the Hershey Trust and is non-executive chairman of the chocolate company, earning hundreds of thousands of dollars a year in Hershey-related directors' fees.

Gilbert Nurick, a partner in the Harrisburg law firm of McNees, Wallace & Nurick, obtained state government and orphans' court approval for diverting Hershey Trust assets to the Hershey medical school. His firm represented Hershey interests for more than 60 years.

John "Johnny" O'Brien, class of 1961, the first Hershey School graduate to attend Princeton University. A corporate consultant, he was hired as president of the Hershey School in late 2002.

Mark A. Pacella, a top official in the Pennsylvania Office of Attorney General, has repeatedly investigated the Hershey Trust.

Rod J. Pera, a partner in McNees, Wallace & Nurick, was the Hershey Trust chairman and interim school president who began the institution's transformation into a school that prepared poor children for college.

Robert Reese, scion of the Reese's peanut butter cup family and former president of the Hershey Trust. He was the Trust board member who filed a petition in Dauphin County Orphans' Court, claiming financial mismanagement of Trust assets and unacceptably high board compensation.

Tom Ridge, former Pennsylvania congressman, governor and director of the Trust-controlled Hershey Chocolate Company.

William "Bill" Scranton, Pennsylvania governor when the Hershey Trust diverted $50 million in Trust assets and more than 500 acres of orphans' land to the Hershey medical school.

Joseph Senser, class of 1974, former tight end for the Minnesota Vikings and a Hershey Trust board member.

John Snyder, Milton Hershey's attorney, helped draft the 1909 Deed of Trust whose beneficiary was the orphanage and school.

Fred Speaker, Pennsylvania attorney general, coauthored a report that cleared the Hershey Trust of wrongdoing in the 1990s.

David Sweitzer, a detective with the Middletown Borough Police Department.

Lee Swope, the Dauphin County Orphans' Court judge who approved the diversion of assets and land to the Hershey medical school, and significant modifications to the 1909 Deed of Trust in the early 1970s.

William "Dick" Thornburgh, U.S. Attorney in western Pennsylvania and former Pennsylvania governor. He coauthored a report clearing the Hershey Trust of conflicts of interest and wrongdoing.

LeRoy S. Zimmerman, a two-term Pennsylvania attorney general, was named to the Hershey Trust board in 2002. He earned more than two million dollars in directors' fees while serving on Hershey-related boards.

SOURCES

CHAPTER 1

Abbott, Grace. *The Child and the State*. Chicago: University of Chicago Press, 1938.

Brace, Charles Loring. Available at http://en.wikipedia.org/wiki/Charles_Loring_Brace.

Castner, Charles S. *One of a Kind: Milton Snavely Hershey, 1857-1945*. Kutztown, PA: Kutztown Publishing Company, 1983.

Certificate of Incorporation with the Secretary of State, Dover, Delaware. The Hershey Corporation, May 5, 1916.

Clark, Dennis. "Babes in Bondage: Indentured Irish Children in Philadelphia in the Nineteenth Century." *Journal of Interdisciplinary History* 2:283-298, 1971.

D'Antonio, Michael. *Milton S. Hershey's Extraordinary Life of Wealth, Empire and Utopian Dreams*. New York: Simon & Schuster, 2006.

Hershey: The Chocolate Town. Hershey, PA: The Hershey Press, ca. 1915.

"The Hershey Industrial School Deed" by Milton S. Hershey and Catharine S. Hershey, notarized November 15, 1909.

Hershey School Chronology. Internal Trust document and decade-by-decade account of the institution that provided information on Kitty Hershey's funeral and burial, hiring of George Copenhaver, and first Home Boys.

Hershey School Indenture, 1910.

High Point Mansion, Hershey Community Archives. Available at http://www.hersheyarchives.org/essay/details.aspx?EssayId=19&Rurl=%2i Fresources%2Fsearch-results.aspx%3FType=BrowseEssay.

Hinkle, Sam. Unpublished and untitled manuscript, 1970.

Hostetter, Herman. *The Body, Mind and Soul of Milton Snavely Hershey*. Self-published, 1971.

Jones, Marshall B. "Decline of the American Orphanage." *Social Service Review*, September 1993.

Milton Hershey School Population Statistics, compiled by Joe Brechbill and submitted to the Dauphin County Orphans' Court, 1999.

Orphanages. Available at http://www.americasfuture.net/1996/june96/6-16-96b.html.

"Our Hershey Heritage." Presentations to the Rotary Club of Hershey, November–December 1983.

"Our Hershey Heritage," Presentations to the Rotary Club of Hershey, October–November 1992.

Snavely, Joseph Richard. *An Intimate Story of Milton S. Hershey.* Hershey, PA: Self-published, 1957.

Snavely, Joseph Richard. *M.S. Hershey Lives On.* Hershey, PA: Self-published, 1947.

Snavely, J.R. *A Chat with Mr. Hershey.* Hershey, PA: Self-published, 1932.

Sorensen, John, with Judith Sealander, editors. *The Grace Abbott Reader.* Lincoln, NE: University of Nebraska Press, 2008.

Wallace, Paul A.W. *The Chocolate King: The Story of M.S. Hershey.* Biography commissioned in the 1950s by the Hershey Trust Company, unpublished.

CHAPTER 2

Castner, Charles S. *One of a Kind: Milton Snavely Hershey, 1857-1945.* Kutztown, PA: Kutztown Publishing Company, 1983.

The Hershey School Chronology, information on Milton Hershey's purchase or construction of student homes in the late 1920s and 1930s.

Klotz, Richard Russell. *The Rise and Demise of the Hershey Junior College: An Historical-Descriptive Study of the Hershey Junior College, Hershey, Pennsylvania, 1938-1965.* Manheim, PA: Stiegel Printing, Inc., 1973.

Milton Hershey School Population Statistics, compiled by Joe Brechbill and submitted to the Dauphin County Orphans' Court, 1999.

Milton Hershey School Population Statistics, compiled by Joe Brechbill and submitted to the Dauphin County Orphans' Court, 1999.

"Our Hershey Heritage," Presentations to the Rotary Club of Hershey, October–November 1992.

"Our Hershey Heritage," Presentations to the Rotary Club of Hershey, November–December 1983.

Sit-down Strike at Hershey chocolate plant. Available at http://explorepahistory.com/hmarker.php?markerId=1-A-320.

Wallace, Paul A.W. *The Chocolate King: The Story of M.S. Hershey.* Biography commissioned in the 1950s by the Hershey Trust Company, unpublished.

CHAPTER 3

Chaisson, John. "Opportunity Farm Thriving." *Lewiston Journal* (Lewiston, ME), April 2, 1983.

Hammond, W. Allen. *A Man and His Boys: 60th Anniversary, 1909-1969.* Manheim, PA: Stiegel Printing Company, 1969.

Hershey, John O. ("J.O."). Dr. Hershey Community Archives Oral History Program, August 1990.

The Hershey School Chronology, information on upgrades to the student homes and release of the admissions-recruitment film *A Living Heritage for Boys.*

Hostetter, Christina J. "Sugar Allies: How Hershey and Coca Cola Used Government Contracts and Sugar Exemptions to Elude Sugar Rationing Regulations." Master's thesis, University of Maryland, 2004.

MacDonald, Dwight. "Our Invisible Poor" (book review). *New Yorker,* January 19, 1963.

Markley, Earle. Hershey Community Archives Oral History Program. Interview, 1982. Available at http://media.hersheyarchives.org/oralhistory/Markley_89OH47.pdf.

Mayo, Leonard W. Available at http://special.lib.umn.edu/findaid/xml/sw0107.xml.

Mayo, Leonard W., Frederick Allen, and Helen C. Hubbell. "Report of the Anniversary Committee to the Milton Hershey School," August 2, 1960.

Milton Hershey School Population Statistics, compiled by Joe Brechbill and submitted to the Dauphin County Orphans' Court, 1999.

New York Times. "Hershey Deal Voted by Sugar Company." March 6, 1946.

Opportunity Farm, history. Available at http://mainedar.org/chapter/marydillingham/opportunityfarm.html.

Patterson, Homer L. *Patterson's College and School Directory of the United States.* Chicago: American Educational Company, 1908.

Saxon, Wolfgang. "Leonard W. Mayo Is Dead at 92; Educator Who Helped Disabled." *New York Times,* September 3, 1992.

Staples, Percy Alexander. Hershey Community Archives. Available at http://www.hersheyarchives.org/essay/details.aspx?EssayId=35&Rurl=%2[Fresources%2F-search-results.aspx%3FType%3DBrowseEssay.

Wallace, Paul A.W. "The Chocolate King: The Story of M.S. Hershey." Biography commissioned in the 1950s by the Hershey Trust Company (unpublished).

Witmer, D. Paul. Hershey Community Archives Oral History Program. Interview, 1975.

Work with Boys. Boston: Federated Boys' Club of Boston, 1911.

CHAPTER 4

Dauphin County Orphans' Court. "Petition for *Cy-près* Award of Portion of Accumulated Income," signed by Judge Lee Swope, August 23, 1963.

Dauphin County Orphans' Court. "Petition of Hershey Trust Company, Trustee for the M.S. Hershey Foundation, for Modification of the Orphans' Court of Dauphin County, Pennsylvania, dated August 23, 1963, to substitute The Pennsylvania State University as trustee," decree signed by Judge Lee Swope, December 17, 1968.

Flint, Peter B. "Samuel F. Hinkle, Developer of WWII K Rations." *New York Times,* April 21, 1984.

Hershey Chocolate military rations, available at http://en.wikipedia.org/wiki/United_States_military_chocolate.

Hinkle, Sam. Private letter to Dr. George T. Harrell, dean and director of the Milton S. Hershey Medical Center, June 10, 1971.

Hinkle, Sam. Speaking of dwindling orphan population, undated, available at http://www.youtube.com/watch?v=TVYbfFV_WcM.

Klotz, Richard Russell. *The Rise and Demise of the Hershey Junior College: An Historical-Descriptive Study of the Hershey Junior College, Hershey, Pennsylvania, 1938-1965.* Manheim, PA: Stiegel Printing, Inc., 1973.

Lang, C. Max. *The Impossible Dream: The Founding of the Milton S. Hershey Medical Center of the Pennsylvania State University.* Bloomington, IN: Author House, 2010.

Legal memorandum (97 pages). "In Re: Hershey Trust Company, Trustee for Milton Hershey School; Proposed Award of a Portion of Accumulated Income Held under Milton Hershey School Trust to the M.S. Hershey Foundation," prepared by law firms Dunnington, Bartholow & Miller of New York and McNees, Wallace & Nurick of Harrisburg (undated). This internal Trust memo argues the case for the *cy-près* petition and contained the financial figures related to the trust fund's surplus.

Milton Hershey School Population Statistics, compiled by Joe Brechbill and submitted to the Dauphin County Orphans Court, 1999.

Nurick, Gilbert. Oral history for the Hershey Community Archives Oral History Program, July 1989.

Nurick, Gilbert. Oral history for the Pennsylvania State University Libraries, July 1984.

Sollenberger, John B., Hershey Community Archives.

Witmer, Helen L. "National Facts and Figures About Children Without Families." *Journal of the American Academy of Child & Adolescent Psychiatry,* April 1965.

CHAPTER 5

Global Nonviolent Action Database, a Swarthmore College project. "Community Members Campaign for Integration of Girard College in Philadelphia, PA, USA, 1965-1968," 2011.

Nurick, Gilbert. Letter regarding admission of non-white orphan boys to the Hershey School to James E. Bobb, chairman of the Board of Managers; Dr. John O. Hershey, president of the Hershey School, and Arthur R. Whiteman, president of the Hershey Trust Company, May 13, 1968.

Philadelphia Inquirer and Philadelphia *Bulletin.* Newspaper morgue files on Walter Alessandroni and Girard College court battles.

Sennett, William C. Office of Attorney General letter with opinion regarding the admission of non-white orphan boys to the Hershey School to James E. Bobb, chairman of the Board of Managers; Dr. John O. Hershey, president of the Hershey School, and Arthur R. Whiteman, president of the Hershey Trust Company, June 4, 1968.

Sims, Gayle Ronan. "Marie Hicks, 83, The Rosa Parks of Girard College." Philly.com, April 21, 2007.

CHAPTER 6

Alpert, Augusta. "Institute on Progress for Children Without Families." *Journal of the American Academy of Child and Adolescent Psychiatry,* April 1965.

Associated Press. "Lepley Resigns as Education Head." *The Daily Reporter* (Columbus, OH), August 10, 1993.

Boyce, Brien T. "Search on for Next School District Head." *The Daily Nonpareil* (Council Bluffs, IA), June 5, 2006.

Business Week. "Hershey's Sweet Tooth Starts Aching; To Cure a Slide in Profits, the Candymaker Finally Tries TV and Diversification," February 7, 1970.

Gula, Martin. *Child-Caring Institutions.* Washington, DC: U.S. Department of Health, Education and Welfare, Children's Bureau, 1958. The publication is available from the Internet Archive at http://archive.org/stream/childcaringinsti00gula/childcaringinsti00gula_djvu.txt.

Hershey, John O. ("J.O."). Dr. Hershey Community Archives Oral History Program, August 1990.

The Hershey School Chronology, information on upgrade to the school campus with new student homes and other buildings related to the medical center investment.

Jones, Marshall B. "Decline of the American Orphanage." *Social Service Review,* September 1993.

Market Plan for Milton Hershey School." Prepared by Rita Borden of Independent School Management of Wilmington, Delaware, November 11, 1988.

Milton Hershey School Population Statistics. Compiled by Joe Brechbill and submitted to the Dauphin County Orphans' Court, 1999.

Morris, Jack H. "Big Chocolate Maker, Beset by Profit Slide, Gets More Aggressive." *Wall Street Journal,* February 18, 1970.

Ross, Jo Anne B. "Fifty Years of Service to Children and Their Families." *Social Security Bulletin,* October 1985.

Schroeder, Alice. *The Snowball: Warren Buffett and the Business of Life.* New York: Bantam Books, 2009.

Time. "Chocolate's Drop," February 9, 1968.

CHAPTER 7

Associated Press. "Associate of Preate Sentenced; Elmo Baldassarri Was Fined and Put on Probation. He Introduced the Ex-Attorney General to a Video Poker Operator," December 31, 1995.

Baer, John M. "Preate Gets 14 Months, Says He Can Do Time Standing on My Head." *Philadelphia Daily News,* December 15, 1995.

Baer, John M. "State Sen. Fisher Declares for AG, Says He'll Restore Integrity to the Office." *Philadelphia Daily News,* November 21, 1995.

Baer, John M. "Attorney General Confirmed; Senate OK of Corbett a Big Win For Guv." *Philadelphia Daily News,* October 3, 1995.

Baer, John M. "Ridge Taps Lawyer to Replace Preate; Thomas Corbett Jr. Helped Guv's Campaign." *Philadelphia Daily News,* June 15, 1995.

Baer, John M. "Preate Admits His Guilt, Atty. General Faces Jail Time for Mail Fraud." *Philadelphia Daily News,* June 14, 1995.

Barasch, David M., Angela Diaz, Jerry Thomas, and David A. Wolf. "Milton Hershey School Blue Ribbon Task Force," *Philadelphia Daily News,* April 9, 2002.

Boston Globe. Obituary for George J. Hauptfuhrer, http://www.legacy.com/obituaries/bostonglobe/obituary.aspx?pid=166207008

Caparella, Kitty. "Preate Haunted from the Grave? Taped Testimony of Deceased Informant Adds Fuel to the Probe." *Philadelphia Daily News,* April 4, 1995.

Cusick, Frederick. "Sarcione Testifies in Probe of Preate and Video Poker." *Philadelphia Inquirer,* April 22, 1995.

Daughen, Joseph R. "Preate's Posh Pen, All Minnesota Prison Camp Is Lacking This Time of Year is Florida's Climate." *Philadelphia Daily News,* December 28, 1995.

Dauphin County Common Pleas Court. Minor boy and his parents vs. Milton Hershey School, Civil Action No. 4965 S 2001, October 19, 2001.

Dauphin County Orphans' Court. Milton Hershey School and Milton Hershey Trust Company, Trustees of the Milton Hershey School Trust, "Petition for *Cy-près* of the

Accumulated Income and Authorization for the Execution and Delivery of Certain Easements *Cy-près*," January 19, 1999.

Dauphin County Orphans' Court. In the Matter of Milton Hershey School, "Transcript of Court Proceedings," June 3, 1999.

Dauphin County Orphans' Court. Milton Hershey School and Milton Hershey Trust Company, Trustees of the Milton Hershey School Trust, "Brief of the Milton Hershey School Alumni Association," July 23, 1999.

Dauphin County Orphans' Court. Milton Hershey School and Milton Hershey Trust Company, Trustees of the Milton Hershey School Trust, "Brief of the Attorney General in Support of the Answer and Objections to the Milton Hershey School and the Hershey Trust Company's Petition for *Cy-près* Award of Portion of Accumulated Income and Authorization for the Execution and Delivery of Certain Easements *Cy-près*," October 1, 1999.

Dauphin County Orphans' Court. Milton Hershey School and Milton Hershey Trust Company, Trustees of the Milton Hershey School Trust, "Reply Brief of Milton Hershey School and Hershey Trust Company to Brief of the Office of Attorney General," October 21, 1999.

Dauphin County Orphans' Court. Milton Hershey School and Milton Hershey Trust Company, Trustees of the Milton Hershey School Trust, "Adjudication," December 7, 1999. Judge Morgan's decision and opinion rejecting the *cy-près* petition.

Dauphin County Orphans' Court. "Petition for Citation for Rule to Show Cause Why the Trust's July 31, 2002 Agreement Should Not be Reinstated, Except as Later Appropriately Modified, and to Appoint a Guardian and a Trustee Ad Litem for Known and Unknown Orphan Beneficiaries, and to Order the Trust Company to Comply with This Court's December 7, 1999 Adjudication," September 4, 2003.

Gleason, Jerry L. "Milton Hershey School Suspends Students." *Patriot-News* (Harrisburg), March 15, 2001.

Hershey School Population Statistics. Compiled by Joe Brechbill and submitted to the Dauphin County Orphans' Court, 1999.

Hershey Trust Company. Restructuring of board. Available at http://www.prnewswire.com/news-releases/milton-hershey-school-board-announces-membership-76838957.html.

Horn, Patricia. "Being Charitable May Get Tougher; A Bill Aimed at Hershey Foods Could Harm Trusts, Experts Say." *Philadelphia Inquirer*, October 18, 2002.

Lipsitz, Joan. Available at http://www.mdcinc.org/about-us/our-people/joan-lipsitz-phd

Moran, Robert. "Preate Gets 14-month Term, $25,000 Fine. The Ex-Attorney General Called It 'The Most Painful Day of My Life.' But He Said Going to Prison Wouldn't Faze Him." *Philadelphia Inquirer*, December 15, 1995.

Moran, Robert. "Jury Indicts Ex-Trooper in Preate Case. State Police Veteran Peter Tonetti Was the First to Publicly Raise Questions About the Then-D.A. Now, Tonetti is Accused of Gambling and Conspiracy." *Philadelphia Inquirer*, November 10, 1995.

Moran, Robert. "Prosecutors Revile Preate as Unrepentant. The U.S. Attorney Took a Hard Line on Sentencing, Complaining That the Ex-State Official Has Been Spinning Lies About His Crime." *Philadelphia Inquirer*, November 7, 1995.

Moran, Robert. "An Uncharacteristic End for Preate; The Attorney General Was Never Known to Back Down, Until Last Week." *Philadelphia Inquirer*, June 18, 1995.

Moran, Robert. "Preate Guilty to Mail Fraud Count; He'll Resign June 23. He Could Get Five Years and a $25,000 Fine." *Philadelphia Inquirer*, June 14, 1995.

Moran, Robert. "Preate Probe Gets Its First Conviction. The Jury Found a Former Operator of Illegal Video-Poker Machines Guilty of Lying to the Grand Jury." *Philadelphia Inquirer*, January 12, 1995.

Moran, Robert. "Court Hears of the Jury Probe of Preate, Details Came in the Trial of Gary Frey. It's the First Official Confirmation of the Grand Jury Probe." *Philadelphia Inquirer*, January 11, 1995.

Moran, Robert, and Russell E. Eshleman Jr. "Preate Gets Target Letter from U.S. Attorney." *Philadelphia Inquirer*, March 23, 1995.

New York Times. "Pennsylvania's No. 3 Official Agrees to Plea on Mail Fraud," June 10, 1995.

Pennington, Hilary. Available at http://www.fordfoundation.org/newsroom/news-from-ford/814.

Pennsylvania election, 2002. Available at http://en.wikipedia.org/wiki/Pennsylvania_gubernatorial_election,_2002.

Philadelphia Daily News. "How the Case Against Preate Unfolded," April 4, 1995.

Raffaele, Martha. "Pa. House Passes Bill to Curb a Hershey Sale; The State Attorney General Could Require Court Review of Deals Involving Publicly Traded Firms That Charitable Trusts Control." Associated Press, October 23, 2002.

Shafer, Raymond P., former Pennsylvania governor. Available at http://en.wikipedia.org/wiki/Raymond_P._Shafer.

Sheffield, Reggie. "Lawsuit Claims Negligence; Family Alleges Son Was Assaulted at Hershey School." *Patriot-News* (Harrisburg), October 26, 2001.

Supreme Court of Pennsylvania. "Brief for Appellant Attorney General of Pennsylvania," January 31, 2006.

Tanaka, Wendy. "Chocolate Town Rallies to Keep Hershey Home." *Philadelphia Inquirer*, August 3, 2002.

Thornburgh, Richard Lewis ("Dick"), former Pennsylvania governor and U.S. Attorney General. Available at http://en.wikipedia.org/wiki/Dick_Thornburgh.

Tresniowski, Alex. "Gratitude's Duty." *People*, January 22, 2001.

White, Dan. "The Milton Hershey School: An Evaluation of Alumni Relations." May 2003. Letter distributed to Hershey School administrators.

Wiggins, Ovetta. "As Legislature Wraps, Schweiker Is the Focus; The Governor's Agenda Will Take Priority, His GOP Colleagues Said. Rendell Wants Big Changes to Wait." *Philadelphia Inquirer*, November 12, 2002.

CHAPTER 8

Ben Richey Boys Ranch. Available at https://mansionkids.org/mission-child-impact/.

Coalition for Residential Education. Available at http://www.residentialeducation.org/.

Dauphin County Orphans' Court. Milton Hershey School and Milton Hershey Trust Company, Trustees of the Milton Hershey School Trust, "Adjudication," December 7, 1999. Judge Morgan's decision and opinion rejecting the *cy-près* petition.

Loyd, E. Christopher, and Richard P. Barth. "Developmental Outcomes After Five Years for Foster Children Returned Home, Remaining in Care, or Adopted," *Children and Youth Services Review*, available online April 14, 2011.

Milton Hershey School Population Statistics. Compiled by Joe Brechbill and submitted to the Dauphin County Orphans' Court, 1999.

Oklahoma Baptist Homes for Children. Available at http://www.obhc.org/.

Rutter, Michael. Available at http://en.wikipedia.org/wiki/Michael_Rutter.

Tupelo Children's Mansion. Available at https://mansionkids.org/mission-child-impact/.

CHAPTER 9

Arias, Jeremy. "Molestation Charges Against Former Milton Hershey School Ice Hockey Coach Held Over for Trial." Pennlive.com, February 20, 2014. Available at http://www.pennlive.com/midstate/index.ssf/2014/02/molestation_charges_against_fo.html.

Bourke, Michael L., and Andres E. Hernandez. "The 'Butner Study' Redux: A Report of the Incidence of Hands-on Child Victimization by Child Pornographer Offenders." *Journal of Family Violence*, published online, December 10, 2008.

Etterman, Joshua, and Eric Stark. MHS Site of Possible Sex Crime." *Hershey Chronicle*, July 2, 2001.

Fernandez, Bob. "Child-Porn Case Led to Hershey School; An Ex-Administrator Heads to Prison. The School Said No Students Were Involved." *Philadelphia Inquirer*, October, 30, 2011.

Fernandez, Bob. "Hershey Pedophile Case Fell Off the Radar." *Philadelphia Inquirer*, May 30, 2010.

Fernandez, Bob. "Sex-abuse Case Shatters Hershey School; The Man Accused of Assaulting the Former Students Is the Son of an Ex-House Parent." *Philadelphia Inquirer*, May 20, 2010.

Johnson, Jeffrey A. "Former Milton Hershey School Hockey Coach Charged with Sexually Assaulting Former Player, Records Say." Pennlive.com, September 6, 2013. Available at http://www.pennlive.com/midstate/index.ssf/2013/09/former_milton_hershey_school_i.html.

Police Criminal Complaint, Dauphin County. "Endangering the Welfare of Child." Docket CR-346-01, August 15, 2001.

United States District Court for the Eastern District of Pennsylvania. *United States v. David Husmann.* "Government's Sentencing Memorandum," June 5, 2013.

CHAPTER 10

ABC News. "Family on Trial; Stepdaughter Turns in Stepmom." *Good Morning America* transcript, July 10, 2012.

ABC News. "Father's Emotional Outburst; Daughter's Testimony Against His Wife." *Good Morning America* transcript, April 28, 2012.

ABC News. "Taking on Her Stepmother; Forces Admission on Hit-and-Run." *Good Morning America* transcript, April 26, 2012.

Chanen, David. "Senser's Appeal Alleges Missteps by Court." *Star Tribune* (Minneapolis), August 11, 2012.

Chanen, David. "Senser's Wife Was Driver in Hit-and-Run." *Star Tribune* (Minneapolis), September 3, 2011.

Hanners, David. "Joe Senser Bashes Media, Hennepin County Attorney Following Court Hearing for His Wife." *St. Paul Pioneer Press* (St. Paul, MN), September 23, 2012.

Hanners, David. "Amy Senser Testifies That She Never Saw Victim of Fatal Hit-and-Run." *St. Paul Pioneer Press* (St. Paul, MN), April 29, 2012.

Hanners, David. "Amy Senser Fatal Hit-and-Run: 'His Blood Was All Over Her Car,' Prosecutor Says." *St. Paul Pioneer Press* (St. Paul, MN), January 22, 2012.

International Business Times News. "Amy Senser Sentenced to 41 Months in Hit-and-Run." IBTN transcript, July 9, 2012.

Mullen, Mike. "Amy Senser, Joe Senser's Wife, Sued for Fatal Hit-and-Run; Anousone Phanthavong Family Asks $50,000 in Wrongful Death." *City Pages* (Minneapolis/St. Paul), September 7, 2011.

Quigley, Rachel. "'Take Responsibility 4 UR Actions': The Tense Text Messages from Ex-NFL Player's Family After Wife Killed Someone in Hit-and-Run as Evidence Is Released by Court." MailOnline.com, May 8, 2012.

Simons, Abby. "Joe Senser Rips Lawyers, Backs Amy." *Star Tribune* (Minneapolis),September 25, 2012.

Simons, Abby. "Senser Texts Reveal a Family Trying to Cope." *Star Tribune* (Minneapolis), May 8, 2012.

Simons, Abby. "Juror: Senser's Story Didn't Add Up." *Star Tribune* (Minneapolis), May 5, 2012.

Simons, Abby, and Matt McKinney. "Brittani Senser Tells of Being 'Furious' After Fatal I-94 Crash." *Star Tribune* (Minneapolis), April 25, 2012.

Simons, Abby. "Senser Driving Details Unfold," *Star Tribune,* January 24, 2012.

Simons, Abby. "In Suing Sensers, Family of Victim Asks 'Why?'" *Star Tribune* (Minneapolis), September 7, 2011.

U.S. Court, Eastern District of Pennsylvania. "Settlement Agreement Between the United States of America, the Milton Hershey School and Mother Smith (on Behalf of Hershey and Abraham Smith), Under the Americans with Disabilities Act." CV-07391, October 10, 2012.

U.S. Court, Southern District of New York. "Opinion and Order," in *Jane Doe v. Deer Mountain Day Camp Inc.* CV-05495, January 13, 2010.

CHAPTER 11

Reporting in this chapter was based entirely on interviews and internal Hershey School documents.

CHAPTER 12

Associated Press. "Dwyer Judge: Jail's a Deterrent." *Philadelphia Daily News,* December 20, 1986.

Beers, Paul B. *Pennsylvania Politics Today and Yesterday: The Tolerable Accommodation.* University Park, PA: Pennsylvania State University Press, 1980.

Cusick, Frederick. "State Finds 2 Cases of Price Fixing in Car Inspections, Suspects More." *Philadelphia Inquirer,* November 16, 1982.

Cusick, Frederick. "Smith: Spoke of a Gift with Zimmerman." *Philadelphia Inquirer,* December 4, 1986.

Cusick, Frederick. "In the Dwyer-Asher Bribery Trial, the Prosecution Completes Its Case." *Philadelphia Inquirer,* December 7, 1986.

Cusick, Frederick. "Dwyer and Asher Found Guilty, Face Prison in Penna. Bribery Case." *Philadelphia Inquirer,* December 19, 1986.

Cusick, Frederick. "Bribery Trial Leaves a Tarnished GOP, Prosecutor says; Case Won't End with Dwyer and Asher." *Philadelphia Inquirer,* December 21, 1986

Cusick, Frederick. "The Last, Dark Days of Budd Dwyer." *Philadelphia Inquirer Magazine,* June 28, 1987.

Cusick, Frederick. "One Year Later, Dwyer Remains Unvindicated." *Philadelphia Inquirer,* January 24, 1988.

Cusick, Frederick, Carol Morello, and Dan Meyers. "Incumbents Win Races Despite Scandals." *Philadelphia Inquirer,* November 8, 1984.

Dauphin County Orphans' Court. "Brief of Milton Hershey School and Hershey Trust Company in Support of Their Preliminary Objections to the Petition of Robert Reese," March 31, 2011.

Dauphin County Orphans' Court. "Petition for Citation for Rule to Show Why (A) Breaches of Trust of the Duty to Loyalty Should Not Be Redressed and (B) Breaches of Trust of the Duty to Exercise Prudence and Due Care, the Duty of Impartiality, the Duty to Administer, the Duty to Use Due Care in Investment Decisions and the Duty to Inform Should Not Be Redressed Pursuant to the Pennsylvania Uniform Trust Act, the Pennsylvania Probate, Estates and Fiduciaries Code and Pennsylvania Common Law," filed by Robert Reese, February 8, 2011.

Fernandez, Bob. "Chocolatetown Meltdown: With the old-fashioned chocolate market stagnant, the Hershey Co. is struggling to hold ground against high-falutin' competition." Philly.com, December 16, 2007.

Fernandez, Bob. "Hershey deal: $12 million profited club, ex-CEO." *Philadelphia Inquirer,* October 3, 2010.

Fernandez, Bob. "Hershey Trust Probe Pits Corbett vs. Ally." *Philadelphia Inquirer,* December 19, 2010.

Fernandez, Bob. "Hershey dinner in question; Corbett feted as he probed charity." Philly.com, February 24, 2011.

Fernandez, Bob. "Hershey School seeks to develop chocolate factory." Philly.com, June 19, 2011.

Fernandez, Bob. "How Hershey charity director fees rose to a half a million." Philly.com, July 20, 2011.

Fernandez, Bob. "High Cost of Hershey School-Related Boards; A Former State Attorney General Received Nearly $500,000. Three Other Republicans Were Well-Paid." *Philadelphia Inquirer,* July 25, 2010.

Ferrick, Thomas Jr. "Convictions of Dwyer and Asher: A Nightmare for the GOP." *Philadelphia Inquirer,* December 19, 1986.

Grotevant, Bob. "Feds Dispute Zimmerman on Bribe Details." *Philadelphia Daily News,* December 18, 1984.

Keisling, William, and Richard Kearns. *The Sins of Our Fathers: A Profile of Pennsylvania Attorney General LeRoy S. Zimmerman and a Historical Explanation of the Suicide of State Treasurer R. Budd Dwyer.* Berkeley, CA: Yardbird, 1988.

Mondics, Chris. "Hershey replaces half its board." Philly.com, November 13, 2007.

Morris, David. "150G Tied to Zimmerman." Associated Press, December 4, 1986.

Onorato, Dan. http://en.wikipedia.org/wiki/Dan_Onorato

Pennsylvania Attorney General. http://en.wikipedia.org/wiki/Pennsylvania_Attorney_General.

Philadelphia Inquirer. "When Gift Offers Are Scams," December 28, 1982.

Roche, Walter F. Jr. "5 Charged in Probe of Computer Contract." *Philadelphia Inquirer,* October 24, 1984.

Spoon, Justin. "Campaign Aims to Curtail Shoplifting." *Philadelphia Inquirer,* November 24, 1982.

Thornburgh, Dick. http://en.wikipedia.org/wiki/Dick_Thornburgh

United Press International. "Debt Agency Fined $6,000." *Philadelphia Inquirer,* December 1, 1982.

CHAPTER 13

Associated Press. "Ex-Hershey Trust Official Robert Reese Gives 100K to AG Candidate Kathleen Kane," October 29, 2012.

Associated Press. "S.E.C. Contends Harrisburg, Pa., Misled Its Bond Investors," May 6, 2013.

Brennan, Chris. "Kane & Corbett Trade Barbs on Sandusky Investigation." Philly.com, October 1, 2012.

Cooper, Michael. "An Incinerator Becomes Harrisburg's Money Pit." *New York Times,* May 20, 2010.

Dauphin County Orphans' Court. In the Matter of the Trust Under Deed of Milton S. Hershey and Catherine S. Hershey, "No Objection to Confirmation of Accounts," May 8, 2013.

Hershey Trust Company. "Hershey Trust Company Reaches Agreement with Attorney General on Reforms to Better Service the Milton Hershey School Mission," May 8, 2013.

Krawczeniuk, Borys. "Kane Says Corbett 'Probably' Played Politics with Sandusky Case." TheTimes-Tribune.com, September 27, 2012.

Krawczeniuk, Borys. "Raising Kane: West Scranton Native Marching Toward Harrisburg." TheTimes-Tribune.com, April 29, 2012.

Krawczeniuk, Borys. "Rendell Endorses Murphy for Attorney General," The Borys Blog, TheTimes-Tribune.com, October 4, 2011.

Malawskey, Nick. "Attorney General Kane on Hershey Trust Reforms: 'A Great Step Forward.'" Pennlive.com, May 7, 2013.

Office of Attorney General. Press release: "AG Kane Announces Reform Agreement with Milton Hershey Trust and Milton Hershey School," May 8, 2013.

Unkovich, David. "David Unkovic: 'Disdain for the Law Is Embedded in Harrisburg's Political Culture.'" Pennlive.com, op-ed, June 10, 2012.

Veronikis, Eric. "Harrisburg Receiver David Unkovic Cites 'Corruption' in Debt Crisis." Pennlive.com, March 22, 2012.

Veronikis, Eric. "Harrisburg Receiver David Unkovic's Resignation Letter Sends Warning." Pennlive.com, April 3, 2012.

CHAPTER 14

Chatterjee, Sumana, and James Kuhnhenn. "House Backs Measure to Label Chocolate as Slave-Free; Hurdles Remain. The Chocolate Industry, Saying Africans Would Be Hurt, Said It Would Fight to Block the Legislation." *Philadelphia Inquirer,* June 29, 2001.

Chatterjee, Sumana, and Tish Wells. "Coffee Beans Often Tainted, Too; There's No Way to Tell Among Shipments. Some Firms Don't Care." *Philadelphia Inquirer*, June 26, 2001.

Court of Chancery of the State of Delaware. *Louisiana Municipal Employees' Retirement System v. The Hershey Company.* "Verified Complaint ursuant to Compel Inspection of Books and Records," October 2012.

Court of Chancery of the State of Delaware. *Louisiana Municipal Employees' Retirement System v. The Hershey Company.* "Defendant Hershey Company's Motion to Dismiss Verified Complaint," November 2012.

Court of Chancery of the State of Delaware. *Louisiana Municipal Employees' Retirement System v. The Hershey Company.* "Master's Report," November 2013.

Court of Chancery of the State of Delaware. *Louisiana Municipal Employees' Retirement System v. The Hershey Company.* "Rulings of the Court from Oral Argument on Exceptions to the Master's Final Report," March 2014.

DePuydt, Peter J. "In the Hearts of Those Whom You Serve: The Teachers for West Africa Program." *Pennsylvania Magazine of History and Biography*, January 2010.

Fernandez, Bob. "Hershey: Slavery a Shock." *Philadelphia Inquirer*, June 24, 2001.

The Hershey Company. *Corporate Responsibility Scorecard, 2012.* Available at http://www.thehersheycompany.com/social-responsibility.aspx

Horn, Patricia. "Being Charitable May Get Tougher; A Bill Aimed at Hershey Foods Could Harm Trusts, Experts Say." *Philadelphia Inquirer*, October 18, 2002.

Payson Center for International Development and Technology Transfer, Tulane University. *Oversight of Public and Private Initiatives to Eliminate the Worst Forms of Child Labor in the Cocoa Sector in Cote d'Ivoire and Ghana, March 31, 2011.*

Raffaele, Martha. "Pa. House Passes Bill to Curb Hershey Sale; The State Attorney General Could Require Court Review of the Deals Involving Publicly Traded Firms That Charitable Trusts Control." Associated Press, October 23, 2002.

Raghavan, Sudarsan. "Where Youths Support Families, Slavery Is More Difficult to Track; Passable Borders and Lax Authorities Help the Practice Persist." *Philadelphia Inquirer*, June 5, 2001.

Raghavan, Sudarsan. "Ivory Coast Officials Aiming to Abolish Child Slavery." *Philadelphia Inquirer*, June 27, 2001.

Raghavan, Sudarsan, and Sumana Chatterjee. "A Slave-Labor Force of Youths Keeps Chocolate Flowing West." *Philadelphia Inquirer*, June 24, 2001.

Securities and Exchange Commission. *The Hershey Company, Form 10-K, February 22, 2013.*

Securities and Exchange Commission. *The Hershey Company, Definitive Proxy, March 19, 2013.*

Securities and Exchange Commission. *The Hershey Company, Definitive Proxy, March 20, 2012.*

Securities and Exchange Commission. *The Hershey Company, Definitive Proxy, March 15, 2011.*

Securities and Exchange Commission. *The Hershey Company, Definitive Proxy, March 22, 2010.*

Securities and Exchange Commission. *The Hershey Company, Definitive Proxy, March 16, 2009.*

Securities and Exchange Commission. *Hershey Foods Corporation, Annual Report to Stockholders, March 15, 2002.*

U.S. Department of State. *Trafficking in Persons Report, June 2007.*

U.S. Department of Labor, Bureau of International Labor Affairs. *2003 Findings of the Worst Forms of Child Labor, 2004.*

Wiggins, Ovetta. "As Legislature Wraps, Schweiker Is the Focus; The Governor's Agenda Will Take Priority, His GOP Colleagues Said. Rendell Wants Big Changes to Wait." *Philadelphia Inquirer,* November 12, 2002.

EPILOGUE

Fernandez, Bob. "Hershey Charity Hires Former Rendell Aide; John H. Estey's Appointment Comes as the State Is Seeking Changes at the Charity." *Philadelphia Inquirer,* October 9, 2011.

Appendix—MILTON HERSHEY SCHOOL ENROLLMENT

In 1999, the Hershey School submitted to the Orphans' Court its historic enrollment as part of a *cy-prés* petition seeking to divert funds into a grant-making research institute. Judge Warren Morgan rejected the request and said the school had to expend its surpluses directly on poor children. The school now enrolls about 1,900 children

YEAR	STUDENTS	
1910	5	
1911	17	
1912	20	
1913	37	
1914	40	
1915	58	
1916	62	
1917	71	
1918	79	*(Milton Hershey puts nearly all assets into school trust.)*
1919	105	
1920	108	
1921	123	
1922	118	
1923	116	
1924	167	

YEAR	STUDENTS	
1925	175	
1926	191	
1927	202	
1928	214	
1929	242	
1930	308	
1931	378	
1932	464	
1933	604	(*Deed changed—age increased to 14 years; fathers could be deceased.*)
1934	740	
1935	880	
1936	941	
1937	1,002	
1938	958	
1939	1,018	
1940	1,004	
1941	982	(*December 7th—U.S. enters World War II.*)
1942	858	
1943	770	
1944	699	
1945	620	(*World War II ends.*)
1946	720	
1947	777	
1948	875	
1949	1,006	
1950	1,056	(*Name changed to Milton Hershey School.*)
1951	1,080	
1952	1,090	
1953	1,077	
1954	1,042	

YEAR	STUDENTS	
1955	1,006	
1956	965	
1957	964	
1958	1,013	
1959	1,033	
1960	1,080	
1961	1,083	
1962	1,120	
1963	1,183	*(Trust sets enrollment goal of 1600 students.)*
1964	1,350	
1965	1,378	
1966	1,417	
1967	1,467	
1968	1,526	*(First nonwhite students are enrolled.)*
1969	1,500	
1970	1,550	*(Deed changed to enroll nonwhite students, age increased to 16 years.)*
1971	1,553	
1972	1,550	
1973	1,506	
1974	1,409	
1975	1,342	
1976	1,216	*(Girls and social orphans are approved by deed.)*
1977	1,162	*(First girls are enrolled.)*
1978	1,305	
1979	1,313	
1980	1,290	
1981	1,234	
1982	1,225	
1983	1,256	
1984	1,157	

YEAR	STUDENTS
1985	1,107
1986	1,113
1987	1,033
1988	1,041
1989	1,024
1990	1,052
1991	1,083
1992	1,104
1993	1,127
1994	1,108
1995	1,082
1996	1,083
1997	1,034
1998	1,037
1999	1,077